# LIVING THE BOOK OF MORMON

# LIVING
# THE BOOK OF
# MORMON
## ABIDING BY ITS PRECEPTS

*edited by*
*Gaye Strathearn and Charles Swift*

THE 36TH ANNUAL
BRIGHAM YOUNG UNIVERSITY
SIDNEY B. SPERRY SYMPOSIUM

RSC
BYU

DESERET
BOOK

The Sperry Symposium is sponsored annually by Brigham Young University and the Church Educational System in honor of Sidney B. Sperry. In the course of his forty-five-year career as a religious educator, Dr. Sperry earned a reputation for outstanding teaching and scholarship. The symposium seeks to perpetuate his memory by fostering continuing research on gospel topics.

Copublished by the Religious Studies Center, Brigham Young University, Provo, Utah, and Deseret Book Company, Salt Lake City, Utah.

**Library of Congress Cataloging-in-Publication Data**

Living the book of Mormon : abiding by its precepts / edited by Gaye Strathearn and Charles Swift.
    p. cm.
    Includes bibliographical references and index.
    ISBN 978-1-59038-799-3 (hardback : alk. paper)
    1. Book of Mormon—Criticism, interpretation, etc.—Congresses. 2. Christian life—Mormon authors.—Congresses. I. Strathearn, Gaye. II. Swift, Charles.
    BX8627.L58 2007
    289.3'22—dc22            2007025719

Printed in the United States of America
Sheridan Books, Chelsea, MI

10  9  8  7  6  5  4  3  2

# CONTENTS

v

# PREFACE

M ark Twain reportedly said, "The man who does not read good books has no advantage over the man who cannot read them." Perhaps a similar statement could be made regarding the Book of Mormon: The person who reads the Book of Mormon but does not follow its teachings is no better off than the person who does not read it. The 2007 Sidney B. Sperry Symposium, *Living the Book of Mormon: "Abiding by Its Precepts,"* focuses on how the Book of Mormon can immeasurably bless our lives as we strive to live what it teaches.

In this volume are papers presented at the Sidney B. Sperry Symposium held on the Provo campus of Brigham Young University, on October 26–27, 2007. The symposium is held each year in honor of one of the great gospel scholars of the Church and provides an excellent opportunity to study particular topics concerning the restored gospel of Jesus Christ. This year the symposium takes its theme from Joseph Smith's statement: "I told the brethren that the Book of Mormon was the most correct of any book on earth, and the keystone of our religion, and a man would get nearer to God by abiding by its precepts, than by any other book" (introduction to the Book of Mormon).

Readers of this book will quickly see that while the topic is centered on *living* the principles, or *application,* one cannot write about application without writing about the doctrines and teachings themselves. Topics include a history of Joseph Smith's statement, the literary power of the book, agency, covenants, the Fall, the Atonement, charity, and the building of Zion. Sometimes authors interpret events or scriptures differently, and we as editors may not always agree with the author's interpretation, but such is the nature of the scholarly endeavor when good students of the gospel seek to pursue and understand truth. It is our hope that while the readers may see differences in understanding, they will also see the great, overarching similarity: the authors love the Book of Mormon and believe in it as divinely inspired scripture that can bless our lives.

We are particularly pleased to have the keynote address of the symposium as the first chapter. In his address, "Abiding by Its Precepts," Elder Joe J. Christensen shares with us his memories of his years in the Church Educational System when the Book of Mormon began to take a more prominent role in CES curriculum. He also discusses particular areas in which following the teachings of the Book of Mormon will help each of us to draw nearer to God. We are grateful to Elder Christensen for his contribution to both the symposium and this volume.

The 2007 Sperry Symposium committee consisted of Patty Smith, Thomas R. Valletta, and Professors John B. Stohlton, Gaye Strathearn, and Charles Swift. Professors Swift and Strathearn carried out the editorial responsibilities. We express our appreciation to each of those who contributed to the Sperry Symposium and to this volume of papers. And we thank our colleagues at Brigham Young University who reviewed the many manuscripts submitted. We consider it a great blessing to have been able to spend such time immersed in studying this great book of scripture, the Book of Mormon.

# 1

# "ABIDING BY ITS PRECEPTS"

## Elder Joe J. Christensen

It is hard for me to believe that fifty-one years ago, in the fall of 1956, I was a very green first-year BYU graduate student. I had been invited to teach two religion classes. The dean assigned me to share office space with Reid Bankhead in the old Joseph Smith Building. The entrance to his office was through the same outer door as that of Dr. Sidney B. Sperry. I had enrolled in religion classes taught by both of these brethren. I felt like a pygmy every time I entered the area. (If Dr. Sperry were still around, I would probably feel the same way today.) I had read and quoted from many of Dr. Sperry's articles and books and had learned to admire him years before having that relatively close geographical proximity for a full academic year. I had several opportunities to visit with him personally on one scriptural or doctrinal question or another. He treated me with courtesy and deference far beyond that which I felt I deserved. He made me feel very much at home. So I doubly consider it a privilege to be here with you today in this symposium that bears his name. He certainly is one of the great pioneer intellectual gospel scholars of our modern era.

---

*Elder Joe J. Christensen is an emeritus member of the First Quorum of the Seventy.*

In the previous thirty-five Sperry symposia, much distinguished scholarly research has been presented and published, adding to the wealth of information benefiting all of us. I pay tribute to those who have made such contributions because they have helped us, as the Apostle Peter said, to "be ready always to give an answer to every man that asketh . . . a reason of the hope that is in [us]" (I Peter 3:15).

This symposium is distinctive in that it centers on the practical application of the precepts taught in the Book of Mormon—precepts that can help us draw nearer to God. My hope is that all of us who hear or read the content of this symposium will be prompted to do some deep soul searching and discover the areas wherein the Book of Mormon provides us the precepts that, if applied in our lives, can bring us closer to God. This is an occasion for all of us literally to be "doers of the word, and not hearers only" (James 1:22).

## THE BOOK OF MORMON IN CES CURRICULUM

The Book of Mormon has not always held the place in our Church Educational System that it does today. For example, I have a seminary graduation pin which, in my day, was commonly worn by those who had completed three high-school years of seminary study. The courses included classes in the Old Testament, the New Testament, and Church history. In some few areas where ninth graders were permitted to take seminary, a Book of Mormon course had been approved, but that didn't happen until 1961—forty-nine years after the first seminary program was initiated adjacent to Granite High School in Salt Lake City in 1912.

Here is a little historical background that those of us who are older may recall. In 1970, when Elder Neal A. Maxwell was appointed commissioner of the Church Educational System, I was called home shortly after beginning to serve as president of the Mexico City Mission to assist as associate commissioner for seminaries and institutes of religion. The Church Board of Education at that time included the entire First Presidency, all of the Quorum of the Twelve, the Presiding Bishop, and Sister Belle Spafford, the general president of the Relief Society. In March 1972, we placed on the board's agenda a quiet yet revolutionary proposal that the graduation requirements for seminary would be increased from three to four years, with the Book of Mormon as one of the required courses. The board approved. I recall a personal conversation with President Spencer W. Kimball, then Acting President of the Quorum of the Twelve Apostles, in which he commented, "I have wondered why we hadn't done this years ago." From that time on, every seminary graduate has had the privilege of completing a course of study in this most important, life-changing volume of scripture—the Book of Mormon. For that I am very grateful.

From the time the Book of Mormon came off the Grandin Press in Palmyra, New York, in 1830—177 years ago—there have been more than 133 million copies distributed around the world, and it has been published in 106 languages with more to come.

## "ABIDING BY ITS PRECEPTS"

The introduction to the Book of Mormon contains this declaration by the Prophet Joseph Smith: "I told the brethren that the Book of Mormon was the most correct of any book on earth, and the keystone of our religion, and a man would get nearer to God by abiding by its precepts, than by any other book."

I searched in the *Oxford English Dictionary* for the definition of key words relating to the Prophet Joseph's statement about the Book of Mormon: *abide, abiding,* and *precept.* Of the more than twenty definitions of the words, the following seem to relate most specifically to what we are discussing today:

*Precept* means "a general command or injunction; an instruction, direction, or rule for action or conduct; [especially] an injunction as to moral conduct; a maxim. Most commonly applied to divine commands."[1]

*Abide* means "to stand firm by, hold to, remain true to."[2]

*Abiding* means "enduring, standing firm" and, with relation to *law-abiding* (or *precept-abiding*), "adhering to the law"[3] (or precepts).

The Book of Mormon is filled with precepts—directions, rules, and commandments—that if applied in our lives will help draw us closer to God than the precepts we will find in any other book.

I submit that anyone who reads the Book of Mormon and receives a testimony of its truthfulness by the power of the Holy Ghost will be motivated to live a life more consistent with the teachings of the Lord

Jesus Christ. He or she will become a better person. The Book of Mormon is action oriented. It is motivational. As long as the Spirit continues to strive with such individuals, their consciences will not let them be completely at peace until they improve their lives. Abiding by the precepts, teachings, and commandments taught so clearly in its pages will help a person proximately in this life and ultimately in the life to come. As a result, I resonate positively to the theme of this symposium: "Living the Book of Mormon: 'Abiding by Its Precepts.'"

## A LIFE-CHANGING EXPERIENCE

Personally, I owe much to the Book of Mormon. To illustrate, permit me to share a simple and yet profound personal experience which I had almost sixty years ago while serving as a newly called missionary in Mexico. In those days, an elder's call to a second-language mission was for two and a half years—allowing an extra six months to work on the language since there was no LTM (Language Training Mission) or MTC (Missionary Training Center) to accelerate language preparation.

After just two months in the field, I was assigned to serve in the beautiful city of Cuernavaca, Morelos, with my senior companion, Elder Bradshaw, who had been in the field just one month longer than I. We were both struggling to unravel what people were saying. They spoke so rapidly that what we heard was like one long, continuous word. Understanding was one thing, but being able to express ourselves was yet another. We were struggling, working, and praying for help to become more competent and comfortable with the language and the message.

We had been out all day, attempting with our very limited Spanish to find someone who would listen to what we had to say. No one had responded. Discouraged and in a gloomy rain, we returned to our apartment, located immediately across the street from the largest Catholic church in the city. There, tacked to the door, we found a note which informed us that as "Mormons" we were not welcome in that city and that for our own safety we should leave as soon as possible.

I went in and slumped down, sitting on the side of my bed. A flood of depressing thoughts and questions went through my mind—what was I doing so far away from home? Even though we had a very important message, no one wanted to hear it, and besides, they spoke a language I was just beginning to speak and understand. We weren't even welcome. Rather than wasting my time here, wouldn't it be better if I were back at the university or home helping Dad on the farm?

I had my triple combination in my hands, and it fell open to Alma chapter 29. The first verses met my gaze, and I read: "O that I were an angel, and could have the wish of mine heart, that I might go forth and speak with the trump of God, with a voice to shake the earth, and cry repentance unto every people! Yea, I would declare unto every soul, as with the voice of thunder [*especially to those inhospitable folks who had written that note!*] repentance and the plan of redemption, that they should repent and come unto our God, that there might not be more sorrow upon all the face of the earth." That was exactly how I felt! Then my eyes fell upon these words: "But behold, I am a man, and do sin in my wish; for I ought to be content with the things which the Lord hath allotted unto me" (Alma 29:1–3).

That was all it took. Then and there, I decided I really *ought to be content with the things the Lord had allotted to me.* From that moment on, I was never discouraged or homesick again. The Book of Mormon's message had changed me for the better—not only for my mission but in many situations in my life since. My whole outlook changed. I committed to being grateful and *content with the things the Lord has allotted to me.*

A few days later, things in our missionary lives began to look up. We met the Jesús Franco family. They listened, and the messages of the gospel and the Book of Mormon touched their hearts. The whole family was baptized. Brother Franco eventually became the branch president, and years later he was ordained to be the first patriarch in their newly created stake. Since then, the message of the Book of Mormon has changed the hearts of many people in Cuernavaca, Morelos, where there are now multiple stakes. That area is the headquarters for one of the newest established missions in the Church.

In August 2005, President Gordon B. Hinckley issued the challenge to all members of the Church to read the Book of Mormon before the end of the year. Near the end of December, several members of the Church were on a Delta Airlines flight returning from their business trips to the East and obviously were attempting to meet the goal of finishing their reading of the Book of Mormon before midnight on New Year's Eve. A flight attendant passed by one of them and said, "I don't know what it is that you all are reading, but those other guys back there are ahead of you."

Now, if we can conservatively assume that just 25 percent of the members of the Church, or one out of four, met President Hinckley's challenge and read the Book of Mormon, that would mean approximately three million members of the Church fulfilled the goal. Susan Easton Black's careful research calculated there are 3,925 references to the Savior in the Book of Mormon. That means on average there is a reference to the Lord every 1.7 verses.[4] If three million members fulfilled the reading assignment, then as a Church we were exposed to about twelve billion references to the Savior, His teachings, His personal ministry, and His revelations to His New World prophets in that six-month period. That could only be a plus to the Church and to the reinforcement in the minds of members that the Book of Mormon is literally another witness that Jesus is the Christ.

## PRESIDENT BENSON'S EMPHASIS

In President Ezra Taft Benson's first general conference address given after he was sustained as President of the Church in 1986, I was impressed with the emphasis he placed on the Book of Mormon. He said: "There is a book we need to study daily, both as individuals and as families, namely the Book of Mormon. I love that book. It is the book that will get a person nearer to God by abiding by its precepts than any other book. (See Book of Mormon, Introduction.) President [Marion G.] Romney recommended studying it half an hour each day. I commend that practice to you. I've always enjoyed reading the scriptures and do so on a daily basis individually and with my beloved wife."[5]

Near the end of his address he mentioned, "The Lord inspired His servant Lorenzo Snow to reemphasize the principle of tithing to redeem the Church from financial bondage. In those days the General Authorities took that message to the members of the Church. Now, in our day, the Lord has revealed the need to reemphasize the Book of Mormon to get the Church and all the children of Zion out from under condemnation—the scourge and judgment. (See D&C 84:54–58.) This message must be carried to the members of the Church throughout the world."[6]

I thought it likely that in President Benson's next conference address he might place emphasis on the Doctrine and Covenants or on the New Testament. But what did he do? He gave another powerful address on the Book of Mormon. We should read that address again and again. In it he said: "My beloved brethren and sisters, today I would like to speak about one of the most significant gifts given to the world in modern times. The gift I am thinking of is more important than any of the inventions that have come out of the industrial and technological revolutions. This is a gift of greater value to mankind than even the many wonderful advances we have seen in modern medicine. It is of greater worth to mankind than the development of flight or space travel. I speak of the gift of the Book of Mormon."[7]

He went on to say: "In 1832, as some early missionaries returned from their fields of labor, the Lord reproved them for treating the Book of Mormon lightly. As a result of that attitude, he said, their minds had been darkened. Not only had treating this sacred book lightly brought a loss of light to themselves, it had also brought the whole Church under condemnation, even all the children of Zion. And then the Lord said, 'And they shall remain under this condemnation until they repent and remember the new covenant, even the Book of Mormon' (D&C 84:54–57)."

He then asked, "Has the fact that we have had the Book of Mormon with us for over a century and a half made it seem less significant to us today?"[8] And he clarified: "The Book of Mormon is . . . the keystone of the doctrine of the Resurrection. . . . The Lord Himself has stated that the Book of Mormon contains the 'fulness of the gospel of Jesus Christ' (D&C 20:9). That does not mean it contains every teaching, every doctrine ever revealed. Rather, it means that in the Book of Mormon we will find the fulness of those doctrines required for our salvation."[9]

We have the book. We are also under condemnation if we do not take it seriously and do all we personally can to apply literally in our lives those precepts contained in the Book of Mormon. We must do this if we are to achieve our ultimate goal of salvation and exaltation.

We live in a world in which we witness much of the "carnal,

sensual, and devilish" nature of so many (Alma 42:10). The media is awash with immoral and violent images. Conflicts and bloodshed are common throughout the world. Christianity is being attacked from all sides. Abortion has depreciated the value of life. Traditional marriage and the family are being attacked on many fronts. Heinous sexual transgressions occur, and many of them are condoned by a public devoid of conscience. War, poverty, genocide, and starvation plague millions around the world. The list could go on and on.

The Book of Mormon has come to us at a critical time in this world's existence. We need all the help we can get on a personal and worldwide scale. This sacred record already helps millions at the deepest level of our personal, practical needs, and I hope in the future its influence will be greatly expanded.

## VALUE TO MEMBERS TODAY

I tried an experiment. I know what the Book of Mormon means to me in my life. I decided that it would be interesting to conduct an informal poll. So I requested that more than one hundred member friends and acquaintances respond to a simple questionnaire: "Please indicate at least one of the scriptures, doctrines, teachings, or experiences you have had with the Book of Mormon that you feel has helped you draw closer to the Lord or to have improved your life."

The responses were enlightening to me for a variety of reasons. There was such a wide diversity in the verses or portions of the Book of Mormon that have had a positive impact in the lives of readers. Their responses came from expected and unexpected areas of the book. It was as though a person could be moved or affected at a life-changing level from something on almost any page in the Book of Mormon.

One of the respondents and her husband had a severe economic disaster, potential loss of their home, and a family member with a life-threatening disease. With permission, I share some of what she wrote of her experience with Mosiah 7:32–33, where she read, "And now, behold, the promise of the Lord is fulfilled, and ye are smitten and afflicted." This family surely was smitten and afflicted. She read on: "But if ye will turn to the Lord with full purpose of heart, and put your trust in him, and serve him with all diligence of mind, if ye do this, he

will, according to his own will and pleasure, deliver you out of bondage."
She wrote:

> That scripture has sustained me during one of the
> lowest points of my life, when things seemed to come crushing
> in on us. Because of the promise in verse 32, I "turned to
> the Lord with full purpose of heart," with absolute confidence,
> and, unconditionally, I "put my trust in him" and tried to serve
> him with "all diligence of mind" and with all my heart and every
> fiber of my being. I relied on the hope that "if ye do this, he will,
> according to his own will and pleasure, deliver you out of
> bondage."
>
> I have felt and seen the fulfillment of this promise, because
> I have felt of His love for us and received the knowledge that
> He is *always* there. I love the Lord with all my heart, and I will
> be forever a debtor, not only for delivering us out of our
> bondage, but primarily for His infinite Atonement. This is my
> testimony.

A sister whose husband walked out on their temple marriage for
another woman, leaving her and their children, wrote about her experience with Nephi's soliloquy in 2 Nephi 4:15–35:

> Each time I read it, the Spirit washes over me and I come
> away feeling my courage refreshed and my commitment
> renewed. When I first read this, I felt that I had been heard—
> not just by our Heavenly Father and Jesus—but somehow, I felt
> that Nephi knew my heart and my feelings. I suppose that the
> comfort I receive from reading his words is much like the com-
> fort he describes in reading the words of Isaiah. . . . Each time I
> read this passage, I realize that everyone struggles—even
> prophets. I see his example of how to pick yourself up out of
> the mire of self-pity and to throw yourself into self-
> improvement. I come away with a desire to be great like Nephi
> was.

She went on to mention her experience with a verse, 2 Nephi 2:2,
which reads, "Nevertheless, Jacob, my first-born in the wilderness, thou

knowest the greatness of God; *and he shall consecrate thine afflictions for thy gain*" (emphasis added). She wrote:

> My mother-in-law brought this to my attention. She had gone through a serious illness for which she was hospitalized. She said one day in the early morning hours she awoke and couldn't sleep. She had a bad feeling and wanted some comfort. She found the copy of the Book of Mormon in her room and flipped it open to read. This verse came to her, and she realized that there must surely be something important for her to learn and that it would be for her gain, just as Jacob's afflictions were to him. She shared this with me because it was the summer when my divorce from her son was happening, and I was truly wondering, "Why me?" "Why this?" "Why now?" and so on. This scripture brought such indescribable peace to my soul. I was led to remember and recognize that Heavenly Father knows me. He knows my trials and consecrates them specifically for my gain. I got a sense of holiness about them. It's not always easy to think of trials in that way, but it always helps when I do.

One of the responses came from a distinguished scientist who had been trained in physics and chemistry at the University of Utah, under the tutelage of Dr. Henry B. Eyring. He then went to the East, where he worked for a leading corporation and became responsible for the work of more than two hundred PhD-level research scientists. He wrote:

> In my early life as a budding scientist, I was constantly challenged by my nonmember colleagues with what they conceived to be the conflicts between science and religion. I had a hard time explaining to them why my scientific training strengthened my belief and why their training destroyed theirs. On several occasions well-known scientists expressed to me privately a desire to believe as I did but professed that their intellectual and cultural upbringings were insurmountable barriers. I found it difficult to explain in scientific terms why I had a testimony of

the gospel and they did not, so I often resorted to citing evidence of the miracles of life and the majesty of the underlying laws of chemistry and physics. These citations proved to be interesting but insufficient to satisfy either me or my fellow scientists. Somehow the key to true belief was missing.

Then one day I came upon these words of the Lord, recorded by Moroni in Ether 4:13–14: "Come unto me, O ye Gentiles, and I will show unto you the greater things, the knowledge which is hid up because of unbelief."

This logically led to the question—unbelief in what? Unbelief in what I had told them? Unbelief in the temporal evidences supporting the scriptures? No, much more than that, as is made clear in the next verse:

"Come, unto me, O ye house of Israel, and it shall be made manifest unto you how great things the Father hath laid up for you, from the foundation of the world; and it hath not come unto you, because of unbelief."

Here was the key! The starting point for a testimony of the gospel is the first principle of the gospel, "faith in the Lord Jesus Christ." This principle is as inviolate as the law of gravity. Defy it and the result is predictable—darkness and unbelief. Follow it and that knowledge hid by unbelief will be revealed.

What he learned from the Book of Mormon helped sustain him and helped him achieve success in his profession, in his family, and in many significant Church callings.

Of the dozens of meaningful responses, here is just one more from a returned mission president about how as a youth he received a confirmation from the Spirit:

The passage that stands out in my experience is 3 Nephi 17, especially verses 13–22. It was as a teenager that I first read the entire Book of Mormon and prayed to receive a testimony. While I was reading this passage, the Spirit witnessed to me that this experience of the Savior with the Nephite people actually happened and was so real that I felt that I was present. I also realized that the reason what happened could not be recorded was that you had to feel it more than hear or see it. I felt that experience and have felt the witness of the Spirit in much the same way each time I have read the Book of Mormon ever since.

The Book of Mormon teaches powerfully, covering a broad range of precepts and doctrines. A presentation such as this can include only a few of a multitude of helpful precepts and doctrines from the Book of Mormon that can help us draw nearer to God. I would like to mention five particular areas.

### 1. Doctrines Resolving the Question "How Are We Saved?"

The Book of Mormon provides us with motivational precepts that help us draw nearer to God. We need to recognize that the Book of Mormon provides any serious student with monumental cognitive, intellectual, and rational insights that provide answers to many of the age-old theological debates—for example, the significant theological question "How are we saved?"

Different answers to this question have caused much dissension and bloodshed over the centuries among those who consider themselves to be Christian. Vestiges of the conflict between Catholics and Protestants exist even to this day in various parts of the world.

The Roman Catholics have essentially taught that for man to be saved, God's saving grace is communicated to man exclusively through the "good offices" of the authorized church that include the sacraments (ordinances) rightly administered by their clergy.

In contrast, Martin Luther, along with others interested in reform, protested against the position that salvation came through the priests, sacraments, indulgences, and "good offices," or works, of the church. He believed and taught that no one stood between a person and the Lord, that every man was his own priest. Of the Apostle Paul's epistles, Luther's favorite was that to the Galatians, where we read, "Knowing that a man is not justified by the works of the law, but by the faith of Jesus Christ, even we have believed in Jesus Christ, that we might be justified by the faith of Christ, and not by the works of the law" (Galatians 2:16). Dr. W. Graham Scroggie stated: "Galatians was the battle axe which Luther brought down with terrific and telling force upon the helmets of his foes [in the Catholic Church]."[10]

Regarding this Protestant doctrine of justification by faith, Paul Tillich wrote that it "has divided the old unity of Christendom; has torn asunder Europe, and especially Germany; has made innumerable martyrs; has kindled the bloodiest and most terrible wars of the past; and has deeply affected European history and with it the history of humanity."[11]

How can a person return to the presence of God justified, cleansed, becoming an heir to the highest blessings God has promised to the faithful? Does this come primarily through the authority of the Catholic Church, its priesthood, and the "good offices," or as the Protestants believe, is it a gift that comes strictly as a result of faith and grace? The differences between the Catholic and Protestant theologies as to how we are saved are yet wide and deep. Never could these polar positions be reconciled without the light of additional revelation.

Fortunately, the revelations of Prophet Joseph Smith and the Book of Mormon shed light on this universally divisive question "How are we saved?" For that we should be eternally grateful.

In a most intellectually satisfying way, the Book of Mormon brings together in just one verse the polar differences that have divided Christianity for centuries. Nephi taught: "For we labor diligently to write, to persuade our children, and also our brethren, to believe in Christ, and to be reconciled to God; for we know that *it is by grace that we are saved,* after all we can do" (2 Nephi 25:23; emphasis added).

Yes, we are saved by the grace of God and do not "earn" salvation, regardless of how many good works we may do. But Nephi included that very important clause: "after all we can do." Our good works, or "all we can do," demonstrate that we are willing to work for and receive the salvation that is offered to us by divine grace.

King Benjamin emphasized the relative position of grace and works in his well known, moving discourse: "I say unto you that if ye should serve him who has created you from the beginning, and is preserving you from day to day, by lending you breath, that ye may live and move and do according to your own will, and even supporting you from one moment to another—I say, if ye should serve him with all your whole souls [that is, do all the good works] yet ye would be unprofitable servants" (Mosiah 2:21).

Even if we served Him with all our whole souls, we would still receive through grace more than we ever could earn. As this doctrine of salvation by grace—so clearly taught in the Book of Mormon—is better understood by Church members, we may observe greater evidences of humility and have fewer problems of reverence in sacrament meetings. We may sing with even more feeling, "I stand all amazed at the love Jesus offers me."[12]

In our teaching, perhaps we should place less emphasis on the idea that we "work out [our] own salvation" (Philippians 2:12; Mormon 9:27) because that is impossible for a human being to do through his own efforts without receiving God's grace. Thus, our position rationally allows us to agree in part with the emphasis the Catholics place on the importance of priesthood authority and the sacraments (ordinances) of the church *rightly* administered.

At the same time, we agree with the Protestants that salvation (and even exaltation) comes to us by grace as a gift from a loving and merciful Heavenly Father. We can, and must, emphasize the importance of grace and works—or obedience to all the commandments—so that "after all we can do," we demonstrate we are willing to receive the blessed gift of salvation by grace and thereby be privileged to return to the presence of our Heavenly Father.

## 2. Dangers Growing from the Sin of Pride

Repeatedly, the Book of Mormon cautions us to avoid the sin of pride. The Book of Mormon describes several cycles in which the Church, after achieving prosperity, was brought down by the pride of its members. President Benson, C. S. Lewis, and others have said that pride is "the universal sin."[13] That means *every one* of us, to one degree or another, suffers from the problem. No one of us is completely free from its effects, but we must do all in our power to overcome its influence in our lives. No book teaches us more effectively than the Book of Mormon about the need to avoid or overcome the negative influence of pride in our lives.

Times of relative prosperity, such as those we are experiencing in our country at this time, are periods of great danger. In 3 Nephi we read a passage that we could easily liken unto our relatively prosperous time:

> And they began again to prosper and to wax great. . . .
>
> And now there was nothing in all the land to hinder the people from prospering continually, except they should fall into transgression. . . .
>
> And it came to pass that there were many cities built anew, and there were many old cities repaired.
>
> And there were many highways cast up, . . . which led from city to city, and from land to land. . . .
>
> But it came to pass . . . there began to be some disputings among the people; and some were lifted up unto pride and boastings because of their exceedingly great riches, yea, even unto great persecutions;
>
> For there were many merchants in the land, and also many lawyers, and many officers.
>
> And the people began to be distinguished by ranks, according to their riches and their chances for learning; yea, some were ignorant because of their poverty, and others did receive great learning because of their riches.
>
> Some were lifted up in pride. . . .
>
> And thus there became a great inequality in all the land, insomuch that *the church began to be broken up.* (3 Nephi 6:4–5, 7–8, 10–14; emphasis added)

It appears that prosperity and peace were destroyed by the disruptive effects of human pride no less than thirty times throughout the Book of Mormon.

Opportunities for education and training, our relative prosperity, and a stratified society make overcoming inappropriate pride a genuine challenge. Our cup of advantages is very full, and as the English proverb states, "A full cup must be carried steadily."

Just after finishing graduate school, I was visiting with an acquaintance. He was much older—probably twice my age. Earlier in his career he had gone back east to a major university and received some graduate training from a few of the scholars in his field. In the course of our conversation, my friend criticized leaders of the Church and some of the policies that he felt should long since have been changed. Then he said the words that still ring in my memory; "You see, Joe, *I* am an intellectual."

In my experience, the genuine intellectual does not need to announce it. Since that time, my friend spent his life on the fringe, speaking, writing, and associating with those who felt they knew more than designated Church leaders. His criticism negatively affected his wife, their children, and their grandchildren.

In my mind, he seemed to become an incarnation of the attitude Nephi described: "O that cunning plan of the evil one! O the vainness, and the frailties, and the foolishness of men! When they are learned they think they are wise, and they hearken not unto the counsel of God, for they set it aside, supposing they know of themselves, wherefore, their wisdom is foolishness and it profiteth them not. And they shall perish. But to be learned is good *if they hearken unto the counsels of God*" (2 Nephi 9:28–29; emphasis added).

Therein lies a challenge for all of us who have received the opportunities of higher education to avoid becoming trapped by the sin of pride. Succumbing to it could cause us to perish spiritually.

Robert J. McCracken wrote:

> If we make a listing of our sins, . . . [pride] is the one that heads the list, breeds all the rest, and does more to estrange us from our neighbors or from God than any evil we can commit. . . .
>
> In this aspect, it is not only the worst of the seven deadly sins; it is the parent sin, the one that leads to every other, the sin from which no one is free. . . .
>
> Pride of rank—the delight taken in status, recognition, honors, in being at the head of the table, the top of the line. . . . Pride of intellect—the arrogance that thinks it knows more than it does, forgets the finiteness of the human mind, talks in terms of morons, smiles at the cultural crudity of contemporaries, and needs to be told what Madame Foch said to one of her sons who was boasting about a school prize: "Cleverness

which has to be mentioned does not exist." Pride of power—the passion to achieve it, to wield more and more of it, to feel superior to others, to give orders with a strident voice and move men about like pawns on a chessboard.[14]

Pride creeps up on us because as human beings we have a remarkable capacity to fall under its influence even when we think we are in the safest of religious settings. A Carthusian monk who was explaining his monastic order to an inquirer said: "When it comes to good works, we don't match the Benedictines; as to preaching, we are not in a class with the Dominicans; the Jesuits are away ahead of us in learning; but in the matter of humility, we're tops."[15]

Even in Church callings there can be danger. We may fall into the trap of aspiring to some position or another. That would be almost like praying, "Father, I want to serve. Use me—in an executive position!" Remember that even the greatest of all—our Savior, Redeemer, and the Creator of worlds without number—set the example of humble service by kneeling and washing His disciples' feet (see John 13). Where we serve does not matter. How we serve matters a great deal.

Many become desirous of being in a position of honor or recognition. I think of the example Nephi set for all of us in terms of humility and not seeking positions of honor. When the Savior appeared to the Nephites at Bountiful, He invited the multitude to come forward one by one and feel His side and the nail prints in His hands and feet so they could receive a tangible witness that He was literally resurrected. He then asked for Nephi, who had not elbowed his way to the front of the group. Where was Nephi? We read: "And it came to pass that he spake unto Nephi (for Nephi was among the multitude) and he commanded him that he should come forth. And Nephi arose and went forth, and bowed himself before the Lord and did kiss his feet" (3 Nephi 11:18–19).

It is always better to be invited to take a place of recognition or honor rather than to assume that we should be there. Book of Mormon precepts teach that we can become overly concerned about organizations we belong to, which side of town we live on, the size of our home, how much money we have, what race or nationality we are, what kind of car we drive, what church we belong to, how much education we have been privileged to acquire, what we wear, and so on. How many times do we read in the Book of Mormon about the spiritually negative consequences of wearing "fine-twined linen" and "costly apparel"? (see Jacob 2:13; Alma 4:6; 5:53). We should place our concern on simple, less worldly things. In our mercenary and materialistic society, we could also learn from what Henry David Thoreau said: "My greatest skill has been to want but little."[16] Precepts taught in the Book of Mormon, more than in any other book, help us overcome these spiritually destructive tendencies of pride.

### 3. The Need to Defend Values, Even to Bloodshed If Necessary

President Benson clearly indicated that one of the reasons we must focus on the Book of Mormon is that "it was written for our day. The Nephites never had the book; neither did the Lamanites of ancient times. It was meant for us. Mormon wrote near the end of the Nephite civilization. Under the inspiration of God, who sees all things from the beginning, he abridged centuries of records, choosing the stories, speeches, and events that would be most helpful to us."[17]

The prophet Mormon abridged many of the Nephite records. With divine guidance, he selected and included those portions of the records that would be most valuable to us in our day.

Frankly, in some of my readings of the Book of Mormon, I would get a little tired of the many pages on the wars between the Nephites and the Lamanites. However, the last time Barbara and I read the Book of Mormon, those turbulent times had more relevance for me in our turbulent, war-torn world today.

Approximately one out of every ten pages of the Book of Mormon deals with the life and times of Captain Moroni, which we read in Alma chapters 43–63. Basically, these were times of war. They were times when enemies arose who wanted to kill those who followed Christ and to wipe them from the face of the earth. There are those in the world today who would like to do the same to us.

Captain Moroni was inspired to know that values of inestimable worth must be preserved, even if it means fighting a defensive war to protect them—even if it means giving up our very lives: "Inasmuch as ye are not guilty of the first offense, neither the second, *ye shall not suffer yourselves to be slain by the hands of your enemies.* And again, the Lord has said that: *Ye shall defend your families even unto bloodshed.* Therefore for this cause were the Nephites contending with the Lamanites, to defend themselves, and their families, and their lands, their country, and their rights, and their religion" (Alma 43:46–47; emphasis added).

We live in a time of prophesied wars and rumors of war. Moroni clearly saw our day and prophesied, "And there shall also be heard of wars, rumors of wars, and earthquakes in divers places" (Mormon 8:30). The Lord, through the Prophet Joseph in our dispensation, made it very clear that "in that day shall be heard of wars and rumors of wars, and the whole earth shall be in commotion, and men's hearts shall fail them" (D&C 45:26). The Lord also said, "And thus, with the sword and by bloodshed the inhabitants of the earth shall mourn; and with famine, and plague, and earthquake, and the thunder of heaven, and the fierce and vivid lightning also, . . . until the consumption decreed hath made a full end of all nations" (D&C 87:6).

The messages contained in the Book of Mormon help prepare our minds and hearts to cope with an era when wars are being fought in many parts of the world. We learn that our challenges are to stand in holy places and to remain firm in defending those values which are more precious than our mortal lives themselves.

## 4. The Need for Heroes Today

The most powerful precepts are taught through the exemplary lives of righteous, capable, and heroic individuals. No other volume of scripture provides us with so many exemplary lives after which to pattern our own as does the Book of Mormon. Example, for good or ill, is the most powerful of precepts. As Ralph Waldo Emerson said, "Who you are speaks so loudly I can't hear what you're saying."

For many, we live in a world lacking genuine heroes. It is has been noted that we live in "a cynical age [which] now accepts the tarnished coin of celebrity in place of heroic virtue."[18] Our young people today need heroes who go beyond the popular rock stars, musicians, comedians, great athletes, the rich, and the famous. They, and all of us, need to come to know of heroic characters such as those in the Book of

Mormon, whose influence will live long after the applause for those who are currently popular has faded away.

Retired brigadier general Joe Foss, a recipient of the Congressional Medal of Honor, said, "America needs a new generation of heroes, . . . people who are ruled by a conscience that doesn't take the Ten Commandments lightly, who have a fundamental reverence for their Creator, and a respect for the people and things He has created."[19]

Anyone who has really studied the Book of Mormon will never lack for heroes to emulate. In fact, a book entitled *Heroes from the Book of Mormon* highlights many individuals' lives, including Nephi, Jacob, Enos, King Benjamin, Abinadi, the two Almas, Captain Moroni, Mormon, and Mormon's son, Moroni.

In this book, Elder Russell M. Nelson summarizes Nephi, the son of father Lehi, as one of the genuine heroes of the Book of Mormon: "Nephi was a multifaceted genius. Endowed with great physical stature, he was a prophet, teacher, ruler, colonizer, builder, craftsman, scholar, writer, poet, military leader, and father of nations. Nephi had a sincere desire to know the mysteries of God. He became a special witness and trusted prophet of the Lord."[20]

And Mormon, describing Captain Moroni, recorded, "If all men had been, and were, and ever would be, like unto Moroni, behold, the very powers of hell would have been shaken forever; yea, the devil would never have power over the hearts of the children of men" (Alma 48:17).

Of the prophet Moroni, who delivered the plates to the Prophet Joseph, President Gordon B. Hinckley wrote, "Of all the characters who walk the pages of the Book of Mormon, none stands a greater hero, save Jesus only, than does Moroni, son of Mormon."[21]

### 5. Our Ultimate Objective: Come unto Christ and Be Perfected in Him

I remember years ago being impressed by a statement made by Truman G. Madsen: "'To be or not to be?' That is *not* the question." The reality is that a part of us is coeternal with God. We are, we live, and we *do* exist. As Brother Madsen went on to say: "What *is* the question? The question is not one of being, but of becoming. 'To become more or not to become more.' This is the question faced by each intelligence in our universe."[22]

What is our ultimate objective? What can we progress to become? What did the Savior mean when He included in the Sermon on the Mount the statement "Be ye therefore perfect, even as your Father which is in heaven is perfect"? (Matthew 5:48). Some scholars claim that when the Savior taught, He often used hyperbole, or exaggeration, to dramatize His demands.[23]

Such interpretations are not found in Elder James E. Talmage's *Jesus the Christ.* Elder Talmage notes, "Our Lord's admonition to men to become perfect, even as the Father is perfect (Matt. 5:48) cannot rationally be construed otherwise than as implying the possibility of such achievement."[24]

Likewise, in *Mormon Doctrine,* Elder Bruce R. McConkie indicates that "any being who becomes perfect—'*even as your Father which is in heaven is perfect*' (Matt. 5:48), that is who has the kind and extent of perfection enjoyed by Deity—must be like God."[25]

So rather than interpreting the Lord's statement in Matthew 5:48 as exaggerated idealism or scriptural hyperbole, we should believe the Lord meant what He said. Our goal is to become perfect, even as our Father in Heaven is perfect. We will not achieve that end in mortality, but through the divine principle of eternal progression we can!

Many outside our faith consider such doctrine blasphemy, but the Book of Mormon helps to clarify the issue. When the Lord appeared in the Western Hemisphere, He reiterated much of the Sermon on the Mount, and in 3 Nephi 12:48 we read, "Therefore I would that ye should be perfect *even as I,* or your Father who is in heaven is perfect" (emphasis added).

Clearly, to achieve such a lofty goal, we need to change our hearts. We need to lose the disposition to do evil, like those who listened to King Benjamin's address (see Mosiah 5:1–2). We need to become the kind of people the Lord intends us to become, as indicated in that rhetorical question He asked of His Nephite disciples: "Therefore, what manner of men ought ye to be? Verily I say unto you, *even as I am*" (3 Nephi 27:27; emphasis added). In other words, we need to do more than just go through the motions and do the works, but literally to *become* as He is.

In a powerful general conference address entitled "The Challenge to Become," Elder Dallin H. Oaks stressed that more is required than just doing a quantity of good works. We must literally be changed—born again. We must *become* what our Heavenly Father desires us to become.[26] Elder Oaks then used a parable to make his point:

> A wealthy father knew that if he were to bestow his wealth upon a child who had not yet developed the needed wisdom and stature, the inheritance would probably be wasted. The father said to his child:
>
> "All that I have I desire to give you—not only my wealth, but also my position and standing among men. That which I *have* I can easily give you, but that which I *am* you must obtain for yourself. You will qualify for your inheritance by learning what I have learned and by living as I have lived. I will give you the laws and principles by which I have acquired my wisdom and stature. Follow my example, mastering as I have mastered, and you will become as I am, and all that I have will be yours."[27]

To become like our Savior and Father in Heaven is the goal of every committed Latter-day Saint. The knowledge of such potential is motivational and makes each day of life more purposeful. That is an idea that merits much more time, effort, thought, and discussion—even a lifetime and on into the eternities.

More than any other book, the Book of Mormon invites us to come unto Christ. As Moroni wrote, "Come unto Christ, and be perfected in him, and deny yourselves of all ungodliness; and if ye shall deny yourselves of all ungodliness, and love God with all your might, mind and strength, then is his grace sufficient for you, that by his grace ye may be perfect in Christ; and if by the grace of God ye are perfect in Christ, ye can in nowise deny the power of God" (Moroni 10:32).

In the last verse of the Book of Mormon, Moroni records: "And now I bid unto all, farewell. I soon go to rest in the paradise of God, until my spirit and body shall again reunite, and I am brought forth triumphant through the air, to meet you before the *pleasing* bar of the great

Jehovah, the Eternal Judge of both quick and dead" (Moroni 10:34; emphasis added).

I am confident that if we abide by the precepts taught in the Book of Mormon, the meeting before that bar will be much more pleasing than if we don't. With President Brigham Young, "I feel like shouting Hallelujah, all the time, when I think that I ever knew Joseph Smith."[28] Through the inspiration he received, he translated and miraculously brought forth the Book of Mormon, which contains the precepts that can bring us nearer to God than any other book. Of that I am thoroughly convinced and eternally grateful.

---

## NOTES

1. *The Compact Edition of the Oxford English Dictionary* (New York: Oxford University Press, 1987), 2:2271.

2. *The Compact Edition of the Oxford English Dictionary,* 1:5.

3. *The Compact Edition of the Oxford English Dictionary,* 1:5.

4. See Susan Easton Black, *Finding Christ through the Book of Mormon* (Salt Lake City: Deseret Book, 1987), 16.

5. Ezra Taft Benson, in Conference Report, April 1986, 99; or *Ensign,* May 1986, 78.

6. Benson, in Conference Report, April 1986, 100; or *Ensign,* May 1986, 78.

7. Benson, in Conference Report, October 1986, 3; or *Ensign,* November 1986, 4.

8. Benson, in Conference Report, October 1986, 3–4; or *Ensign,* November 1986, 4.

9. Benson, in Conference Report, October 1986, 5; or *Ensign,* November 1986, 5–6.

10. W. Graham Scroggie, as quoted in Sidney B. Sperry, *Paul's Life and Letters* (Salt Lake City: Bookcraft, 1955), 171.

11. Paul Tillich, as quoted in Sperry, *Paul's Life and Letters,* 172.

12. "I Stand All Amazed," *Hymns* (Salt Lake City: The Church of Jesus Christ of Latter-day Saints, 1985), no. 193.

13. Ezra Taft Benson, in Conference Report, April 1989, 6; or *Ensign,* May 1989, 6.

14. Robert J. McCracken, *What Is Sin? What Is Virtue?* (New York: Harper & Row, 1966), 11–13; see also the author's chapter on pride in *To Grow in Spirit* (Salt Lake City: Deseret Book, 1983), 46–53.

15. McCracken, *What Is Sin? What Is Virtue?* 14.

16. Henry David Thoreau, *Walden* (New York: HarperCollins, 2000), 79.

17. Ezra Taft Benson, in Conference Report, October 1986, 5; or *Ensign,* November 1986, 6.

18. Pete Axthelm, as quoted in Joe J. Christensen, "Captain Moroni, an Authentic Hero," in *Heroes from the Book of Mormon* (Salt Lake City: Bookcraft, 1995), 128.

19. Joe Foss, as quoted by Tim Kimmel in the foreword to *Home-Grown Heroes: How to Raise Courageous Kids* (Portland, OR: Multnomah Press, 1992).

20. Russell M. Nelson, "Nephi, Son of Lehi," in *Heroes from the Book of Mormon*, 15.

21. Gordon B. Hinckley, "Moroni," in *Heroes from the Book of Mormon*, 195.

22. Truman G. Madsen, *Eternal Man* (Salt Lake City: Deseret Book, 1966), 31–32.

23. See C. Milo Connick, *Jesus: The Man, the Mission, and the Message*, 2nd ed. (Englewood Cliffs, NJ: Prentice-Hall, 1974), 261. In making this observation, Connick cites Harvey K. McArthur, *Understanding the Sermon on the Mount* (Westport, CT: Greenwood Press, 1940), 105–27.

24. James E. Talmage, *Jesus the Christ*, 3rd ed. (Salt Lake City: Deseret Book, 1916), 248.

25. Bruce R. McConkie, *Mormon Doctrine*, 2nd ed. (Salt Lake City: Bookcraft, 1966), 568.

26. See Dallin H. Oaks, in Conference Report, October 2000, 40–44; or *Ensign*, November 2000, 32–34.

27. Oaks, in Conference Report, October 2000, 41; or *Ensign*, November 2000, 32.

28. Brigham Young, *Discourses of Brigham Young*, comp. John A. Widtsoe (Salt Lake City: Bookcraft, 1954), 458.

## 2

# USING THE BOOK OF MORMON TO MEET TODAY'S CHALLENGES

## Clyde J. Williams

After more than thirty-two years of teaching and studying the Book of Mormon, I have gained a profound appreciation for the importance of this book in preparing us to meet the challenges of our day. Several Book of Mormon prophets left us clues indicating awareness that their writings would be very important for people of another time. While Mormon is credited with editing this work, he specifically told us, "I, Mormon, do write the things which have been commanded me of the Lord" (3 Nephi 26:12). Moreover, Mormon said of his impression to include the small plates of Nephi, "The Lord knoweth all things which are to come; wherefore, he worketh in me to do according to his will" (Words of Mormon 1:7). Nephi knew the Lord would preserve his words to go forth "from generation to generation as long as the earth shall stand" (2 Nephi 25:22). Therefore, he counseled all Israel, not just his own people, to liken the scriptures unto themselves that they might have hope (see 1 Nephi 19:23–24).

Writing after his people were destroyed, Moroni spoke to us personally, explaining, "I speak unto you as though I spake from the

*Clyde J. Williams is a professor of ancient scripture at Brigham Young University.*

dead; for I know that ye shall have my words" (Mormon 9:30). On another occasion he declared why he knew so much about the latter days and those who would live at that time: "Behold, the Lord hath shown unto me great and marvelous things concerning that which must shortly come, at that day when these things shall come forth among you. Behold, I speak unto you as if ye were present, and yet ye are not. But behold, Jesus Christ hath shown you unto me, and I know your doing" (Mormon 8:34–35). Clearly, Moroni knew that we would need to learn to be more wise than his people had been (see Mormon 9:31).

Prophets and apostles have counseled us how to use the Book of Mormon. In April 1986, President Ezra Taft Benson pleaded: "I would particularly urge you to read again and again the Book of Mormon and *ponder* and *apply* its teachings. . . . [One] who knows and loves the Book of Mormon, who has read it several times, who has an abiding testimony of its truthfulness, and who *applies its teachings* will be able to stand against the wiles of the devil and will be a mighty tool in the hands of the Lord."[1]

At the Mexico City Temple dedication in 1983, Elder Richard G. Scott had what he described as "one of those singular experiences that readjusts the course of a life."[2] Having been impressed with profound feelings about the Book of Mormon he said, "It is not sufficient that we should treasure the Book of Mormon, nor that we testify that it is of God. We must *know* its truths, *incorporate* them into our lives, and *share* them with others."[3] President Benson added: "If they [the Book of Mormon writers] saw our day and chose those things which would be of greatest worth to us, is not that how we should study the Book of Mormon? We should constantly ask ourselves, 'Why did the Lord inspire Mormon (or Moroni or Alma) to include that in his record? What lesson can I learn from that to help me live in this day and age?'"[4]

Our charge is not only to read and understand the scriptures but, more importantly, to apply them to the social, emotional, and spiritual challenges of our day. As parents, teachers, and individuals, we will find the Book of Mormon useful in a variety of settings and on virtually every major issue we may face. What follows is a discussion of how the truths of the Book of Mormon can help us face issues today.

## CHALLENGES WITHIN THE FAMILY

*Siblings*

Many families have or will face the challenges associated with sibling rivalries or quarrels. Several helpful lessons can be learned from the Book of Mormon. When children rebel as did Laman and Lemuel, parents sometimes feel helpless because wayward children cannot be forced to change. Their rebellion brings suffering and challenges to their parents and other siblings. Lehi promised his son Jacob, who had suffered unjustly at the hands of his brothers Laman and Lemuel, that the Lord would "consecrate thine afflictions for thy gain" (2 Nephi 2:2). A belief in this divine principle can help sustain the innocent in times of suffering and trial.

When Nephi frankly forgave his brothers for the terrible things they had done to him (see 1 Nephi 7), he set an example of how family members should treat each other, which is helpful in a time when unwillingness to forgive is the standard. Later in Nephi's life, before he was commanded to leave Laman and Lemuel, he records how he allowed his brothers to "destroy my peace" and let the "evil one have place in my heart" until he was angry with them. Surely, few families could have harder challenges than those presented by Laman and Lemuel (see 2 Nephi 4:27). Yet Nephi responded to discouragement and "slacken[ing of his] strength" by pleading with the Lord for help and remembering all that the Lord had done and could do (see 2 Nephi 4:29–35). Nephi's commitment to trust in the Lord and not the arm of flesh is a worthy example for all who face family stress.

In today's world, with so much abuse and anger occurring in families, we may wonder why the Lord permits tragic things to happen. We can recall that even though Nephi was righteous and faithful, the Lord did not take Laman and Lemuel's agency from them. However, even though Nephi was tied up, mocked, and threatened with death by his brothers, he was sustained by the Lord and given power to overcome his trials (see 1 Nephi 7:17; 17:47–48; 2 Nephi 5:4–5). Nephi's example of dealing with the injustices imposed on him by family members is impressive. He recorded, "I did look unto my God, and I did praise him all the day long; and I did not murmur against the Lord because of mine afflictions" (1 Nephi 18:16). Nephi understood that while the Lord did not take away the agency of his brothers, He still loved him and would help him in his times of trouble.

The Book of Mormon also provides us with positive lessons that come through the influences of righteous siblings. Because of Nephi's faithful example, Lehi could promise his youngest son: "Blessed art thou, Joseph. Behold, thou art little; wherefore hearken unto the words of thy brother, Nephi, and it shall be done unto thee even according to the words which I have spoken" (2 Nephi 3:25). Alma the Younger, who apparently knew he was soon to be "taken up by the Spirit," told his wayward son Corianton to "counsel with [his] elder brothers in [his] undertakings." Alma further reminded him that he stood "in need to be nourished by [his] brothers. And give heed to their counsel" (Alma 45:19; 39:10). The powerful influence of righteous siblings should not be underestimated.

### Parents

When young people see their parents struggle or manifest weakness, what direction does the Book of Mormon provide? A classic lesson may be drawn from Nephi's experience with the broken bow in 1 Nephi 16. With the Liahona recently discovered, the prospect for family unity seemed to be brighter. However, when everyone's bows broke or failed, the family was thrown into a crisis for food. Even Lehi, who felt a sense of responsibility for the whole journey, began to "murmur against the Lord" (1 Nephi 16:20). Nephi's response illustrates the best way for any child to respond. He could have criticized his father for murmuring. He could have questioned the kind of example his father was setting. He could even have determined to take over the spiritual leadership of the family because he might have felt Lehi was suffering from the effects of old age. However, Nephi chose none of these approaches. He simply went to work to prepare a new bow and then ask his father to inquire where he should go to obtain food (see 1 Nephi 16:23). In this manner Lehi was reminded of his responsibility as the spiritual head of their family. It was thus the Lord, as it should have been, who chastised Lehi and provided him correction (see 1 Nephi 16:25).

The danger of failing to heed the counsel of a wise parent is presented in the tragic story of Corianton, who forsook his mission and committed fornication (see Alma 39:2). In contrast, Helaman and Shiblon both followed their father's counsel to "learn of me; for I know that whosoever shall put their trust in God shall be supported in their trials, and their troubles, and their afflictions, and shall be lifted up at the last day" (Alma 36:3). Consequently, their influence for good among their people increased.

In a similar way, Nephi and Lehi remembered their father's counsel, which led them to remember their heritage and to build their lives on the foundation of Christ (see Helaman 5:5–15).

### Individual Testimony and Conviction

The Book of Mormon illustrates that the family can and should be a setting in which individual testimony and conviction can grow and flourish. Some readers of 1 Nephi chapters 1 and 2 might think of Nephi as a young man just following his father without ever questioning. However, 1 Nephi 2:16 helps us see even he had questions and doubts, yet, following his father's example, the resolution of his questions came by having "great desires to know" and by "cry[ing] unto the Lord." Nephi's example is contrasted with Laman and Lemuel, who did not understand the dealings of God, did not believe, and did not seem interested in seeking an answer from the Lord (see 1 Nephi 2:12–13).

After his father's death, Enos recalled how consistently he had listened to his father's words and remembered his teachings, thus leading him to develop a closer relationship with his Father in Heaven (see Enos 1:1, 3). Alma the Younger also indicated that it was eventually his father's words that led him to have a hope in Christ and to make a dramatic change in his life (see Alma 36:17–24).

## CHALLENGES WITH MORALITY AND LOVE

### Dealing with Pornography and Immorality

President Gordon B. Hinckley warned us to avoid pornography as we would a plague. He has described it as a "great disease that is sweeping over the country and over the entire world." He called it a "vicious brew of slime and sleeze."[5] While printed pornography was not the problem in Book of Mormon times, there were still problems with the same passions and resulting improprieties. One of the major sins of Jacob's day was the infidelity of brethren who rationalized their actions using the excesses of David and Solomon as a justification (see Jacob 2:23–24). The effects of unfaithfulness are the same in any society. Jacob described the sorrow, mourning, and suffering that come in the wake of such moral abandonment, including the broken hearts of tender wives and the loss of children's confidence (see Jacob 2:31, 33, 35). We see this same plague today as some parents are unfaithful to their covenants and leave their children wondering about the sacredness of broken temple covenants. Jacob's warning still applies today—that immoral behavior would also lead to a curse on the land (see Jacob 3:3).

Alma warned Corianton of the grievous effects of his immoral conduct. He masterfully balanced emphasis on the seriousness of the transgression with the hope to be found in the Atonement of Christ (see Alma 39:5–7). The sins of murder and adultery both have to do with the giving or taking of life. With adultery or fornication, a child could be brought into the world in unfavorable circumstances and the life of all involved may be severely affected because of these decisions. To tamper with the wellspring of life is to commit a grievous sin. In Alma's counsel to his son were instructions to do several things to avoid repetition of his serious moral transgressions: "Repent and forsake your sins, and go no more after the lusts of your eyes, but cross yourself in all these things. . . . Counsel with your elder brothers. . . . Acknowledge your faults [to those you have offended]. . . . And seek not after riches nor the vain things of this world" (Alma 39:9–10, 13–14). To "cross yourself" means to stop, cancel, and erase the effects of inappropriate behavior from one's life.[6]

In His sermon at the temple in Bountiful, the Savior established the higher law among the Nephites. In doing so, He shifted the focus from outward actions—such as killing or adultery—to the thoughts preceding such actions (see 3 Nephi 12:27–28). Therefore, we too must move the battleground from outward actions, striving to maintain control of our thoughts and desires. Indeed, President Benson taught that "some of the greatest battles you will face will be fought within the silent chambers of your own soul."[7]

### Helping Victims

Today, as in Jacob's day, we have far too many who are victims of abuse or abandonment. Parents, spouses, siblings, and others perpetrate numerous forms of abuse upon the innocent. I know of no more tender and touching promises to those who have been victimized than the words of the Lord given by Jacob to those in his day who had been victims of immorality or infidelity. The following are eight promises or invitations offered to those who innocently suffer because of the choices or abuses of others.

1. Be pure in heart themselves (see Jacob 3:1).

2. Look to God with firmness of mind (see Jacob 3:1; D&C 6:36; Alma 58:11–12).

3. Pray for help with exceeding faith (see Jacob 3:1).

4. He will console you *in* your afflictions (the Lord generally does not immediately remove afflictions or their causes because of the principle of agency; see Jacob 3:1).

5. Avoid feelings of anger or revenge—the Savior will plead our cause before the Father (see Jacob 3:1).

6. God will send down justice upon those who seek your spiritual destruction (see Jacob 3:1).

7. Receive the pleasing word (scriptures) from the Lord (see Jacob 3:2).

8. Feast upon His love forever—He will not betray you (see Jacob 3:2).

### Repentance and Forgiveness

How does one repent and receive forgiveness when guilty of immorality or other serious sins? The sons of Mosiah forsook their sins and felt the need to repair the injuries they had caused wherever possible (see Mosiah 27:35). A barrier that often faces those who are confronted with the need to repent and receive forgiveness is the question of whether confession to the Lord is sufficient. As a former stake president, I often had individuals who questioned why they must go to their bishop or stake president to confess their sins. They wondered why they couldn't just take care of the matter with the Lord if they were truly sorry.

The Book of Mormon contains the answer. In Mosiah 26, Alma the Elder was struggling with his new assignment as head of all the Church in Zarahemla. He feared he would do wrong as he dealt with the people and their iniquities. The Lord gave Alma the specific pattern that was to be followed. It included confessions to Alma and the Lord and forgiveness by both. Concerning matters that could affect one's standing in the Church, Alma was told by the Lord that "whosoever transgresseth against me, him shall ye judge according to the sins which he has committed; and if he *confess* his sins *before thee* and *me,* and repenteth in the sincerity of his heart, him shall *ye forgive,* and *I will forgive* him also" (Mosiah 26:29; emphasis added). The Lord has established the need for both confession to the priesthood leader and to Him. When the transgressor has had sufficient time to demonstrate to himself, to the priesthood leader, and to the Lord that he has truly repented or forsaken his sin, then the priesthood leader will forgive the individual so far as his standing in the Church is concerned. He may now exercise all the blessings of full membership in the Church. The Lord is the one who bestows the ultimate forgiveness, which includes peace of conscience and spiritual joy.

## Mighty Change

Another important aspect of repentance that the Book of Mormon emphasizes is the "mighty change" that must occur (see Mosiah 27:25–26). After having been taught, warned, and prepared for some time by King Benjamin and many "holy prophets," his people were ready to take upon themselves the name of Christ (Words of Mormon 1:17–18). The scriptures describe their experience as a "mighty change . . . in our hearts, that we have no more disposition to do evil" (Mosiah 5:2). It would be hard to better describe the type of change that must occur in true repentance. It is not, as Mormon witnessed, the sorrow of the "caught" or the damned, who are sad because they cannot sin and still prosper (see Mormon 2:12–13). We see much of this attitude today as people lament, for example, contracting a disease as a result of leading a lifestyle in direct conflict with the laws of God. Instead, they must realize that a mighty change in values is required to bring the blessings of heaven into their lives.

Alma the Younger was prompted to ask the people at Zarahemla if they had experienced the kind of mighty change of heart that their fathers had in the land of Lehi-Nephi and if they had experienced such a feeling, could they feel so now (see Alma 5:13–14, 26). It is also apparent that once one has experienced a mighty change, retaining that spiritual rebirth requires vigilance in keeping the commandments, which many in Zarahemla at that time had failed to do.

### How Can I Know I Am Forgiven?

People often ask how they can know if they are forgiven. President Harold B. Lee told of an experience he and President Marion G. Romney had with a young man who came to them seeking to know that the Lord had truly forgiven him of his past mistakes. President Lee indicated:

> As we pondered for a moment, we remembered King Benjamin's address contained in the book of Mosiah. Here was a group of people who now were asking for baptism, and they said they viewed themselves in their carnal state: "And they all cried aloud with one voice, saying: O have mercy, and apply the atoning blood of Christ that we may receive forgiveness of our sins, and our hearts may be purified. . . . After they had spoken these words the Spirit of the Lord came upon them, and they were filled with joy, having received a remission of their sins, and having peace of conscience" (Mosiah 4:2, 3.) There was the answer. If the time comes when you have done all that you can to repent of your sins, whoever you are, wherever you are, and have made amends and restitution to the best of your ability; if it be something that will affect your standing in the Church and you have gone to the proper authorities, then you will want that confirming answer as to whether or not the Lord has accepted of you. In your soul-searching, if you seek for and you find that peace of conscience, by that token you may know that the Lord has accepted of your repentance.[8]

Thus, Mosiah 4 offers one of the clearest descriptions of what one may expect from the Lord when He has extended forgiveness: a peace of conscience and fulness of joy because of what the Father and the Son have made possible for us.

## What Is Real Love?

The moral condition of the world today calls to mind the question "what is love and how is it perceived?" It would surely puzzle many in the world if they read Alma's counsel to his son Shiblon to bridle his passions so that he can be filled with love (see Alma 38:12). Many in the world would likely say, "No, you unbridle your passions so you can be filled with love." However, this is because many equate love and lust. It is vitally important for the world to understand what love really is and what its source is. Mormon wrote a sobering epistle to his son, Moroni, describing his people as being so angry and hard in their hearts that "the Spirit of the Lord hath ceased striving with them" (Moroni 9:4). He wrote that, as a result, his people had "lost their love, one towards another" (Moroni 9:5). In an earlier epistle to his son, Mormon taught clearly the power and influence that comes from the Holy Ghost, "which Comforter filleth with hope and perfect love, which love endureth by diligence unto prayer, until the end shall come" (Moroni 8:26). To maintain this love, Moroni declared, we must pray with all the energy of heart. He also stated that it is bestowed only on those who are true followers of Jesus Christ (see Moroni 7:48). The lesson to be learned here is that a young person who wants to marry someone who will be faithful and enduring must find one who has the Spirit and desires to maintain that relationship with the Lord. True love is a gift of the Spirit, so some people may never experience this divine gift in this life.

## OTHER PERSONAL AND SOCIAL ISSUES

### Use of the Scriptures

The Book of Mormon is replete with examples of the importance of using the scriptures and the dangers that arise when one does not use them. In Jacob's day, it was their failure to understand the scriptures that led some Nephites to justify serious moral transgressions (see Jacob 2:23). We learn that the people's failure to search the scriptures contributed significantly to the ability of Sherem to lead the people astray (see Jacob 7:3, 23).

We also learn that one reason the city of Ammonihah had gone into such a spiritual decline was that the people and their leaders had begun to "wrest," or distort, the scriptures for their own unrighteous purposes (see Alma 13:20). Only after solemn warnings from Alma and Amulek did some of the people begin to repent and search the scriptures (see Alma 14:1).

Similarly, the Zoramites had been led astray because they had not been searching the scriptures (see Alma 33:2). Perhaps the most devastating doctrinal problem that arose from this failure to search the scriptures was the people's inability to accept and understand the Atonement of Jesus Christ (see Alma 33:14–17). Because of this dilemma, Amulek posed the "great question," whether the word of salvation is in Christ (see Alma 34:5–6). Today, this same great question must be asked when scholars and others have relegated the Old and New Testaments to the realm of fiction.

In light of these illustrations, it is clear that the message from the Book of Mormon is the same given by the Savior near the end of His mortal ministry: "And whoso treasureth up my word shall not be deceived" (Joseph Smith—Matthew 1:37).

## Boasting and Arrogance

We live in a society that is full of boasting and arrogance. This attitude is contradictory to the Spirit of the Lord. The sports and entertainment world is overrun with these negative characteristics. Mormon reminds us that it is man's nature to boast (see Helaman 12:5). He speaks of self-righteous pride, of boasting that often comes when we are victorious, which reflects the attitude of trusting in one's own wisdom and power (see Mosiah 11:19; Mormon 3:9). Such a prevalent attitude was reflected by Korihor when he said, "Every man prospered according to his genius, and that every man conquered according to his strength" (Alma 30:17). In essence, Korihor was the ax boasting of itself and disregarding the one who swings the ax (see 2 Nephi 20:15). Another type of arrogance prevalent in society today comes in the form of youth who decide they know more than their parents and choose to ignore their counsel, as Corianton chose to ignore Alma's counsel to his regret (see Alma 39:2).

## Social Classes

Social classes generally become a characteristic of any society. They are closely associated with pride and arrogance. Class distinctions seem to have been a major disease that brought Nephite society down to destruction (see 3 Nephi 6:12). Even with the Zion society established by Christ among Lehi's descendants, the rise of social classes became a key factor in breaking up the law of consecration that had united the people for over one hundred and sixty years (see 4 Nephi 1:26). It should come as no surprise that many of our current societal problems have their roots in the inequities of class distinctions that thrive in modern societies.

## Appearance and Marking Oneself

In a world where immodesty, extreme appearance, body piercing, and tattooing are prominent, insights from the Book of Mormon are most helpful. From Enos 1:20–23 we learn that one of the signs of the loss of the Spirit is a dramatic change in one's apparel. Often immodesty or other extremes in appearance are manifested. Frequently, those who have lost the Spirit begin to take on outlandish, even fearful-looking attire to intimidate others (see 3 Nephi 4:7). A classic illustration of marking oneself is found in the example of the Amlicites. They did not want to appear as Nephites and "marked themselves with red in their foreheads after the manner of the Lamanites" (Alma 3:4). The modern application of this type of practice is reflected in the sociological principle, "Appearance affects attitude, and then it reflects attitude." Just as these Amlicites began to take on the appearance of the Lamanites, they also began to take on their attitudes. The spiritual principle is, "You can't act like, think like, and dress like the world. It will cost you spiritually."[9]

## CHALLENGES WITH THE PROPER USE OF OUR TIME

### The Sabbath and Worship

The Book of Mormon gives us significant insights in teaching the proper use of the Sabbath and proper worship. In Alma 31:9–25, we learn about Zoramite worship and Sabbath habits. Their prayer was a single, set prayer, offered only once a week and given only in a designated place—the Rameumpton. This prayer was primarily a brief verbal boasting session in which the Zoramites declared their prideful and narrow attitude that they had been "elected" while the rest of humanity was doomed "to be cast by [God's] wrath down to hell" (Alma 31:17). Clearly, these Zoramites worshiped weekly (as well as weakly), never speaking about God until the next Sabbath.

Their misguided worship practices further led them to use their time in many other wasteful and inappropriate ways. They shunned the poor, wore all manner of costly apparel, set their hearts on riches and were lifted up in their pride (see Alma 31:24–28).

Do these sound at all familiar? They are some of the same dangers we experience today. Confining our religious activities and thoughts to only three hours on Sunday, becoming prideful that we are the chosen people, and neglecting the poor while we accumulate material possessions is a real danger for Latter-day Saints today. Religion needs to be a daily concern. Jacob taught his people to "remember the words of your God; pray unto him *continually* by day, and give thanks unto his holy name by night" (2 Nephi 9:52; emphasis added). In further affirmation of this, we need to use more of our time in reflecting on the goodness of God. Amulek counseled that we should "live in thanksgiving daily, for the many mercies and blessings which [God] doth bestow upon you" (Alma 34:38).

## Idleness

Idleness is a pernicious habit that destroys our personal incentive for excellence and progression. Some years ago, I had the opportunity to visit communities in a developing country in Central America. I was struck with the fact that all of the children labored to help in the support of their families. This was starkly contrasted one summer evening when I returned home to see youth who were wandering around aimlessly looking for something to do. While the idle time may have seemed nice to them, I wondered how having so few responsibilities or obligations may eventually affect their character. Nephi described how the Lamanites became an idle people, which led them to be "full of mischief and subtlety" (2 Nephi 5:24). In Alma 1, we find an interesting pairing of words describing those who were becoming wicked. They are described as engaging in "idolatry or idleness" (Alma 1:32). The implication may be that idleness is more than sitting around. It is a compulsive or almost worshipful involvement in things that are vain and of no eternal worth.

As a stake president, I counseled returning missionaries to "refrain from idleness" (Alma 38:12). This can obviously be a danger to missionaries who have been involved in full-time service to the Lord and are then released. They suddenly have much more discretionary time and must make great efforts to use their time wisely and productively. One of the impressive lessons we learn from the people of Ammon, the Anti-Nephi-Lehies, is that their wholehearted acceptance of the gospel led them to turn from a life of "idleness" to "labor[ing] abundantly with their hands" (Alma 24:18).

## DEALING WITH LIFE'S TESTS AND CHALLENGES

In the first verse of the Book of Mormon, Nephi speaks of having suffered many afflictions yet being highly favored of God. How can this be? Similarly, Lehi refers to his travels from Jerusalem as "the wilderness of mine afflictions" (2 Nephi 3:1). To his son Jacob, Lehi had promised that the Lord would "consecrate thine afflictions for thy gain" (2 Nephi 2:2). It becomes apparent from the Book of Mormon that life will have tests and trials in spite of our righteousness or having found favor with God. One of the obvious lessons is that we can grow by overcoming afflictions. However, the Book of Mormon also teaches us that we may also impact to some extent those trials we face.

Describing the difficulty of Lehi's journey, Alma noted that the Lord had prepared a way for the journey to be pursued in the most efficient way. However, because "they were slothful, and forgot to exercise their faith and diligence and then those marvelous works ceased, and they did not progress in their journey; therefore, they tarried in the wilderness, or did not travel a direct course, and were afflicted with hunger and thirst, because of their transgressions" (Alma 37:41–42). Alma indicated that the problems Lehi's family experienced had direct application to things that are spiritual. Our journey through life is similar to this Book of Mormon account. How will our journey in life look compared to Lehi's family's journey? Will our path through life look like a straight, steadfast course, or will it be a meandering path with lengthy delays and side trips and ultimately a different destination than we originally intended?

The Book of Mormon is clearly one of the greatest sources we have to prepare us for today's challenges and for exaltation in the kingdom of God. Speaking of using the scriptures to meet the problems we face, President Howard W. Hunter encouraged people "to have confidence in the strength and truths of the scriptures, confidence that their Heavenly Father is really speaking to them through the scriptures, and confidence that they can turn to the scriptures and find answers to their problems and their prayers, . . . [confidence] that the scriptures hold the answers to many—indeed most—of life's problems."[10]

---

NOTES

1. Ezra Taft Benson, "To the 'Youth of the Noble Birthright,'" *Ensign,* May 1986, 43; emphasis added.

2. Richard G. Scott, "True Friends That Lift," *Ensign,* November 1988, 76.

3. Scott, "True Friends That Lift," 76; emphasis added.

4. Ezra Taft Benson, in Conference Report, October 1986, 5.

5. Gordon B. Hinckley, *Teachings of Gordon B. Hinckley* (Salt Lake City: Deseret Book, 1997), 463-64.

6. *Noah Webster's First Edition of An American Dictionary of the English Language,* facsimile of 1828 edition (San Francisco: Foundation for American Christian Education, 1985) includes each of the definitions used.

7. Ezra Taft Benson, *The Teachings of Ezra Taft Benson* (Salt Lake City: Bookcraft, 1988), 401.

8. Harold B. Lee, *The Teachings of Harold B. Lee* (Salt Lake City: Bookcraft, 1996), 119.

9. Boyd K. Packer, Sandy Utah Stake Conference, January 8, 1984, notes in author's possession.

10. Howard W. Hunter, *The Teachings of Howard W. Hunter,* ed. Clyde J. Williams (Salt Lake City: Bookcraft, 1997), 186.

# 3

# GETTING "NEARER TO GOD": A HISTORY OF JOSEPH SMITH'S STATEMENT

## Scott C. Esplin

The Prophet Joseph Smith's statement, "I told the brethren that the Book of Mormon was the most correct of any book on earth, and the keystone of our religion, and a man would get nearer to God by abiding by its precepts, than by any other book,"[1] may be one of his most recognizable quotes. Millions of readers of the Book of Mormon find it in the sixth paragraph of the book's introduction. Hundreds of thousands of general conference participants hear it cited repeatedly from the pulpit.[2] Books, articles, and even entire symposia use it as a theme. However, how many people familiar with the quote understand its context? For example, why did Joseph say what he did regarding the Book of Mormon? Who were "the brethren" to whom he made the statement? What sparked the declaration? How has it been used over time? Answers to these important historical questions help us better appreciate the power and application of Joseph's prophetic statement in our modern day.

---

*Scott C. Esplin is an assistant professor of Church history and doctrine at Brigham Young University.*

## HISTORICAL CONTEXT FOR THE STATEMENT

Putting Joseph Smith's statement in its historical context includes examining the audience, the nature of the surrounding discussion, and the Prophet's original intent. Understanding these things helps the reader appreciate the breadth of the quote's application. Robert J. Matthews observed, "If we examine [the statement] in its historical context, our understanding and appreciation of this declaration will increase, we will be more able to defend it against critics and non-believers, and we will be in a better position to explore the reasons why the Book of Mormon is indeed the 'keystone of our religion.'"[3]

### Audience and Setting

Looking first at its audience, the statement begins with "I told the brethren." Who were the brethren to whom Joseph made this declaration and what was the occasion for their gathering? Examining the context of the original statement reveals these answers. Before the Prophet made the declaration on November 28, 1841, Joseph's history records, "I spent the day in the council with the Twelve Apostles at the house of President [Brigham] Young, conversing with them upon a variety of subjects. Brother Joseph Fielding was present, having been absent four years on a mission to England."[4]

Though the Prophet clearly states where the occasion took place and who was present, some clarification may be necessary. For example, the Brigham Young home mentioned in the statement was not the brick home with which modern visitors to Nauvoo are familiar. That more spacious structure was not completed until 1843. Rather, it was what President Young called his "small unfinished log-cabin, situated on a low, wet lot."[5] This original log home occupied the same block as the later brick structure.[6]

Joseph's statement further records that the assembled meeting was a council with the Twelve Apostles and Joseph Fielding. However, like the location of the Brigham Young home, the actual assemblage needs explanation. Not all of the Twelve Apostles were present. While an exact listing is problematic, we can be certain of a few who were absent from Nauvoo in 1841. For example, Parley P. Pratt was still in Great Britain after his fellow quorum members and mission companions left him to preside over that mission until 1843.[7] At the time of the council meeting, Orson Hyde was on a ship returning from Jerusalem, having fulfilled his mission to the Holy Land.[8] The Prophet's brother William Smith was on a mission to Ohio, Pennsylvania, and New Jersey, gathering funds for the construction of the Nauvoo Temple and Nauvoo House.[9] Finally, John E. Page was presiding over a conference of the Church held in New York City the same weekend.[10] The remaining eight members of the Quorum, namely Brigham Young, Heber C. Kimball, Willard Richards, Orson Pratt, Lyman Wight, John Taylor, Wilford Woodruff, and George A. Smith, were all living in Nauvoo and were likely present.[11] The journal entries of Brigham Young, Willard Richards, and Wilford Woodruff mention the meeting.

Regarding the discussion at this meeting, the Prophet's record simply indicates that they conversed upon "a variety of subjects."[12] Brigham Young adds little detail, merely recording, "Brother Joseph and the Twelve spent the day in council at my house."[13] Willard Richards's daily journal adds the phrase, "law of tything [sic]," apparently one of the topics discussed.[14] Wilford Woodruff gives the greatest detail, calling it an "interesting day."[15] Like Joseph Smith, he also emphasizes the presence of Joseph Fielding, adding that they "saw a number of english [sic] Brethren."[16] He also records nearly word for word Joseph Smith's statement about the Book of Mormon.

### Joseph Fielding's Possible Influence

The presence of Joseph Fielding, as emphasized by both Wilford Woodruff and Joseph Smith, may hold a key to understanding the context of the statement. As noted in the Prophet's record, Elder Fielding had been absent four years preaching the gospel in England. In fact, he had only been in Nauvoo four days.[17] This information immediately precedes Joseph's statement regarding the Book of Mormon, almost as if prompted. Possibly, Joseph Fielding and the British Mission had some tie to Joseph's statement regarding the power of the Book of Mormon.

Joseph Fielding went to his native Great Britain as part of the original British Mission in 1837. Elders Heber C. Kimball and Orson Hyde assigned him to remain, and he presided over the mission from 1838 until the arrival of Brigham Young in April 1840. Though replaced as presiding officer, Elder Fielding continued his missionary labors in England until the Twelve left for Nauvoo in the summer of 1841. Joseph Fielding followed them later that fall, arriving four days before this council. The meeting was likely a missionary reunion of sorts for the group, much like modern missionaries reporting before their leaders. Joseph Fielding's missionary experiences may have been one of the "variety of subjects" discussed by the brethren. If so, it may explain the Prophet's statement regarding the Book of Mormon, especially because the book played a prominent role in Elder Fielding's mission.

The missionary diary of Joseph Fielding emphasizes the importance he placed on the Book of Mormon and its power to bring men "nearer to God."[18] It begins with detailing his own personal conversion with Elder Parley P. Pratt, who "laid before [him] the Ordinances of the Gospel, which were very plain, being perfectly in accordance with the Scriptures, being still more clearly expressed in the Book of Mormon."[19] On his mission, Elder Fielding attempted to use the same pattern, teaching the gospel from the scriptures, especially the Book of Mormon. Early in his preaching, he recorded, "On Sunday Evening I spoke in the Cock Pit on the coming forth of this Work, the first Ministration of the Angel, and of the truth of the Book of Mormon, and it appears that several of the members of the Church were hurt at my setting it on a Level with the Bible. It grieves me to see some of the Church so weak in the Faith of the Church. It is Difficult to bring them to believe in their hearts that God has spoken as in Days of old, and that his Word is as important as it was then."[20] Later, when preaching with John Taylor, Elder Fielding encountered people who wanted proof of the truthfulness of the Book of Mormon. He recorded, "One of them stayed after the others, and I told him about the Book of M [Mormon] & talked to him about their Pride & their Conduct in general, that they were casting away a precious Pearl before they had looked at it."[21]

Another especially poignant experience Joseph Fielding had in bringing men closer to God through the power of the Book of Mormon occurred after the Twelve left England. Before departing for Nauvoo himself, Elder Fielding went on a preaching tour on the Isle of Man. As in earlier missionary experiences, the Book of Mormon was a central part of his message. Following a day of preaching, he recorded,

"Preached in the Morning on 'Beloved now are we the Sons of God,' etc. Had liberty, and the People felt well. In the Eve on Joseph's Dreams and the Book of Mormon. The Lord was with me today, but the Church here are dull."[22]

The inability to impress the people with the message of the Book of Mormon weighed on Elder Fielding. Two weeks later, he recorded in his journal his feelings, including a recommitment to the importance of the Book of Mormon:

> In the Eve I took a Walk on the high Mountain, with a great desire to have some Blessing from Heaven. I have long desired to behold some heavenly Messenger or some Ray of the Glory of God, and have often prayed for it, and often laid and watched for it by night, or stopped on the Road to look for some thing from the Heavenly World. We read of the Saviour, after he had through the Day taught the People, at night [would] go to the Mountain and spend [the] whole Night in Prayer to his Heavenly Father. But I feared lest I should ask for things which were not right, and while seated on the Ground, I opened the Book of Doctrine and Covenants and began to read the Instructions there: to be diligent in the Work of God, to teach from the Book of Mormon, etc. I saw that I had not been giving due heed to that Book, and I felt that I was not prepared to hold that Converse with the Angels as I thought. I began to pray for the Church. I felt humbled before the Lord. I feel indeed a strong desire after him, for he is my God, and my chief Joy.[23]

Recommitted to the converting power of the Book of Mormon, Elder Fielding wrote in his journal the following day: "Preached in the Even here in Douglas. Spoke of the Book of Mormon. Felt well, and the People, too."[24]

## Importance of Abiding

Though the message of the Book of Mormon caused some people to rejoice, others were embittered by it. A portion of Joseph Smith's statement may relate to this. The Prophet stressed that the Book of

Mormon would bring men nearer to God "by abiding by its precepts." Merely hearing the message was not enough; to enjoy the full benefit of the book, the reader must apply it. The Savior taught a similar principle during His ministry in Jerusalem, "If any man will do his will, he shall know of the doctrine, whether it be of God, or whether I speak of myself" (John 7:17). Living the message of the gospel brings conversion. In the Book of Mormon, Alma taught the same idea. Comparing the word of God to a seed, he stressed that nourishing it with faith, diligence, and patience brought forth fruit (see Alma 32:38–43).

Again, this may relate to Joseph Fielding and his experience in Britain. Undoubtedly some members of the Twelve, and possibly even Joseph Smith himself, were familiar with the opposition Elder Fielding experienced on his mission. Time and again, this opposition related to the Book of Mormon. On one occasion, he recorded, "A man named Giles is lecturing against us, the Book of Mormon, etc. He treats us all with great contempt and Ridicule, and often makes his hearers laugh."[25] Later, he continued, "Three different Priests of the Sects were lecturing against us last Sabbath Week. . . . One named Dent, of the Church of England, held up the Book of Mormon to his Congregation as an object of Scorn and laughter. Another named Worrell of the Methodists, did the same, calling us imposters."[26]

The opposition was especially strong from Joseph Fielding's brother James. Initially friendly to the missionaries, the relationship soured as James's Primitive Episcopal congregation increasingly left to join the Saints.[27] In August 1838, James wrote his brother, forcefully accusing him of stealing his flock. Again, the Book of Mormon was central to the attack. "You were certainly the *aggressor*," James wrote. "Your business was not to tell me 'in plain terms that the Book of Mormon was the word of God'—this was *assuming* the thing—I want something to convince my judgment."[28] James further charged Joseph, "Now I do not believe at all that you were sent of God to rend my little Church to pieces—Were I to speak as 'plain' as you do I should boldly declare that it was not God but Satan as an angel of light sent you here—However, I do seriously declare that that is my sincere belief."[29]

The attack from his brother hurt Elder Fielding significantly, but he stood by the message of the Restoration. In his journal, he recorded,

"[James] was very much opposed to us. In the Morning as we were sitting down to Breakfast he began to say very hard things of us and the Book of Mormon. I was much grieved and it appeared that I could not eat. I got up from the Table, took the Book in my Hand and declared to all, to him in particular, that what we had told them was the Truth, that that Book was of God, and that he would have to repent, and then left the House, from which time I have not been much in his Company. When I go to his house he will scarcely speak to me."[30] These and other experiences undoubtedly influenced Joseph Fielding as a missionary. Though details of the meeting are scarce, it is possible that upon his return Elder Fielding shared some of these encounters, leading Joseph Smith to emphasize that a man comes nearer to God only by abiding by the Book of Mormon message.

### "Most Correct"

Another part of the statement, that the Book of Mormon is "the most correct of any book on earth," can also be better understood in its historical context. By "most correct," did Joseph's original intent mean "without error"? Hugh Nibley observed, "What is a 'correct' book? One with properly cut margins, appropriate binding, a useful index, accurately numbered pages? Not at all; these are mere mechanical details, as are also punctuation, spelling, and even grammar—those matters about which the critics of the Book of Mormon have made such a to-do. . . . The most correct book in the world is the one that will be found to contain the fewest untrue statements after all the books in the world have been checked and compared."[31]

Book of Mormon prophets understood that "most correct" did not mean without error. Beginning the record, Nephi acknowledged that if he erred, it was "because of the weakness which [was] in [him]" (1 Nephi 19:6). Concluding his record, Mormon himself wrote, "And if there be faults they be the faults of a man" (Mormon 8:17). Later, Moroni lamented his own "weakness in writing" (Ether 12:23). In light of these disclaimers, it is apparent that Joseph Smith's statement regarding the accuracy of the Book of Mormon likely referred to content and message rather than grammar and style. In fact, the reality that the Book of Mormon was not grammatically perfect was evident at the time the statement was made. Joseph Smith himself had recently gone through the text, making changes for the third published edition. These corrections included editorial changes to improve grammar and the restoration of phrases lost when the printer's manuscript was produced.[32] Though he called the book the "most correct," Joseph was apparently not satisfied with its typographical flaws.

Similarly, the Twelve had published a British edition of the Book of Mormon earlier in 1841. Done with the permission of Joseph Smith, it reproduced the earlier 1837 edition with British spellings.[33] This later version of the Book of Mormon was an important part of the Twelve's mission to Britain. Seeking permission to print it, Brigham Young even wrote Joseph Smith that "[the British saints] beg and plead for the Book of Mormon."[34] Similarly, Parley P. Pratt lobbied for its printing, observing that the book "was not to be had in this part of the vineyard for love or money. Hundreds are waiting in various parts here about but there is truly a famine in that respect."[35] Publishing the Book of Mormon in Britain, even though it didn't match the most recent Nauvoo edition, satisfied the need. Discussion regarding these recent editions of the Book of Mormon, especially as they differed in their slight grammatical corrections, may relate to why Joseph called it "the most correct of any book on earth."

## Preserving the Statement

A final observation regarding the context of Joseph Smith's statement is its recording itself. Though presented in the *History of the Church* as if it were recorded by Joseph Smith, the statement was likely not personally preserved by him. In reality, no personal journal entry for the Prophet exists for November 28, 1841. In fact, more than two years separate Joseph's 1839 Illinois journal and his later December 1841 writings.[36] This period was marked by the untimely death of one scribe, Robert B. Thompson, and the appointment of Willard Richards as his replacement. Summarizing these record-keeping difficulties, Joseph observed:

> Since I have been engaged in laying the foundation of the
> Church of Jesus Christ of Latter-day Saints, I have been

prevented in various ways from continuing my journal and history in a manner satisfactory to myself or in justice to the cause.
Long imprisonments, vexatious and long-continued law-suits,
the treachery of some of my clerks, the death of others, and the
poverty of myself and brethren from continued plunder and
driving, have prevented my handing down to posterity a connected memorandum of events desirable to all lovers of truth;
yet I have continued to keep up a journal in the best manner
my circumstances would allow, and dictate for my history from
time to time, as I have had opportunity so that the labors and
suffering of the first Elders and Saints of this last kingdom
might not wholly be lost to the world.[37]

How, then, was Joseph Smith's statement preserved? The answer
lies in the compilation of the manuscript version of *History of the Church,*
where the statement initially appeared. This document was begun in
1839 and continued sporadically throughout Joseph Smith's lifetime.
Nauvoo's newspaper, the *Times and Seasons,* began publishing it in serial
form in March 1842. By the time of Joseph's death, the manuscript was
complete through August 5, 1838, and published through December
1831.[38] Under the direction of Willard Richards, work continued on the
document even as the Saints prepared to leave Nauvoo in 1846. By
the time of their departure, the manuscript was complete through
March 1, 1843, including the famous 1841 statement by Joseph Smith
calling the Book of Mormon the keystone of our religion.

Without the aid of Joseph Smith himself or a personal journal to
fill in missing details, Willard Richards was forced to rely on other
records to craft the history. In 1845, he pled with the Saints, "All those
who have letters, or documents of any kind in their possession, which in
any way relate to the History of the Church of Jesus Christ of Latter-
day Saints, are requested to leave them with the historian."[39] The Joseph
Smith statement, as we have it today, likely comes from individuals who
heard the Prophet say it and submitted their record as requested. In
fact, Wilford Woodruff's journal itself may be the statement's source,
since it nearly identically matches the statement found in *History of the
Church.* The authors of *History of the Church* likely changed Wilford
Woodruff's third-person account to sound like Joseph's first-person

record. Regarding this process, historian Dean C. Jessee observed, "To further complicate the question of authorship, since Joseph Smith's diary did not provide an unbroken narrative of his life, gaps were bridged by using other sources, changing indirect discourse to direct as if Joseph had done the writing himself. Not uncommon according to the editorial practices of the day, this method of supplying missing detail had the effect of providing a smooth-flowing, connected narrative of events."[40] Joseph Smith's keystone statement regarding the Book of Mormon likely comes to us this way.

## MODERN USE OF JOSEPH SMITH'S STATEMENT

Though Joseph Smith's statement is well known today, it has not always been so recognized. Probably due to the small audience who first heard it and the inaccessibility of Joseph's history to the early Church, the statement was rarely quoted during the first hundred years of the Church. The earliest print version of the statement likely appeared in Salt Lake City in the *Deseret News* as part of the serialized printing of "Joseph Smith's History."[41] In Great Britain, the *Latter-day Saints' Millennial Star* likewise published it as part of their series "History of Joseph Smith."[42] In the early twentieth century, B. H. Roberts first included the statement in book form in the multivolume *History of the Church.* However, the sheer size of this work may have deterred readers from finding the statement, since isolating one paragraph buried in six volumes spanning 3,285 pages is problematic. Edwin F. Parry may have helped bring the statement to light by including it in his 1912 work, *Joseph Smith's Teachings,* a brief collection of statements by the Prophet culled from *History of the Church.* Undoubtedly Joseph Fielding Smith's 1938 publication, *Teachings of the Prophet Joseph Smith,* which included the statement under the title, "Perfection of the Book of Mormon," aided in its dissemination.[43]

### General Authority Use of the Quotation

With its increased publication, General Authorities began using the keystone statement in their addresses and writings. One early authority to use the statement was Elder John A. Widtsoe, who used it in articles in the *Improvement Era* in 1937 and again in 1952.[44] The statement was also included as part of a lesson in the official 1942 Melchizedek

Priesthood study outline, a course which used *Teachings of the Prophet Joseph Smith* as its text. In April 1949, Elder Bruce R. McConkie became the first to quote it in general conference.[45]

With the statement's increased familiarity, more and more individuals began citing it. In the April 1961 general conference, Elder McConkie delivered a powerful address on the Book of Mormon and its ability to bring men and women to Christ. Citing the "keystone statement," he declared, "The Book of Mormon is the means, the tool, the way which has been ordained and given so that men can get their hearts and souls in a frame of mind, in a condition where they can hearken to the testimony of the Spirit."[46]

Ironically, Elder Marion G. Romney apparently intended to speak on the same topic. In the closing session of the same conference, he declared:

> I have a prepared talk in my pocket, which took me five months to prepare, titled "The Book of Mormon—The Keystone of Our Religion." You, of course, know what Brother McConkie did to it. He has made me feel towards it as the player on a boys' baseball team felt towards left field. This player was taken out of a game to give Jimmy from the second string a chance to play. As luck would have it, Jimmy dropped the first two balls hit into left field. He was therefore taken out, and the left fielder put back in. The next two balls hit also went to left field, and the regular player dropped them. When he came off the field at the end of the inning, the coach said, "I wasn't surprised when Jimmy fumbled the ball, but I was surprised at you." "Well, Coach," said the player, "I'll tell you, Jimmy messed up left field so badly that no one can play it."

Though he changed his address, Elder Romney still urged all members, and especially Melchizedek Priesthood holders studying it that year, to read the Book of Mormon, promising that "the Prophet knew what he was talking about when he said that ' . . . a man would get nearer to God by abiding by its precepts, than by any other book.'"[47] A year later, Elder Romney happily reported that 59,740 bearers of the Melchizedek Priesthood had accepted the challenge.[48]

*President Benson's Use of the Statement*

While General Authorities like Elder McConkie and Elder Romney used Joseph Smith's statement in their addresses, President Ezra Taft Benson seems to be the quote's chief advocate. Over a period of nearly thirty years, he repeatedly returned to the statement in his addresses. Quoting it as early as the October 1963 general conference, President Benson famously emphasized the importance of the Book of Mormon and its power to bring Church members closer to Christ. In fact, in conference President Benson used Joseph Smith's quote regarding the Book of Mormon ten different times from 1984 to 1988 alone, including twice in his first conference as Church President (April 1986) and three more times in his second (October 1986). After quoting the Joseph Smith statement, President Benson declared, "[The Book of Mormon] is the keystone of our religion. It is the keystone of our doctrine. It is the keystone of our testimony. It is a keystone in the witness of Jesus Christ. It is a keystone in helping us avoid the deceptions of the evil one in these latter days. . . . The Book of Mormon must be reenthroned in the minds and hearts of our people. We must honor it by reading it, by studying it, by taking its precepts into our lives and transforming them into lives required of the true followers of Christ."[49]

The final step in bringing Joseph Smith's statement to the general recognition of Church membership was its inclusion in the 1981 edition of the Book of Mormon. "One of the significant additions of the 1981 edition of the Book of Mormon," observed Robert J. Matthews, "is a one-page introduction that briefly explains what the Book of Mormon is."[50] A complete revision from earlier introductory pages to the Book of Mormon, the text was apparently drafted by Elder McConkie, a member of the Scriptures Publication Committee.[51] As shown, Elder McConkie was an advocate of Joseph Smith's statement and thus was instrumental in including it for the first time in the book's introduction. Since 1981, Book of Mormon readers have been introduced to Joseph Smith's famous statement early in their reading of its inspired pages.

## CONCLUSION

The story of Joseph Smith's keystone statement regarding the Book of Mormon is a fascinating case study in the use of his teachings.

Though delivered to a small audience of Church leaders, its preservation, publication, and citation have helped the statement become one of the Prophet's most easily recognizable declarations. Understanding the historical context of the statement, including the individuals present at its delivery, the possible nature of their discussion, and the Prophet's original intent, helps the reader appreciate its significance. These men and others early in this dispensation were brought closer to God through the message of the Book of Mormon. Responding to the call of their Lord, they traveled the world, seeking a similar blessing for others. Today, millions of readers worldwide apply the message these early brethren received from the Prophet, likewise relying on his promise that abiding by the precepts of the Book of Mormon will bring them closer to God.

---

## NOTES

1.  Joseph Smith, *History of the Church of Jesus Christ of Latter-day Saints,* ed. B. H. Roberts, 2nd ed. rev. (Salt Lake City: Deseret News, 1957), 4:461.

2.  A simple search of general conference reports from 1971 to 2006 shows that Joseph Smith's "keystone" statement has been quoted in one form or another thirty-one times. Nearly as well known, his statement that "happiness is the object and design of our existence" was used twenty-three times in general conference over a similar period. The Prophet's statement, "I teach them correct principles and they govern themselves" has appeared thirteen times in general conference, while the declaration "A religion that does not require the sacrifice of all things never has power sufficient to produce the faith necessary unto life and salvation" has been used ten times.

3.  Robert J. Matthews, *A Bible, A Bible!* (Salt Lake City: Bookcraft, 1990), 69.

4.  Smith, *History of the Church,* 4:461.

5.  Elden Jay Watson, ed., *Manuscript History of Brigham Young, 1801–1844* (Salt Lake City: Smith Secretarial Service, 1968), 109.

6.  Craig J. Ostler, "Brigham Young Lot," *Virtual Historian: Doctrine and Covenants,* CD-ROM.

7.  See Parley P. Pratt, *Autobiography of Parley P. Pratt* (Salt Lake City: Deseret Book, 1985), 276; see also James B. Allen, Ronald K. Esplin, and David J. Whittaker, *Men with a Mission: The Quorum of the Twelve Apostles in the British Isles, 1837–1841* (Salt Lake City: Deseret Book, 1992), 307–8.

8.  See Smith, *History of the Church,* 4:454–59.

9.  William Smith was likely in New Jersey in November 1841. Early in August of the same year, he wrote Joseph, informing him he was leaving Pennsylvania for New Jersey within the week (see *History of the Church,* 4:391). On January 1, 1842,

Joseph recorded that William was still in New Jersey (see *History of the Church,* 4:490). William's whereabouts are complicated somewhat by his name appearing with those of eight other Apostles in epistles written from Nauvoo on November 15, 1841, and December 13, 1841 (see *History of the Church,* 4:453, 475). However, it is doubtful William returned to Nauvoo between August and January. More likely, his name was included by the other members of the Twelve in his absence, much like the Apostolic letter of December 1, 1841, also written from Nauvoo with all twelve names appended (see *History of the Church,* 4:466). Clearly, Parley P. Pratt and Orson Hyde could not have signed the letter, as they were assigned overseas.

10.  See Smith, *History of the Church,* 4:462.

11.  A similar council of the Twelve Apostles held at Brigham Young's home two days later lists seven apostles present (see *History of the Church,* 4:463). George A. Smith was absent for this later meeting but did record in his journal being in Nauvoo during this time (see "Memoirs of George A. Smith," December 12, 1841, George A. Smith Papers, Church Archives, The Church of Jesus Christ of Latter-day Saints, Salt Lake City).

12.  Smith, *History of the Church,* 4:461.

13.  Watson, *Manuscript History of Brigham Young,* 112.

14.  Willard Richards Journal, November 28, 1841, Willard Richards Papers, Church Archives.

15.  Scott G. Kenney, ed., *Wilford Woodruff's Journal* (Midvale, UT: Signature Books, 1983), 2:139.

16.  Kenney, *Wilford Woodruff's Journal,* 2:139.

17.  Smith, *History of the Church,* 4:460.

18.  Smith, *History of the Church,* 4:461.

19.  Joseph Fielding, *Diary of Joseph Fielding,* book 1:7, L. Tom Perry Special Collections, Harold B. Lee Library, Brigham Young University, Provo, UT.

20.  Fielding, *Diary of Joseph Fielding,* book 1:73–74.

21.  Fielding, *Diary of Joseph Fielding,* book 2:117.

22.  Fielding, *Diary of Joseph Fielding,* book 4:33.

23.  Fielding, *Diary of Joseph Fielding,* book 4:38–39. It is unclear which passage in the Doctrine and Covenants inspired this recommitment on the part of Elder Fielding. Both Doctrine and Covenants 42:12 and 84:57 instruct the elders to preach from the Book of Mormon.

24.  Fielding, *Diary of Joseph Fielding,* book 4:39.

25.  Fielding, *Diary of Joseph Fielding,* book 1:50–51.

26.  Fielding, *Diary of Joseph Fielding,* book 1:54.

27.  Allen, Esplin, and Whittaker, *Men with a Mission,* 31–33, 329.

28.  James Fielding to Joseph Fielding, August 27, 1838, in Joseph Fielding Correspondence, 1837–1842, MSS 670, L. Tom Perry Special Collections.

29.  James Fielding to Joseph Fielding, August 27, 1838, in Joseph Fielding Correspondence, 1837–1842, MSS 670, L. Tom Perry Special Collections.

30.  Joseph Fielding, *Diary of Joseph Fielding,* book 1:25, L. Tom Perry Special Collections.

31.  Hugh Nibley, *Since Cumorah,* 2nd ed. (Salt Lake City: Deseret Book, 1981), 8.

32. Dennis L. Largey, ed., *Book of Mormon Reference Companion* (Salt Lake City: Deseret Book, 2003), s.v. "Book of Mormon, editions of."

33. Daniel H. Ludlow, ed., *Encyclopedia of Mormonism* (New York: Macmillan, 1992), s.v. "Book of Mormon Editions (1830–1981)."

34. Brigham Young to Joseph Smith, May 7, 1840, cited in Allen, Esplin, and Whittaker, *Men with a Mission,* 250.

35. Parley P. Pratt to Joseph Smith, November 22, 1839, cited in Allen, Esplin, and Whittaker, *Men with a Mission,* 249n53.

36. Dean C. Jessee, ed., *The Papers of Joseph Smith* (Salt Lake City: Deseret Book, 1992), 2:334.

37. Smith, *History of the Church,* 4:470.

38. Dean C. Jessee, "The Reliability of Joseph Smith's History," *Journal of Mormon History* 3 (1976): 34.

39. Smith, *History of the Church,* 7:526.

40. Jessee, "The Reliability of Joseph Smith's History," 37.

41. Ronald W. Walker, David J. Whittaker, and James B. Allen, *Mormon History* (Urbana: University of Illinois Press, 2001), 8.

42. "History of Joseph Smith," *Millennial Star,* December 13, 1856, 790.

43. Joseph Fielding Smith, comp., *Teachings of the Prophet Joseph Smith* (Salt Lake City: Deseret Book, 1973), 194.

44. See John A. Widtsoe, "The Articles of Faith," *Improvement Era,* September 1937, 535; see also Widtsoe, "May God's Word Be Interpreted?" *Improvement Era,* August 1952, 567.

45. Bruce R. McConkie, in Conference Report, April 1949, 91.

46. Bruce R. McConkie, in Conference Report, April 1961, 38.

47. Marion G. Romney, in Conference Report, April 1961, 116–17.

48. Marion G. Romney, in Conference Report, April 1962, 19.

49. Ezra Taft Benson, "The Gift of Modern Revelation," *Ensign,* November 1986, 80. Of the emphasis President Benson placed on the Book of Mormon during his early presidency, his biographer observed, "During his first year as president, he delivered some twenty major addresses on the Book of Mormon. In a temple meeting of the General Authorities in early February 1986, President Hinckley told the Brethren that President Benson would become the Church's greatest proponent of the Book of Mormon" (Sheri L. Dew, *Ezra Taft Benson: A Biography* [Salt Lake City: Deseret Book, 1987], 491).

50. Robert J. Matthews, "The New Publications of the Standard Works—1979, 1981," *BYU Studies* 22, no. 4 (Fall 1982): 393.

51. Robert J. Matthews, interview with author, January 8, 2007.

# 4

# "THE MOST CORRECT BOOK": JOSEPH SMITH'S APPRAISAL

## Robert L. Millet

On November 28, 1841, the Prophet Joseph Smith met with the Nauvoo City Council and members of the Quorum of the Twelve in the home of President Brigham Young. *History of the Church* records that he conversed "with them upon a variety of subjects. Brother Joseph Fielding was present, having been absent four years on a mission to England."[1] It was in that setting, at the Sunday city council meeting in the Youngs' residence, that Joseph Smith made what has come to be one of the most axiomatic and memorable statements in Mormon literature: "I told the brethren," he said, "that the Book of Mormon was the most correct of any book on earth, and the keystone of our religion, and a man would get nearer to God by abiding by its precepts, than by any other book."[2] In what follows, we will consider the possible meaning and implications of the various parts of this rather bold declaration about this extrabiblical document. We will consider the nature of the Book of Mormon's correctness, how it is the keystone, the precepts it contains, the poignancy of those precepts, its importance

*Robert L. Millet is a professor of ancient scripture at Brigham Young University.*

to the world, and finally, its prophetic destiny as a book of holy scripture.

## "THE MOST CORRECT BOOK"

How is it that the Book of Mormon is correct—in fact, the *most* correct of any book? In Joseph Smith's day the adjective *correct* was understood to mean "set right, or made straight," "conformable to truth, rectitude or propriety, or conformable to a just standard; not faulty; free from error." Likewise, to correct something was "to amend" or to "bring back or attempt to bring back to propriety in morals," to "obviate or remove whatever is wrong," or to "counteract whatever is injurious."[3] In our day we would say that something is correct if it is "free from error; accurate; in accordance with fact, truth, or reason."[4] In the action sense of the word, the Book of Mormon was given to us to set things straight, to make things right, to bring our thinking into conformity with truth, to see things as they really are (see Jacob 4:13; D&C 93:24), to bring back or restore to propriety, and to counteract ideas or teachings or practices that are harmful.

Nephi beheld in vision that after plain and precious truths had been taken away or kept back from the Bible and the gospel, the Lord would bring forth the Book of Mormon and "other books" (1 Nephi 13:39). "And in them shall be written my gospel, saith the Lamb, and my rock and my salvation . . . unto the convincing of the Gentiles and the remnant of the seed of [Nephi's] brethren, and also the Jews . . . that the records of the prophets and of the twelve apostles of the Lamb are true" (vv. 36, 39). In short, the Restoration scriptures "shall establish the truth of the first" and "shall make known the plain and precious things which have been taken away from them [the Bible]; and shall make known to all kindreds, tongues, and people, that the Lamb of God is the Son of the Eternal Father, and the Savior of the world; and that all men must come unto him, or they cannot be saved" (v. 40).

We are all acquainted with Ezekiel's grand prophecy that the stick of Judah and the stick of Ephraim would become one in the hand of Jehovah, a prophecy that was a poignant symbol of the ultimate gathering and uniting of the two formerly estranged nations (see Ezekiel 37:15–22). We learn from a lengthy prophecy of Joseph who was sold into Egypt these words from Jehovah, words later excerpted by Lehi in counseling his young son Joseph: "The fruit of thy loins shall write [the Book of Mormon]; and the fruit of the loins of Judah shall write [the Bible]; and that which shall be written by the fruit of thy loins, and also that which shall be written by the fruit of the loins of Judah, shall grow together." And why would they grow together? For the purpose of "the confounding of false doctrines and laying down of contentions, and establishing peace among the fruit of thy loins, and bringing them to the knowledge of their fathers in the latter days, and also to the knowledge of my covenants, saith the Lord" (2 Nephi 3:12; see also Joseph Smith Translation, Genesis 50:31).

I believe the Bible to be the word of God and a marvelous witness of the Almighty's love and tender mercies; of His eagerness to bless and prosper those who put their trust in Him; and of the central, saving significance of the Messiah, the Christ, the Anointed One. I love the Bible, especially the New Testament, for the manner in which it beckons me to submit to the divine will and surrender my hopes and dreams to Him who can do far more with my life than I can. I believe with all my heart that the Bible is meant to be read and pondered and memorized and applied by the Latter-day Saints and by all of God's children. Having affirmed my love for the Bible, I hasten to add, that as the Book of Mormon teaches, I do not believe it has come down to us in its pristine purity as it was written by the original authors.[5] This perspective does not, however, weaken my faith in its essential and central messages. Instead, it makes me that much more grateful for the scriptures of the Restoration that strive to prove "to the world that the holy scriptures are true" (D&C 20:11).

Why work so hard to prove the truthfulness of the Bible? Simply because a growing percentage of people in our world have begun to discount, belittle, or deny those elements of holy scripture that make the scriptures matter—divine intervention, miracles, and prophecy. And because the "quest for the historical Jesus" has retrogressed to the point of an outright rejection of our Lord's divinity and His bodily Resurrection from the dead on the part of people who still desire to be known as Christians. In 1966 Elder Gordon B. Hinckley said: "Modern theologians strip [Jesus] of his divinity and then wonder why men do not worship him. These clever scholars have taken from Jesus the mantle of godhood and have left only a man. They have tried to accommodate him to their own narrow thinking. They have robbed him of his divine sonship and taken from the world its rightful King."[6] Some five years later, President Harold B. Lee explained to a group of students at Utah State University: "Fifty years ago or more, there were the unmistakable evidences that there was coming into the religious world actually a question about the Bible and about the divine calling of the Master himself. Now, fifty years later [this was in 1971], our greatest responsibility and anxiety is to defend the divine mission of our Lord and Master, Jesus Christ, for all about us, even among those who claim to be professors of the Christian faith, are those not willing to stand squarely in defense of the great truth that our Lord and Master, Jesus Christ, was indeed the Son of God."[7]

From my perspective (and I quickly acknowledge my bias), the Book of Mormon is the most correct of any book on earth because of the undiluted and penetrating message it presents—the way it establishes in no uncertain terms "that there is a God in heaven, who is infinite and eternal, from everlasting to everlasting the same unchangeable God, the framer of heaven and earth, and all things which are in them" (D&C 20:17); the way it highlights the nature of fallen humanity; the way it focuses repeatedly upon man's utter inability to forgive or cleanse or resurrect or save himself; the way it places Jesus Christ on center stage and testifies of the infinite and eternal scope of His atoning sacrifice. In the Book of Mormon, Christ is the Lord God Omnipotent, who saves "not only those who believed after he came in the meridian of time, in the flesh, but all those from the beginning, even as many as were before he came, who believed in the words of the holy prophets, . . . as well as those who should come after" (D&C 20:26–27). For me the Book of Mormon is the most correct book on earth because it teaches us who God is, what the Godhead is, how they are infinitely more one than they are separate, and how the love and unity between the Father, Son, and Holy Ghost is of such magnitude that the Nephite record speaks of them several times simply as "one God, without end" (2 Nephi 31:21; see also D&C 20:28; Alma 11:44; 3 Nephi 9:15; 11:27, 36; 28:10; Mormon 7:7). I believe the Book of Mormon is the most correct book because it presents with consistent clarity the delicate balance between the mercy and grace of our Lord and God and the works of righteousness that must always characterize and identify true disciples of the Master (see 2 Nephi 2:2–8; 25:23; 31:19; Alma 22:14; Helaman 14:13; Moroni 6:4).

I believe the Book of Mormon to be the most correct scriptural book because it assists us in spanning the Testaments and consequently spanning the chasm that many feel exists between the God of the Old and the God of the New Testament. "I make my own heartfelt declaration of God, our Eternal Father, this morning," Elder Jeffrey R. Holland stated, "because some in the contemporary world suffer from a distressing misconception of Him. Among these there is a tendency to feel distant from the Father, even estranged from Him, if they believe in Him at all. And if they do believe, many moderns say they might feel comfortable in the arms of Jesus, but they are uneasy contemplating the stern encounter of God."

Elder Holland further observed that "one of the remarkable contributions of the Book of Mormon is its seamless, perfectly consistent view of divinity throughout that majestic book. Here there is no Malachi-to-Matthew gap, no pause while we shift theological gears, no misreading the God who is urgently, lovingly, faithfully at work on every page of that record from its Old Testament beginning to its New Testament end. Yes, in an effort to give the world back its Bible and a correct view of Deity with it, what we have in the Book of Mormon is a uniform view of God in all His glory and goodness, all His richness and complexity—including and especially as again demonstrated through a personal appearance of His Only Begotten Son, Jesus Christ."

Finally, Elder Holland pointed out that "Jesus did not come to improve God's view of man nearly so much as He came to improve man's view of God and to plead with them to love their Heavenly Father as He has always and will always love them. The plan of God, the power of God, the holiness of God, yes, even the anger and the judgment of God they had occasion to understand. But the love of God, the profound depth of His devotion to His children, they still did not fully know—until Christ came."[8]

Our belief as Latter-day Saints in the supreme correctness of this other testament of Jesus Christ is neither a denunciation nor a denial of the Bible, not a statement that the former is wholly correct and the latter is wholly incorrect. Moroni himself acknowledged that the Book of Mormon may contain human error (see title page; Mormon 8:17). The very fact that we study and teach the Bible in our own homes and in the meetings of the Church, general and local, is statement enough that we treasure its content and seek to conform our lives with its timeless counsel.

## THE KEYSTONE

Let us now examine the Prophet Joseph's characterization of the Book of Mormon as the keystone of our religion. Elder Holland explained, "A keystone is positioned at the uppermost center of an arch in such a way as to hold all the other stones in place. That key piece, if removed, will bring all of the other blocks crashing down with it."[9] What does this mean in regard to the Book of Mormon? President Ezra Taft Benson explained that the Book of Mormon is the keystone of our witness of Christ, the keystone of our doctrine, and the keystone of our testimony.[10] He taught:

> The Book of Mormon is the keystone in our witness of Jesus Christ, who is Himself the cornerstone of everything we do. It bears witness of His reality with power and clarity. Unlike the Bible, which passed through generations of copyists, translators, and corrupt religionists who tampered with the text, the Book of Mormon came from writer to reader in just one inspired step of translation. Therefore, its testimony of the Master is clear, undiluted, and full of power. But it does even more. Much of the Christian world today rejects the divinity of the Savior. They question His miraculous birth, His perfect life, and the reality of His glorious resurrection. The Book of Mormon teaches in plain and unmistakable terms about the truth of all of those. It also provides the most complete explanation of the doctrine of the Atonement.[11]

Regarding the Book of Mormon as the keystone of our doctrine, President Benson reminded us that it contains what the scriptures call "the fulness of the gospel" (D&C 20:9; see also D&C 27:5; 42:12; 135:3). It is not the case that this scriptural record contains the fullness of Latter-day Saint doctrines, for there is no mention in the Book of Mormon of such matters as eternal marriage, the three degrees of glory, or the corporeality of God. The Book of Mormon is what it is and teaches what it teaches. It contains the fullness of the gospel in the sense that it declares and elevates the core verity of salvation in Christ—including the good news or glad tidings of the Atonement (see 3 Nephi 27:13–14), as well as the means by which we incorporate the Atonement through the first principles and ordinances (see 2 Nephi 31; 3 Nephi 27:15–21). In short, "in the Book of Mormon we will find the fullness of those doctrines required for our salvation. And they are taught plainly and simply so that even children can learn the ways of salvation and exaltation. The Book of Mormon offers so much," President Benson continued, "that broadens our understandings of the doctrines of salvation. Without it, much of what is taught in other scriptures would not be nearly so plain and precious."[12]

Simply stated, if either the origins or the message of the book is false, the whole religious system that is built upon and flows from the book, including our individual and collective testimonies of the Restoration, is false, misleading, and thus spiritually destructive. "The enemies of the Church understand this clearly," President Benson noted. "This is why they go to such great lengths to try to disprove the Book of Mormon, for if it can be discredited, the Prophet Joseph Smith goes with it. So does our claim to priesthood keys, and revelation, and the restored Church."[13] Elder Holland likewise has written: "To consider that everything of saving significance in the Church stands or falls on the truthfulness of the Book of Mormon and, by implication, the Prophet Joseph Smith's account of how it came forth is as sobering as it is true. It is a 'sudden-death' proposition. Either the Book of Mormon is what the Prophet Joseph said it is, or this Church and its founder are false, a deception from the first instance onward."

"Not everything in life is so black and white," Elder Holland went on to say, "but the authenticity of the Book of Mormon and its keystone role in our religion seem to be exactly that."[14] If Moroni did not truly appear to the seventeen-year-old Joseph Smith Jr. on September 21, 1823; if Joseph and the witnesses did not handle tangible metal plates with the appearance of gold; if Joseph and his scribes did not translate the Book of Mormon by the gift and power of God through the Urim and Thummim, Joseph "would not be entitled to the reputation of New England folk hero or well-meaning young man or writer of remarkable fiction. No, nor would he be entitled to be considered a great teacher, a quintessential American religious leader, or the creator of great devotional literature. If he had lied about the coming forth of the Book of Mormon, he would certainly be none of these."

"I am suggesting," Elder Holland stated soberly, "that one has to take something of a do-or-die stand regarding the restoration of the gospel of Jesus Christ and the divine origins of the Book of Mormon. Reason and righteousness require it. Joseph Smith must be accepted either as a prophet of God or else as a charlatan of the first order, but no one should tolerate any ludicrous, even laughable middle ground about the wonderful contours of a young boy's imagination or his remarkable facility for turning a literary phrase. That is an unacceptable position to take—morally, literarily, historically, or theologically."[15]

## OBEDIENCE TO ITS PRECEPTS

A *precept* is a command, a mandate, an order pertaining to proper behavior.[16] It is "a general instruction or rule for action, a maxim, *esp.* an injunction regarding moral conduct."[17] Joseph Smith's statement avers that a person will draw nearer to God by abiding by the precepts of the Book of Mormon than by any other book. It would seem that attending scrupulously to and abiding by the ever-present "and thus we see" or "and thus we can plainly discern" statements would be a significant part of our obedience. These appear to be Mormon's means of stating to the reader: "In case you didn't get the point of this story or that episode or this tragedy or that happy ending, let me make it clear by formulating it into a maxim or a memorable saying. It is something that should not be ignored or forgotten."

Precepts could obviously take the form of "thou shalts" and "thou shalt nots," warnings against violating the Ten Commandments, as well as such sins as pride, greed, immorality, arrogance, indifference, profanity, rebellion, and failure to remember. On the positive side, there are precepts that invite us to give mind and heart to transcendent truths—liberating and lasting lessons. These demand an explanation that is reasonable. Where did they come from? Who wrote them? Was Joseph Smith really that bright, that articulate, that eloquent, that polished in his presentation of sacred truths? Someone noted to me recently that it takes too much faith to be an atheist. I agree wholeheartedly. I am persuaded—setting aside the living witness I have within my mind and heart of the truthfulness of the Book of Mormon—that it is much easier to believe in angels and golden plates and seer stones than some of the ridiculous explanations that critics of the book offer. "If Joseph Smith did not translate the Book of Mormon as a work of ancient origin," Elder Holland has written, "then I would move heaven and earth to meet the 'real' nineteenth-century author. After one hundred and fifty years, no one can come up with a credible alternative candidate, but if the book were false, surely there must be someone willing to step forward—if no one else, at least the descendants of the 'real' author—claiming credit for such a remarkable document and all that has transpired in its wake. After all, a writer that can move millions can make millions. Shouldn't someone have come forth then or now to cashier the whole phenomenon?"

Elder Holland concluded, "There is no other clandestine 'author,' no elusive ghostwriter still waiting in the wings after a century and a half for the chance to stride forward and startle the religious world. Indeed, that any writer—Joseph Smith or anyone else—could create the Book of Mormon out of whole cloth would be an infinitely greater miracle than that young Joseph translated it from an ancient record 'by the gift and power of God.'"[18]

As the Apostle Paul taught, the things of God are known only by the power of the Spirit of God (see 1 Corinthians 2:11–14). The *truthfulness* of a religious matter is known by the quiet whisperings of the Spirit. But the *significance* of a religious matter—such as the Book of Mormon or temples or the nature of God—may often be discerned by the loud janglings of opposition from those who are somehow threatened and offended by them. In other words, if I did not already know, by the power of the Spirit, that the Book of Mormon is indeed the word of God and another testament of Jesus Christ, I might suspect that it is holy writ by the intensity and even rabidity of those who attack it. Nephi warned: "Wo be unto him that saith: We have received, and we need no more! And in fine, wo unto all those who tremble, and are angry because of the truth of God! For behold, he that is built upon the rock receiveth it with gladness" (2 Nephi 28:27–28).

If those who rail against and battle the Book of Mormon would spend a fraction of their time and energy seeking to discover and fathom the *fruits* of the Book of Mormon as they do in conjuring up a new angle every month to explain the *roots* of it, they just might come to different conclusions. People must judge for themselves. As President Benson observed, "The Book of Mormon is not on trial—the people of the world, including the members of the Church, are on trial as to what they will do with this second witness for Christ."[19]

## POIGNANT PRECEPTS

We are given little indication in the biblical record that the prophet-writers delivered and preserved their messages for any day other than their own. There is no doubt that Isaiah, Jeremiah, Ezekiel, Daniel, Malachi, Peter, Paul, John, and others spoke of the distant future; by the power of the Spirit, they saw and described the doings of peoples of another time and place. Their words were given to the people of their own time. Their words have and will yet find application and fulfillment for future times. And yet we never see a particular prophet from the stick of Judah addressing himself directly to those who will one day read his pronouncements.

How very different is the Book of Mormon! It was prepared and preserved by men with seeric vision who wrote and spoke to us; they saw and knew our day and addressed themselves to specific issues that a people in the last days would confront. The poignant words of Moroni point us to the contemporary relevance of the Book of Mormon: "Behold, I speak unto you as if ye were present, and yet ye are not. But behold, Jesus Christ hath shown you unto me, and I know your doing" (Mormon 8:35). Later Moroni said: "Behold, I speak unto you as though I spake from the dead; for I know that ye shall have my words" (Mormon 9:30). In the words of President Benson, the Book of Mormon "was written for our day. *The Nephites never had the book; neither did the Lamanites of ancient times.* It was meant for us. Mormon wrote near the end of the Nephite civilization. Under the inspiration of God, who sees all things from the beginning, he abridged centuries of records, choosing the stories, speeches, and events that would be most helpful to us. . . . If they saw our day, and chose those things which would be of greatest worth to us, is not that how we should study the Book of Mormon? We should constantly ask ourselves, 'Why did the Lord inspire Mormon (or Moroni or Alma) to include that in his record? What lesson can I learn from that to help me live in this day and age?'"[20]

Do I desire to know how to handle wayward children, how to deal justly yet mercifully with transgressors, how to bear pure testimony, how to teach and preach in such a manner that people cannot go away unaffected, how to detect the enemies of Christ and how to withstand those who seek to destroy my faith, how to discern and expose secret combinations that seek to destroy the works of the Lamb of God, how to deal properly with persecution and anti-Mormonism, and how to establish Zion? Then I must search and study the Book of Mormon.

Do I desire to know more about how to avoid pride and the perils of the prosperity cycle; how to avoid priestcraft and acquire and embody charity, the pure love of Christ; how my sins may be remitted and how I can know when they have been forgiven; how to retain a remission of sins from day to day; how to come unto Christ, receive His holy name, partake of His goodness and love, be sanctified by His Spirit, and eventually be sealed to Him? Do I desire to know how to prepare for the Second Coming of the Son of Man? Then I must search and study the Book of Mormon. This volume of holy writ is without equal. It is the most relevant and pertinent book available to humankind today.

The Book of Mormon is different from the other books of scripture. They are true, and they are inspired. They come from God. But the Book of Mormon has a spirit all its own. "Not all truths are of equal value," President Benson has taught, "nor are all scriptures of the same worth." This modern prophet explains further:

It is not just that the Book of Mormon teaches us truth, though it indeed does that. It is not just that the Book of Mormon bears testimony of Christ, though it indeed does that, too. But there is something more. There is a power in the book which will begin to flow into your lives the moment you begin a serious study of the book. You will find greater power to resist temptation. You will find the power to avoid deception. You will find the power to stay on the strait and narrow path. The scriptures are called "the words of life" (see D&C 84:85), and nowhere is that more true than it is of the Book of Mormon. When you begin to hunger and thirst after those words, you will find life in greater and greater abundance.[21]

But there is more. The Book of Mormon is far more than a theological treatise, more than a collection of great doctrinal sermons. (It would be worth its weight in gold even if that was all it were!) It is not just a book that helps us feel good; it is a heavenly document that has been given to help us *be* good. It is as if the Nephite prophet-leaders were beckoning and pleading to us from the dust: "We sought for the Lord. We found him. We applied the gospel of Jesus Christ and have partaken of its sweet fruits. We know the joy of our redemption and have felt to sing the song of redeeming love. And now, O reader, go and do thou likewise!" The Book of Mormon is not only an invitation to come unto Christ but also a pattern for the accomplishment of that consummate privilege. That invitation is extended to all, the rank and file as well as the prophets and apostles. The Book of Mormon does more than teach with plainness and persuasion the effects of the Fall and the absolute necessity for an atonement; it cries out to us that unless we acknowledge our fallen state, put off the natural man, apply the atoning blood of Christ, and be born again, we can never be with or become like our Lord, worlds without end. Nor can we ever hope to establish Zion, a society of the pure in heart. Stated differently, this volume is not just a book about religion. It *is* religion. Our challenge, therefore, is not just to read and study the Book of Mormon; we must live it and accept and apply its doctrines and philosophy.

## IMPORTANCE TO THE WORLD

Too much effort has been expended over too many centuries, too much blood has been shed, too many tears have watered the pillows, too many prayers have ascended to the ears of the Lord of Sabaoth, too great a price has been paid for the Book of Mormon record to be destroyed. Or discarded. Or ignored. No, it must not be ignored, either by the Latter-day Saints (the present custodians of the stick of Joseph) or by a world that desperately needs its message and transforming power. No less than God Himself has borne witness of the Book of Mormon. To Oliver Cowdery, who was raised up to serve as scribe in the translation, the Lord affirmed: "I tell thee, that thou mayest know that there is none else save God that knowest thy thoughts and the intents of thy heart. I tell thee these things as a witness unto thee—that *the words or the work which thou hast been writing are true*" (D&C 6:16–17; emphasis added; see also 18:2). The Almighty set His own seal of truthfulness with an oath upon the Nephite record when He said: "And he [Joseph Smith] has translated the book, even that part which I have commanded him, and *as your Lord and your God liveth it is true*" (D&C 17:6; emphasis added). In the words of a modern Apostle: "This is God's testimony of the Book of Mormon. In it Deity himself has laid his godhood on the line. Either the book is true or God ceases to be God. There neither is nor can be any more formal or powerful language known to men or gods."[22]

For those outside the faith, the Book of Mormon presses for a decision. It forces an issue. One cannot simply dismiss it with a wave of the hand and a turn of the head; it must be explained. Thus, as Elder Bruce R. McConkie declared, "the time is long past for quibbling about words and for hurling unsavory epithets against the Latter-day Saints. These are deep and solemn and ponderous matters. We need not think we can trifle with sacred things and escape the wrath of a just God. Either the Book of Mormon is true, or it is false; either it came from God, or it was spawned in the infernal realms. . . . It is not and cannot be simply another treatise on religion; it either came from heaven or from hell. And it is time for all those who seek salvation to find out for themselves whether it is of the Lord or of Lucifer."[23] And as far as members of the Church are concerned, President Benson has declared boldly: "Every Latter-day Saint should make the study of this book a lifetime pursuit. Otherwise he is placing his soul in jeopardy and neglecting that which could give spiritual and intellectual unity to his whole life."[24]

## ITS PROPHETIC DESTINY

So here we are today. In compliance with the prophetic mandate, millions of Latter-day Saints across the world have begun to search and pray over and teach from the Book of Mormon. Because of their study of the Book of Mormon, many Saints have already begun to find answers to their problems; many have come alive to the scriptures and have begun to understand many of the more mysterious passages in the Bible. Many have begun to feel that sometimes subtle but certain transforming influence that flows from the Book of Mormon—they have begun to sense its sanctifying power. Theirs is a greater yearning for righteousness and the things of the Spirit, a heightened sensitivity to people and feelings, and a corresponding abhorrence for the sins of the world. Many have come to the point where they honestly and truly desire to surrender to the Lord and His ways, to know and abide by His will, and to keep an eye single to His glory. For such devotees of the Book of Mormon, surely the condemnation spoken of in Doctrine and Covenants 84 is no more.

I believe this pattern will continue. In regard to the future, President Benson said:

> I have a vision of homes alerted, of classes alive, and of pulpits aflame with the spirit of Book of Mormon messages.
>
> I have a vision of home teachers and visiting teachers, ward and branch officers, and stake and mission leaders counseling our people out of the most correct of any book on earth—the Book of Mormon.
>
> I have a vision of artists putting into film, drama, literature, music, and paintings great themes and great characters from the Book of Mormon.
>
> I have a vision of thousands of missionaries going into the mission field with hundreds of passages memorized from the

Book of Mormon so that they might feed the needs of a spiritually famished world.

I have a vision of the whole Church getting nearer to God by abiding by the precepts of the Book of Mormon.

Indeed, I have a vision of flooding the earth with the Book of Mormon.[25]

Such a day will not come to pass without opposition. But amid it all, the work of the Lord, with the Book of Mormon held high as an ensign to the nations, will go forward. As Moroni explained to Joseph Smith: "Those who are not built upon the Rock will seek to overthrow this church; but it will increase the more [it is] opposed."[26]

I know that the Book of Mormon is the word of God. I know that the Lord God is its author. It speaks peace and joy to my soul. It is a quiet, steadying influence in my life. Many of our longings for another time and place, those vague but powerful feelings that we have wandered from a more exalted sphere, are satisfied and soothed when we read the Book of Mormon. Reading it is like coming home. It is a gift of God that we are expected to receive, understand, and experience. I feel a deep sense of kinship with its writers, particularly Mormon and Moroni. I think they are as concerned now, if not more, with what is done with their book than when they etched their messages onto the golden plates some sixteen centuries ago. I know that the Almighty expects us to read and teach from the Book of Mormon and to devote significant time to the consideration and application of the doctrines and principles it contains.

"Its appeal is as timeless as truth," President Hinckley declared, "as universal as mankind. It is the only book that contains within its covers a promise that by divine power the reader may know with certainty of its truth. Its origin is miraculous; when the story of that origin is first told to one unfamiliar with it, it is almost unbelievable. . . . No one can dispute its presence. All efforts to account for its origin, other than the account given by Joseph Smith, have been shown to lack substance. It is a record of ancient America. It is a scripture of the New World, as certainly as the Bible is the scripture of the Old. Each speaks of the other. Each carries with it the spirit of inspiration, the power to convince and convert. Together they become two witnesses, hand in hand, that Jesus is the Christ, the resurrected and living Son of the living God."[27]

God grant that we might be wise in the day of our probation. God grant us strength in our sacred care and keeping of the timely and timeless Book of Mormon. Then, having done all in this regard, we will rest our souls everlastingly with those who paid such a dear price to write and preserve and bring it forth.

———————————

NOTES

1. Joseph Smith, *History of the Church of Jesus Christ of Latter-day Saints,* ed. B. H. Roberts, 2nd ed. rev. (Salt Lake City: Deseret Book, 1957), 4:461.

2. Smith, *History of the Church,* 4:461; see also Joseph Smith, *Teachings of the Prophet Joseph Smith,* comp. Joseph Fielding Smith (Salt Lake City: Deseret Book, 1976), 194.

3. *Noah Webster's First Edition of An American Dictionary of the English Language,* facsimile of 1828 edition (San Francisco: Foundation for American Christian Education, 1985), s.v. "correct."

4. *The New Shorter Oxford English Dictionary,* ed. Lesley Brown (Oxford: Clarendon Press, 1993), s.v. "correct."

5. See Smith, *Teachings of the Prophet Joseph Smith,* 9–10, 61, 327.

6. Gordon B. Hinckley, in Conference Report, April 1966, 85.

7. LDS Student Association fireside, Utah State University, October 10, 1971, as quoted in *The Book of Mormon: The Keystone Scripture,* ed. Paul R. Cheesman (Provo, UT: BYU Religious Studies Center, 1988), 23–24.

8. Jeffrey R. Holland, in Conference Report, October 2003, 73–75.

9. Jeffrey R. Holland, *Christ and the New Covenant* (Salt Lake City: Deseret Book, 1997), 344–45.

10. Ezra Taft Benson, *A Witness and a Warning* (Salt Lake City: Deseret Book, 1988), 18–19.

11. Benson, *A Witness and a Warning,* 18.

12. Benson, *A Witness and a Warning,* 18–19.

13. Benson, *A Witness and a Warning,* 19.

14. Holland, *Christ and the New Covenant,* 344–45.

15. Holland, *Christ and the New Covenant,* 345–46.

16. *Webster's 1828 Dictionary,* s.v. "precept."

17. *The New Shorter Oxford English Dictionary,* s.v. "precept."

18. Holland, *Christ and the New Covenant,* 347, 349.

19. Benson, *A Witness and a Warning,* 13.

20. Benson, *A Witness and a Warning,* 19–20; emphasis added.

21. Benson, *A Witness and a Warning,* 10, 21–22.

22. Bruce R. McConkie, in Conference Report, April 1982, 50.

23. McConkie, in Conference Report, October 1983, 105–6.

24. Benson, *A Witness and a Warning,* 7–8.

25. Benson, in Conference Report, October 1988, 4–5.

26. *Messenger and Advocate,* October 1835, 2:199; as quoted in Francis W. Kirkham, *A New Witness for Christ in America* (Independence, MO: Zion's Printing, 1942), 100.

27. Gordon B. Hinckley, *Teachings of Gordon B. Hinckley* (Salt Lake City: Deseret Book, 1997), 38.

## 5

# THE LITERARY POWER OF THE BOOK OF MORMON

## *Charles Swift*

Although the Book of Mormon is composed of such literary elements as stories, poetry, symbolism, letters, archetypes, typology, and allegories, it is not just literature; it is sacred literature, and millions of people with open hearts have found the power behind the Prophet Joseph Smith's inspired words that "a man would get nearer to God by abiding by its percepts, than by any other book" (introduction to the Book of Mormon). For believers, there is no question that the Book of Mormon has the power to change the lives of those who are willing to let it. What believers may not so readily understand, however, is the powerful role that the book's literary features play in changing their lives. These literary elements are not decorative add-ons included by the prophets merely to make reading the book more interesting. Often the literary nature of the Book of Mormon conveys the doctrine and other life-changing precepts in ways that help us better abide by them and experience their power in our lives.

---

*Charles Swift is an assistant professor of ancient scripture at Brigham Young University.*

## LITERATURE

When we say that the Book of Mormon is sacred literature, we are not equating this book of scripture with a novel, nor are we saying that it is in any sense a work of fiction or merely the product of human intellect and effort. To appreciate the Book of Mormon through a literary lens does not require us to see it as anything less than scripture. What one scholar wrote about the Gospel of John applies to all scripture: "One can call attention to the gospel's literary features because the author used standard literary conventions in order to make his gospel interesting and lively. In no way does the use of literary criticism suggest that his gospel is 'only' a story; but it is no less than that."[1]

Philosophers, scholars, and writers have debated for thousands of years about the meaning of the word *literature.* If we define *literature* so broadly to mean anything that is written, then a grocery list can be seen as poetry. However, if we define it too narrowly, then the field of literature will be so small that finding patterns and themes to help us understand what we read will be almost impossible. The description offered by Leland Ryken, a scholar of the Bible as literature, is useful in our discussion of some of the literary parts of the Book of Mormon: "A working definition of literature, is that it is an interpretive presentation of experience in an artistic form. This means that there are two criteria that must be insisted on if we are to distinguish between the literary and nonliterary parts of the Bible: (1) literature is experiential rather than abstract, and (2) literature is artistic, manifesting elements of artistic form."[2] The literary parts of the Book of Mormon manifest a certain aesthetic care about the diction, and they help us to *experience* the people, action, ideas, and feelings in the book rather than merely read about them. As important as it is to read "Thou shalt not kill" (Exodus 20:13), we find additional power and insight when we read stories that involve that commandment, such as Nephi's being commanded to take the life of Laban (see 1 Nephi 4).

The Book of Mormon has so many literary elements that it would be impossible to touch on even one of each kind in such a brief study. However, discussing just a few elements is helpful in understanding how the literature of the book can convey the doctrines and principles of the gospel.

## DIALOGUE

Writers often reveal characters and their natures through dialogue. Rather than having a narrator comment on a character's motivation or intentions, for example, a skillful author will often have the characters speak for themselves, thereby allowing us to see more fully into the characters. Instead of being told everything by the narrator, we have the satisfaction of gaining insights on our own. This masterful use of dialogue to reveal truths is often used in the Book of Mormon.

In discussing dialogue in the Bible, the biblical scholar and literary critic Robert Alter writes that "the very occurrence of extended dialogue should signal the need for special attentiveness as we read."[3] We certainly find this to be the case in the amazing encounter between the prophet Alma and the anti-Christ Korihor. Of course, their dialogue provides a direct account of much of what each of these men believes. While there is a narrative description of what Korihor believes (see Alma 30:17–18), we also learn through his dialogue what Korihor believes: "Behold, these things which ye call prophecies, which ye say are handed down by holy prophets, behold, they are foolish traditions of your fathers"; and "Ye cannot know of things which ye do not see" (Alma 30:14–15). In contrast, we know from Alma's own words, among many other things, that he knows "there is a God, and also that Christ shall come" (Alma 30:39).

What is not so obvious, however, are the characteristics that are revealed about these men by closely examining the dialogue. For example, we hear Korihor apparently splitting hairs when he says, "I do not deny the existence of a God, but I do not believe that there is a God" (Alma 30:48). This is a significant distinction to make, though, because people in that society were not punished for their beliefs but only for the crimes they committed (see vv. 11–12). In addition, Alma has just told him that if he does "deny again, behold God shall smite" him and take away his ability to speak (Alma 30:47). Korihor wants to make clear that while he does not believe there is a God (a belief, for which one cannot be punished), he is not denying the existence of God (an act that could lead to his being smitten by God). What principle can be learned from this insight that is revealed by looking more closely at dialogue? There is a difference between an honest person who seeks the truth but may have some doubts, and the kind of person Korihor is—a man who merely plays with words and who is not interested in finding truth as much as he is in covering it up. His motives are not sincere; his methods are not honorable.

For his part of the dialogue, Alma speaks of his personal testimony, the testimony of people in the community, the testimony of the holy prophets, and even the testimony of the natural world (see Alma 30:29, 44). In contrast to Korihor, Alma is a man who is rooted in testimony. This is a man who indeed knows things he may not be able to see. Among the many principles we learn from Alma's dialogue is that one of the best approaches to take in such discussions is to rely on testimony.

Many other examples of dialogue appear in the Book of Mormon. For example, we read of dialogues between Nephi and the Spirit of the Lord (see 1 Nephi 11), between Nephi and an angel (see 1 Nephi 11), between Jacob and Sherem (see Jacob 7), between Ammon and King Limhi (see Mosiah 8), between Amulek and Zeezrom (see Alma 11), and between Ammon and King Lamoni (see Alma 17–18). Each dialogue reveals principles of the gospel as well as character traits of the men who participate in the discussions.

Sometimes, however, the absence of dialogue teaches us. For example, in the first chapter in the Book of Mormon that offers an account of the Savior's physical appearance to the Nephites (3 Nephi 11), we have no account of any dialogue—of any conversation between two or more people. We hear the voice of Heavenly Father introducing the Son, and we hear the Son teach the people, but there is no dialogue. We never read in this chapter of the Lord speaking to anyone and that person, in turn, speaking to Him. This chapter is not an account of a sermon; it is not like the chapters in the New Testament, for example, that provide us with the Sermon on the Mount. It makes sense that people are not going to interrupt the Savior as He delivers a sermon. In this Third Nephi chapter, though, there are many times in which it would make sense that there would be some dialogue. Everyone present comes forth and touches the Lord, feeling the wound in His side and the prints of the nails in His hands and feet (see 3 Nephi 11:15). This is an experience that must have taken hours, yet we have no record of anyone saying anthing to Him in dialogue during this time. Also, there is no account of dialogue when He calls Nephi and others to Him and gives them power to baptize.

We do hear the voice of the people: "Hosanna! Blessed be the name of the Most High God!" (3 Nephi 11:17). But, of course, this is not a dialogue but a beautiful, spontaneous expression of worshipful joy from the Nephites. They are not entering into a conversation with the Lord; they are praising Him.

From a historical perspective, the reason we have no recorded dialogue from this experience may be that no one said anything to Him in any form of discussion. It is difficult to imagine that in all that time, no one asked a question or entered into a simple conversation with Him, but it is not impossible. However, that approach is looking at the chapter through a historical lens. If we study it through a literary lens, we may see that the absence of dialogue helps to create a beautiful and powerful image of the Lord as one who blesses and teaches but is not our equal. The focus of the chapter is on the Savior and on His words and actions, not on anything or anyone else. I believe we can learn from this the importance of coming to the Lord not as His equal but as disciples who hunger to be taught and blessed by Him. We do not enter into negotiations with the Savior; we follow Him.

If we look at 3 Nephi as a whole, we read very little dialogue with the Savior in the entire book. When we compare the account of the Lord's visit to the Nephites with those accounts in the Gospels of His mortal interactions with others, it is amazing how little dialogue there is. Could it be that the people who surrounded Him during His mortal ministry had more to say to Him than those in His Nephite ministry? Perhaps. But, once again, if we look at the text through a literary lens, we can see that there is a difference between how the people of Palestine treated the mortal Jesus of the Gospels and how the Nephites treated the resurrected, glorified Christ of 3 Nephi. And it is not just a difference between a people who had evil among them and a people who were more righteous in general. Righteous people can have dialogues with the Savior, but those in 3 Nephi rarely do. As we look at the text, we see that these Nephites worship Him, adore Him, quietly listen to His teachings, and follow Him. From a literary perspective, the

3 Nephi account portrays the Savior in ways that help readers *experience* Him as an elevated, superior Being whom we are to worship.

## METAPHOR

While many metaphors in the Book of Mormon communicate essential doctrinal truths, it may be most helpful to select one and study it in some depth. In Alma's sermon to the members of the Church in Zarahemla, we find this example: "I say unto you, ye will know at that day that ye cannot be saved; for there can no man be saved except his garments are washed white; yea, his garments must be purified until they are cleansed from all stain, through the blood of him of whom it has been spoken by our fathers, who should come to redeem his people from their sins" (Alma 5:21). Alma is using the image of a person possessing a white garment that has been stained and cleansing it in blood. In fact, the garments are actually "washed white" from being soaked in the blood. This metaphor is more than just a poetic way in which to portray the Atonement, but a powerful way to convey one of the most important truths about the Atonement. No one can wash any garment in blood and have it become clean. More emphatically, no one can wash a white garment in blood and have it turn out white. It is simply impossible—it would take a miracle for such a phenomenon to occur. And this is an essential doctrine that is communicated by means of this metaphor: the Atonement accomplishes the impossible; it is a miracle beyond human comprehension.

Alma could have taught the members of the Church accurately without metaphorical language that if they repent they would be forgiven through the Atonement of Christ. And, though that teaching would have been true, it also would have been missing the significant aspect of how the Atonement is miraculous. Alma's metaphor sends a special message to all those who are struggling to repent and who doubt that the Atonement can reach them in their need. They may feel that it's impossible for them to be forgiven for what they did. What is the message they can receive from Alma's metaphor? To the human mind, it is impossible for justice to be satisfied by what someone else does. But the Lord's Atonement does the impossible. "It would take a miracle for me to be forgiven," we may cry out in anguish. And a miracle is exactly what we can receive.

## SIMILE

After the dramatic, catastrophic destruction among the Nephites and Lamanites because of the Crucifixion, the Savior speaks to the remaining people, giving an account of what happened and why it happened. Then there is silence for many hours. The silence is finally broken by the voice of the Savior once more, and this time the Lord uses a literary device—a simile—as he speaks to His people: "How oft have I gathered you as a hen gathereth her chickens under her wings" (3 Nephi 10:4). He states the simile four different times, perhaps leading the casual reader to infer that His message is the same each time and that He is repeating it for emphasis. However, upon closer examination, we see that while the simile is the same, it is used in three different contexts.

1. "O ye people of these great cities which have fallen, who are descendants of Jacob, yea, who are of the house of Israel, how oft have I gathered you as a hen gathereth her chickens under her wings, and have nourished you" (3 Nephi 10:4). He speaks in the past tense, indicating that there were previous times when He gathered His people.

2. "And again, how oft would I have gathered you as a hen gathereth her chickens under her wings, yea, O ye people of the house of Israel, who have fallen; yea, O ye people of the house of Israel, ye that dwell at Jerusalem, as ye that have fallen; yea, how oft would I have gathered you as a hen gathereth her chickens, and ye would not" (3 Nephi 10:5). Now He speaks not in the past tense but conditionally, referring to the times He would have gathered His people if they had been willing to follow Him.

3. "O ye house of Israel whom I have spared, how oft will I gather you as a hen gathereth her chickens under her wings, if ye will repent and return unto me with full purpose of heart" (3 Nephi 10:6). In this third iteration, He speaks in the future tense, indicating that He will gather them in the future if they will repent and return to Him.

Once again, this literary element helps to convey a doctrine that would not otherwise have been communicated with more direct language. He could have spoken of the gathering by saying something like, "How often I would bring you all together if you would just repent and follow me." However, by using the simile of the hen gathering her chicks under her wings, He is also using the image of *kaphar*. This is the "basic word for atonement" with "the same basic meaning in Hebrew, Aramaic, and Arabic." That meaning includes the act of bending, arching over, or covering.[4] The simile of a hen gathering her chickens under her wings refers not only to the gathering of the house of Israel but also to the great work of His Atonement, which is fully efficacious to those who repent and return to Him "with full purpose of heart." Just as the hen's wings embrace her chickens and protect them, the Lord embraces and protects us through His Atonement.

## ALLEGORY

Much has been written about Zenos's allegory of the olive tree in the fifth chapter of Jacob. If we think of an allegory as an extended metaphor in which elements correspond to a meaning outside of the actual narrative,[5] we can see other "allegories" in the Book of Mormon. The detailed story of the Jaredites crossing the ocean in their unique barges, though an account of an actual, historical event, can also be read in such a way that we see gospel principles and basic truths of the kind of life disciples lead. A modern example of this idea that actual events can have symbolic meaning happened years ago. When President Boyd K. Packer was in a sacrament meeting in Peru, a little native boy came inside off the streets. President Packer held his arms out to him, and the little boy ran to him. After the boy sat on his lap for a period of time, President Packer set him on the chair previously occupied by Elder A. Theodore Tuttle, president of the South America West Area, an act that was "something symbolic." Later, when President Packer shared this experience, President Spencer W. Kimball told him the experience had "far greater meaning than [he had] yet come to know" and that he had held a nation on his lap.[6] We will certainly miss much meaning in life if we assume that only fictitious works can have symbolic significance.

As we study the Jaredite record of their historical journey, it is important to realize that journeys across oceans in literature are often symbolic of mortality, with the ocean representing the many great unknowns in life and with the final destination of the oceanic voyage representing where we wish to be when mortality has come to a close. The Jaredites begin their journey by placing stones that have been blessed by the Lord's touch in their ships so that they might have light: "And thus the Lord caused stones to shine in darkness, to give light unto men, women, and children, that they might not cross the great waters in darkness" (Ether 6:3). As a historical record, this chapter mentions stones because that is what was used for light. As an allegory, however, this chapter presents a significant image of light coming from Christ through stones. Of course, the Lord could have provided light for the travelers by many other methods, but He used the stones the brother of Jared brought to Him. These stones may serve to remind those in the barges, and us as well, that all light comes from the Savior, that He is the rock of our salvation (see Psalm 89:26; 2 Nephi 4:30), and that He is the rock upon which we should build the foundation for our lives (see Helaman 5:12). The Church, after all, is built upon the rock of revelation (see Matthew 16:18).

Notice the careful language used in this verse to explain the purpose of these stones. The essence of the message could have been conveyed more simply and less emphatically: the Lord caused stones to shine so everyone would have light for the voyage. Why say that these stones will shine "in darkness" when that is obvious? Perhaps the writer includes the phrase to remind us of what darkness symbolizes: "misfortune, spiritual need," or "ignorance,"[7] as well as "chaos, mystery, [and] the unknown."[8] In religious terms, darkness is "a silencing of prophetic revelation" and "the state of the human mind unilluminated by God's revelation."[9] The stones give light not just to people but specifically to "men, women, and children," as if to emphasize that this light from Christ is much like the Light *of* Christ given to each individual person (see Moroni 7:18–19; D&C 88:7). Because of the Light of Christ, no man, woman, or child faces having to cross the "great waters" of mortality in darkness.

The Jaredites make extensive preparations, making certain that they will have the food they need as well as the food their animals will need, and then they commend "themselves unto the Lord their God" (Ether

6:4). Once again, we have a historical account of something the people actually did. But it also serves in the allegory to teach us that while we are to fully prepare ourselves in this life, we are not to ignore the Lord and His hand in our affairs. In fact, even after our preparations, we are to rely on Him.

One of the most interesting elements in this allegorical account is the wind. It becomes a character in the narrative; it is caused by the Lord, and it is a "furious wind" whose "fierceness" brings about "great and terrible tempests" (vv. 5–6). Even though at times the wind appears to be no friend to the travelers, from a broader perspective it ends up being one of their greatest allies, for it "did never cease to blow towards the promised land" (v. 8). Just as the wind seems to cause problems for the Jaredites in certain moments but actually helps them arrive at the promised land, the trials and challenges in this mortal life that often cause us to despair can help us get to our promised land (if we have open minds and hearts so we can see our trials for what they truly are).

For the Jaredites, the ocean both blesses their lives as the means by which they travel to the promised land and makes their lives more difficult as it "buries" them under the water. The ocean threatens them with "mountain waves" and "great and terrible tempests," yet when they are "buried in the deep," no water "could hurt them" because of the tightness of their vessels. At these difficult times, the Jaredites remember on whom they rely: "When they were encompassed about by many waters they did cry unto the Lord, and he did bring them forth again upon the top of the waters" (v. 7). Once again, the imagery teaches us principles that can help us grow closer to the Lord as we abide by them.

Despite the difficulty of their journey, the voyagers remain steadfast in their faith and also grateful to the Lord: "And they did sing praises unto the Lord; yea, the brother of Jared did sing praises unto the Lord, and he did thank and praise the Lord all the day long; and when the night came, they did not cease to praise the Lord" (v. 9). This spirit of gratitude to the Lord at all times, and especially during challenging times, is central to a happy, fulfilling life. "Gratitude is a sign of maturity," President Gordon B. Hinckley writes. "It is an indication of sincere humility. It is a hallmark of civility. And most of all, it is a divine principle. I doubt there is anything in which we more offend the

Almighty than in our tendency to forget His mercies and to be ungrateful for that which He has given us."[10]

After a treacherous journey of almost a year, the Jaredites arrive in the promised land, bow themselves in humility, and "shed tears of joy before the Lord, because of the multitude of his tender mercies over them" (v. 12). Like all those who endure to the end, they are protected throughout their journey from all things that mean them harm. Just as "no monster of the sea could break them, neither whale that could mar them" (v. 10), nothing can break disciples of Christ who remain true to their covenants. It is true that these disciples will not live lives free of mortal trials—there will be sickness, death, and heartache—but such trials will not have the power to break or mar them if they are faithful to the Lord. The Jaredites had "light continually, whether it was above the water or under the water" (v. 10). We too can have the comfort and guidance of the Light of Christ and the Holy Spirit in our lives, both in times of happiness and in times of sorrow.

## TRAGEDY

If we look at the entire Book of Mormon through a literary lens, it is worthwhile to ask what kind of book it is. As we ask ourselves that question, we may be quick to conclude that if it is anything, it is not a tragedy. The individual heroes of the book—Lehi, Sariah, Nephi, King Benjamin, Alma, Moroni, Mormon, and many more—do not have tragic flaws, characteristic of heroes in a tragedy, which bring them down and ultimately destroy them. However, if we take the large view, we see that there is a tragic hero in the book: the Nephite civilization. The Nephite civilization is, in essence, a heroic character in the book, and it is a hero with a tragic flaw: pride. Traditionally, the tragic heroes in literature have had to fight their hubris and have lost. So it is with the Nephites. They constantly struggle against their pride—against their desires to follow their own vain ways and rebel against God—and as a people they ultimately lose this struggle.

The climax of this tragedy is found in the record of Mormon. In Mormon we have an account of the fall of the now-wicked Nephites and of their righteous general, Mormon, who leads them with love but without faith (see Mormon 3:12). We read Mormon's tragic lamentation: "O ye fair ones, how could ye have departed from the ways of the Lord! O ye fair ones, how could ye have rejected that Jesus, who stood with open arms to receive you! Behold, if ye had not done this, ye would not have fallen. But behold, ye are fallen, and I mourn your loss. O ye fair sons and daughters, ye fathers and mothers, ye husbands and wives, ye fair ones, how is it that ye could have fallen! But behold, ye are gone, and my sorrows cannot bring your return" (Mormon 6:17–20). We experience Mormon's pain as we read these words. The power of the doctrine of obedience, and the tragedy of disobedience to God, strikes our hearts through this lamentation and through the story of the fall of this great hero, the Nephite civilization. We see the same tragedy as we read of the Jaredite civilization in Ether. The message is not just taught by the text but also experienced through the literature: obedience to God ensures joy in this life and the life to come.

While the Book of Mormon has tragic elements, its overall message is not one of tragedy but of hope. As scripture, the book delivers a great message of hope—*the* great message of hope that we need to come unto Christ and be saved. In the last chapter of the Book of Mormon, we do not find a lamentation over a fallen people. Instead we find a promise to those who receive the book and read, ponder, and pray that they will know the truth (see Moroni 10:3–5). The Book of Mormon does not focus on the fall of the Nephite civilization so much as it concentrates on the faith and hope the reader can nurture through reading the book and by living what it teaches.

## CONCLUSION

Though the Book of Mormon can be seen as literature, it stands apart from works of literature because it is holy scripture, the word of God. The book is not bound by the constraints of other literary works that are primarily the product of human efforts, even if some of the principles in those works are inspired. The literary qualities of the book not only help us love reading it but also convey this message of hope and faith in Christ in a memorable way.

―――――――――――

NOTES

1. Marianne Meye Thompson, "John," in *A Complete Literary Guide to the Bible,* ed. Leland Ryken and Tremper Longman III (Grand Rapids, MI: Zondervan, 1993), 409.

2. Leland Ryken, *The Literature of the Bible* (Grand Rapids, MI: Zondervan, 1974), 13–14.

3. Robert Alter, *The Art of Biblical Narrative* (New York: Basic Books, 1981), 182.

4. Hugh Nibley, *Approaching Zion,* ed. Don E. Norton (Salt Lake City and Provo: Deseret Book, FARMS, 1989), 558. On the following page, Nibley offers this relevant description: "It was the custom for one fleeing for his life in the desert to seek protection in the tent of a great sheik, crying out, 'Ana dakhiluka,' meaning 'I am thy suppliant,' whereupon the Lord would place the hem of his robe over the guest's shoulder and declare him under his protection. . . . This puts him under the Lord's protection from all enemies."

5. William Harmon and Hugh Holman, *A Handbook to Literature,* 10th ed. (Upper Saddle River, NJ: Pearson/Prentice Hall, 2006), 12.

6. Boyd K. Packer, "Children," *Ensign,* May 2002, 7, 9.

7. Ad de Vries, *Dictionary of Symbols and Imagery* (London: North-Holland, 1974), 129.

8. Wilfred L. Guerin, Earle G. Labor, Lee Morgan, Jeanne C. Reesman, and John R. Willingham, eds., *A Handbook of Critical Approaches to Literature,* 4th ed. (Oxford: Oxford University Press, 1999), 161.

9. Leland Ryken, James C. Wilhoit, and Tremper Longman III, eds., *Dictionary of Biblical Imagery* (Downer's Grove, IL: InterVarsity Press, 1998), 192.

10. Gordon B. Hinckley, *Standing for Something: Ten Neglected Virtues That Will Heal Our Hearts and Homes* (New York: Three Rivers Press, 2000), 106.

# 6

## AGENCY—IT'S OUR CHOICE: BOOK OF MORMON INSIGHTS

### Victor L. Ludlow

One enduring precept governing our relationship to God is the issue of free will, including why and how we submit our will to His. *Agency* is the key word Latter-day Saints use to describe this free-will nature of our beings. Readers of the Book of Mormon are aware of the lasting effects of agency in the pervasive struggles between the Nephite and Lamanite descendants of Lehi. Some readers may wonder, what if Laman and Lemuel had chosen not to come with their family to the promised land? Would a much more peaceful society have developed? Actually, the two rebellious brothers had such a choice when they could have returned to Jerusalem rather that staying with their family (see 1 Nephi 7:6–21, especially v. 15). However, they exercised their agency and made choices that forever affected Book of Mormon history.

The choices we make may not affect the future history of our nation, but they do impact our personal destiny and influence those in our families and other circles of influence. Indeed, the cause-effect

---

*Victor L. Ludlow is a professor of ancient scripture at Brigham Young University.*

relationship of our choices is a major message of the Book of Mormon. In its pages, we learn about the nature of human agency and the enduring consequences of our choices. This chapter will discuss what agency is; how, where, and by whom various principles of agency are taught; and how understanding and applying the basic elements of agency will bring us nearer to God.

The English word *agency* derives from the Latin root *agere*, meaning "to act" and the Greek root *agein*, meaning "to drive." These linguistic roots emphasize the *action* of actually using our opportunity to exercise our free will. This emphasis on action is also found in dictionary definitions of *agency*. Agency, as it applies to the moral dimensions of our lives, is defined as:

> An active force, action, or power
> That by which something is done; a means or instrumentality[1]
> An action or intervention to produce a particular result[2]

The word *agency* does not appear in the King James Bible, and many Latter-day Saints would be surprised to note that the word *agency* also is not in the Book of Mormon. Rather, it is a philosophical-doctrinal term found in the Restoration scriptures.[3] However, valuable teachings and clear examples of agency are found throughout the Book of Mormon.

## SCRIPTURE PASSAGES ON AGENCY

Synonyms of *agency* and the principles and applications of agency are found throughout the Book of Mormon. An easy way to locate these passages is to refer to scripture aids, particularly the Topical Guide to the LDS scriptures. Under the term *agency*, eighteen Book of Mormon references are shown.[4] The common Topical Guide synonyms for *agency* are words such as *will, choose, free,* and *act*.[5] The scripture passages highlight the use of our *will* to follow God or the devil, our opportunity to *choose* spiritual life or death as we either serve the Lord or pursue works of wickedness; and they emphasize our being *free* to *act* for ourselves. Often two of the key words are combined in phrases like "free to choose," "free to act," "do according to your will," or "act according to their wills."

A second helpful reference resource is the *Encyclopedia of Mormonism.*[6] The *Encyclopedia of Mormonism* entry on agency shows eight citations from the Book of Mormon.[7] The focus of this chapter is to highlight essential insights about agency as found in the Book of Mormon passages highlighted in these two resources. As a starting point, the twenty-four particular references associated with agency are listed in the following chart:

| PASSAGE | REF.* | AGENCY-RELATED INSIGHTS |
|---|---|---|
| 2 Nephi 2:11 | TG | There is an opposition (or different choices) in all things. |
| 2 Nephi 2:11–13 | EM | There must be things (beings) to act and not just be acted upon. |
| 2 Nephi 2:16 | TG | God gave unto man that he should act for himself. |
| 2 Nephi 2:23 | EM | Joy is impossible without opposite choices. |
| 2 Nephi 2:26 | EM (2X) | Individuals are free to act for themselves. |
| 2 Nephi 2:27 | TG | People are free to choose liberty/eternal life or captivity/death. |
| 2 Nephi 2:27–29 | EM | We choose eternal life by following the will of God's Holy Spirit. |
| 2 Nephi 10:23 | TG, EM | We can act for ourselves and choose the way of death or life. |
| 2 Nephi 26:10 | TG | Those who choose works of darkness must go down to hell. |
| Mosiah 2:21 | TG | God gives us life that we can do according to our own will. |
| Mosiah 2:33 | TG | Woe is pronounced upon him who chooses to obey the evil spirit. |
| Mosiah 5:2 | EM | We can have a disposition to do good continually. |
| Mosiah 5:8 | TG | We are made free as covenant children of Christ. |
| Mosiah 16:4 | EM | Sin limits the agency of sinners as they become lost and fallen. |

| Mosiah 28:4 | TG | God's mercy can spare us from the consequences of our evil acts. |
| Alma 3:26 | TG | We are rewarded according to the good or evil spirit that we obey. |
| Alma 12:31 | TG | God places us in a state to act according to our wills. |
| Alma 13:3 | TG | Men who choose good over evil can receive the priesthood. |
| Alma 13:10 | TG | Men can choose to repent and work righteousness. |
| Alma 29:4 | TG | God decrees, according to people's wills, salvation or destruction. |
| Alma 30:8 | TG | People can choose whom they will serve. |
| Alma 41:7 | TG | People stand or fall according to whether they do good or do evil. |
| Helaman 14:30 | TG | God made us free; we are permitted to act for ourselves. |
| Moroni 7:15 | TG | We can judge, with perfect knowledge, to know good from evil. |

* TG = Topical Guide; EM = *Encyclopedia of Mormonism*

## KEY INSIGHTS ABOUT AGENCY

These two dozen key passages provide valuable insights into some essential elements about agency. They can be summarized into seven statements:

1. There are two types of entities—those that can make choices and act and those that are acted upon; God would that we should act for ourselves.

2. Those who choose to act for themselves need to know good from evil because various opposing forces seek to influence and act upon them.

3. People should appreciate that there are natural opposites in the many choices they confront and that opposition is a necessary part of existence.

4. God has given us the opportunity and gift to exercise our own wills and He encourages us to act and to use our agency in righteousness, which leads to greater growth and opportunity.

5. There are natural consequences to our choices, some good and others bad, and one must learn to act wisely if one wants to enjoy the blessings of God and ongoing freedom of choices.

6. Even though we may choose to act in wickedness or ignorance, the merciful and redemptive acts of God can redeem us from the negative consequences of our actions.

7. The challenges and opportunities of agency define our eternal existence, and our choices determine our relationship with God and others.

In turn, these seven statements can be condensed into seven key terms that describe agency:

*Identity*—each entity or being is either one who acts or one who is acted upon.

*Knowledge*—one should learn to identify truth and to distinguish right from wrong.

*Choices*—many influences act upon us and many decisions lay before us.

*Actions*—one needs to do something to gain further experience and understanding.

*Consequences*—a variety of positive and/or negative results follow any action.

*Efficacy*—one can learn and grow from these consequences, especially with God's help.

*Unity*—one should become a child of God who lives in harmony with His will.

Let us first describe some essential precepts associated with each of these seven elements, and then we will review how some Book of Mormon prophets teach and testify about these terms.

*Identity* defines the human capacity to think and choose. Referred to in the scriptures and by philosophers as our "will" and by social scientists as our "personality," identity is the core element that makes each person original, unique, and distinct. Before we can act as "free agents," we must first "be," or exist as independent beings. The Prophet Joseph Smith revealed that the essential unique element of our being is our *intelligence,* which is coeternal with God. This "light of truth" within each of us cannot be created or destroyed, but it can be strengthened by obedience to God's laws until one "is glorified in truth and knoweth all things." Indeed, there is no existence without all intelligence being free to act for itself (see D&C 93:27–30).

*Knowledge,* both its acquisition and its application, is one of the primary purposes of this earth life. We, as spirit children of God, came to earth to receive physical bodies, to develop our ability to choose good from evil, and to grow in knowledge and understanding. Greater knowledge expands the range of our potential choices. Eventually our knowledge should encompass all physical, moral, and spiritual truths. Then, as Jesus promised His disciples, we can "know the truth, and the truth shall make you free" (John 8:32).

*Choices,* especially those in opposition to each other, provide multiple opportunities to exercise agency. Opposition is a natural part of life in God's universe. Different forces and entities work for and against each other and us. Various influences motivate us toward a great variety of choices and decision-making patterns. Freedom of discernment is a divine gift that God expects us to apply in righteousness. As we make internal decisions to obey spiritual, moral, and physical laws, we choose a path that allows us to maintain and expand our freedom to make future choices.

*Action* is the central focal point and function of agency. Agency, as defined in its linguistic roots ("to act" and "to drive"), is an active force or power by which something is done. Having the gift of moral agency but not using it is like having a spiritual toolbox but not opening it— eventually the gift "rusts away" and becomes stagnant and useless. Additionally, action is the means by which we transform our dreams, hopes, and expectations into reality. Through action, our agency remains vibrant and fulfilling.

*Consequences* follow every action. We may choose the actions, but we cannot control all the consequences. When we exercise our freedom to act, the results of our actions are based upon eternal laws governing our existence. Because the consequences of all actions are based on unalterable and dependable laws, we can confidently move forward toward our chosen goals with less fear of failure. Consequences also lead to feelings and experiences ranging from joy and happiness to sorrow and misery. God's will is that we experience the joy that follows actions of righteousness.

*Efficacy* is a formal term describing our ultimate effectiveness to produce intended results. Since no human is completely powerful and free, each of us must learn to do the best with our available resources. Efficacy is the capacity, with the divine help of God's grace and Christ's Atonement, to produce continuous and lasting righteous results that will bless the lives of others and ourselves. We produce success best when we choose the right. But we can also learn from our mistakes and be redeemed from our sins if we access the mercy and powers of God.

*Unity* is the essential element of agency that unites those entities and forces that want to work together to preserve agency. Since there are forces and beings that seek to limit or destroy agency, the wise and righteous who want to preserve it must work in unison and harmony to guarantee the blessings of agency throughout eternity. God Himself acts as the ultimate preserver of our agency, promising that the consequences of our actions will be fair, consistent, and eternal. He solicits that our will becomes united with His, furthering His works of righteousness.

The Book of Mormon prophets place these philosophical precepts into practical examples of agency. They emphasize that in the moral realm of our free will, just as in the physical world for our bodies, God has provided a wonderful environment for us to learn and grow as His children. Thus, we can learn how to apply these principles of agency in our lives, using the Book of Mormon as a helpful resource. Several Book of Mormon prophets enrich and amplify our insights into agency's seven key words and elements.

## PERSPECTIVES ON AGENCY

The selected Book of Mormon passages highlighted earlier also help identify the Book of Mormon spokesmen who teach the precepts associated with agency, as seen in the following chart:

| PASSAGE | SPOKESMAN |
| --- | --- |
| 2 Nephi 2:11 | Lehi |
| 2 Nephi 2:11–13 | Lehi |
| 2 Nephi 2:16 | Lehi |
| 2 Nephi 2:23 | Lehi |
| 2 Nephi 2:26 | Lehi |
| 2 Nephi 2:27 | Lehi |
| 2 Nephi 2:27–29 | Lehi |
| 2 Nephi 10:23 | Jacob |
| 2 Nephi 26:10 | Nephi |
| Mosiah 2:21 | Benjamin |
| Mosiah 2:33 | Benjamin |
| Mosiah 5:2 | People |
| Mosiah 5:8 | Benjamin |
| Mosiah 16:4 | Abinadi |
| Mosiah 28:4 | Mormon (editor) |
| Alma 3:26 | Mormon (editor) |
| Alma 12:31 | Alma, the Younger |
| Alma 13:3 | Alma, the Younger |
| Alma 13:10 | Alma, the Younger |
| Alma 29:4 | Alma, the Younger |
| Alma 30:8 | Mormon (editor) |
| Alma 41:7 | Alma, the Younger |
| Helaman 14:30 | Samuel |
| Moroni 7:15 | Moroni |

The nine prophets who provide insights about agency range from Lehi, the founder of the main Book of Mormon community, to Moroni, the last Nephite prophet. In 2 Nephi 2, we can find almost one-third of the key Book of Mormon insights about agency. In this single, profound chapter, Lehi teaches his family (and us) about eternal principles of agency, especially the need and consequences of opposition in all things.

The primary spokesman in the Mosiah passages is Benjamin, the prophet and king, as he gives his farewell address to the multitudes assembled at Zarahemla.

Forty to fifty years later, Alma, the son of Alma, provides some precepts of agency as he teaches various Nephite audiences as recorded in the book of Alma.

About a half-century later, another famous Book of Mormon prophet, Samuel, gives powerful teachings about agency to the citizens of Zarahemla (see Helaman 14:30–31).

Lastly, Moroni gives us, the future readers of his exhortations, important incentives and promises for properly applying our agency, as found in the last chapters of the Book of Mormon.

We will carefully review the Lehi passages to model how we can locate and personalize the precepts of agency. Then we will highlight the words and witnesses of Samuel and Moroni about agency.

## LEHI'S DOCTRINAL TEACHINGS

We will both review a sequential summary of Lehi's teachings and also answer some key topical questions about agency. Beginning in 2 Nephi 2:5, Lehi teaches his son Jacob some foundational doctrines about agency. He reminds Jacob that men are instructed to know good from evil and that they have received temporal and spiritual laws that cut them off from God (because they choose to break them).

Lehi testifies that the Messiah, being full of grace and truth, brings redemption and offers Himself as a sacrifice for their sins to answer the demands of the law. He promises that they who believe in Him shall be saved (see vv. 6–9).

Lehi then addresses all his sons as he highlights the necessity of opposites in all things, giving examples of righteousness and wickedness, life and death, and happiness and misery. He categorizes all entities of the universe into two great opposites—the active (things or beings to act) and the passive (things or beings to be acted upon). And unto mankind, Lehi continues, God gave to them that they should act for themselves, being enticed by good or evil (see vv. 10–16). Lehi reviews, on one hand, how the devil enticed Adam and Eve and brought about the Fall and, as an opposite, how God provided repentance to rescue mankind from their fallen state (see vv. 17–21).

With profound insight, Lehi teaches that the resulting benefits of the Fall are of great value because mankind moved out of a state of innocence and stagnancy into one of wisdom and progression. After the Fall, humans could now experience joy, having known misery; they could do good, having known sin. All this was done in the wisdom of God (see vv. 22–24).

Lehi then delivers his famous quote that "Adam fell that men might be; and men are, that they might have joy" (v. 25). This joy and the accompanying freedoms are brought about through the redemptive acts of the Messiah, which moves mankind to a new level of lasting freedom where they can "act for themselves and not be acted upon"! (v. 26). They are now "free according to the flesh" and "free to choose liberty and eternal life" (v. 27). Lehi concludes with an exhortation to his sons to hearken to the great Mediator and to choose eternal life according to His divine will (see v. 28).

These two dozen verses, more than any other block of scripture, provide profound insight, deep meaning, and eternal context into mankind's free-will relationship with God. The prophet Lehi truly helps us understand the divine gift, nature, and purpose of agency.

## INSIGHTS FROM LEHI

Next, by asking ourselves some key questions about what we have learned about agency from the words of Lehi, we can discover ways that we can apply these precepts in our lives. We particularly want to know how these agency precepts will enhance our relationship with God. We will use the seven key words and elements of agency as our reference points.

### Identity

*Who are the essential free-will persons involved in our relationship with God?*

God the Father grants us freedom to act for ourselves. He encourages us to exercise our agency in righteousness. He also has provided a Savior for us to recover from our misuse of agency.

Jesus the Christ, as the great Mediator, redeems us from our errors and sins. He restores and helps maintain our freedoms. He has shown us the way to eternal life if we choose to follow Him.

We, the children of God on earth, are free to choose eternal life or lasting captivity. We, as eternal intelligent beings, can follow light and truth as we obey God's will.

## Knowledge

*What critical truths do we need to know as we develop our relationship with God?*

God has given us the gift of agency; we are not to be forced either to sin or to do good.

We can gain knowledge of eternal truths and learn to distinguish good from evil.

The Holy Spirit will help us to discern truth from error and to make wise and righteous choices.

## Choices

*What key influences and opportunities affect our relationship with God?*

Opposing forces of good (God) and evil (Satan) constantly act upon us.

We, as accountable children of God, ultimately have to decide what we think, say, and do.

The extremes of eternal life with God or spiritual death with Satan await our choices.

## Action

*What significant acts must we do as we build our relationship with God?*

We need to come to God with faith in Him, His goodness, His plan, and His Son.

We need to repent of our sins and failures.

We need to come unto Christ in a covenant relationship.[8]

## Consequences

*What eternal laws and consequences apply to our relationship with God?*

Obedience to God's eternal laws brings blessings that result in joy and happiness.

Disobedience to God's eternal laws brings punishments that result in misery and sorrow.

God's mercy has provided a means of redemption, *if* we meet His conditions.

## Efficacy

*How can our relationship with God be improved and enhanced?*

We need to *know,* recognizing truth and learning to discern good from evil.

We need to *do,* following the Master in acts of faithfulness and righteousness.

We need to *be,* becoming more like the Father and Son in love, testimony, and service.

## Unity

*What could and should be our ultimate relationship with God and His will?*

We should return to God the Father with wisdom, integrity, and virtue like that of God's Son.

Ultimately, we should be in harmony and unison with God, His Son, and the celestial hosts.

Surely each of us, as we study and ponder the above list of questions and answers, will find a number of areas in our personal lives that need to be strengthened so that we can improve our relationship with God.

## SAMUEL'S POWERFUL INSIGHTS AND WITNESS

To reinforce our understanding about agency and to add a second prophetic witness to the teachings of Lehi, we will highlight the words of the great Lamanite prophet, Samuel. After foretelling the signs of Jesus's birth, Samuel testifies that whosoever will believe might be saved and whosoever will not believe will bring upon themselves their own condemnation (see Helaman 14:28–29). Then in two concise, powerful verses, the prophet reviews the basic elements of agency and accountability in the following words:

> And now remember, remember, my brethren, that whosoever perisheth, perisheth unto himself; and whosoever doeth iniquity, doeth it unto himself; for behold, ye are free; ye are permitted to act for yourselves; for behold, God hath given unto you a knowledge and he hath made you free.
>
> He hath given unto you that ye might know good from evil, and he hath given unto you that ye might choose life or death;

and ye can do good and be restored unto that which is good, or have that which is good restored unto you; or ye can do evil, and have that which is evil restored unto you. (Helaman 14:30–31)

We could easily have inserted the key words describing agency in this passage. Samuel testifies to his audience of their *identity* as free individuals and that God has given them *knowledge* of good from evil. They are free to make their own *choices*, and he encourages them in their *action* to do good. Samuel reminds them of the opposite life-or-death *consequences* of their choices and how, in a process of *efficacy*, they can have either good or evil restored unto them. He continues in the following verses and admonishes them toward repentance as they follow the righteous examples of those, especially the Lamanites, among them. All are invited to come to their Redeemer and, in *unity*, to be numbered among His sheep. As in other Book of Mormon passages, the word agency or even the key words describing agency are often not in the text of the prophetic messages. However, the essential precepts, principles, and practices of agency are taught by the Book of Mormon prophets.

## MORONI'S FINAL EXHORTATION

As a third and final witness, the concluding words of the last prophet in the Book of Mormon provide insightful and encouraging instruction that applies to agency. Moroni, as recorded in Moroni 10, reminds us that every good gift (such as agency) comes from God (see v. 18). He encourages us to act in faith (as we apply our agency) to "do all things which are expedient" for our salvation (v. 23). He exhorts us to "lay hold upon" the good gifts of God and to "touch not the evil gift, nor the unclean thing"—using our agency wisely and always choosing the right and good (v. 30). Finally, the great prophet Moroni invites us to exercise our agency to "come unto Christ, and be perfected in him." As we deny ourselves of ungodliness and love God with all our hearts, then by the grace of God we become perfect in Christ (v. 32). The ultimate reward of the wise use of our agency is to be sanctified in Christ by the grace of God so we may become "holy, without spot" (v. 33).

## IT IS OUR CHOICE

Wise use of agency helps fulfill the two key purposes of the Book of Mormon, as cited on its title page—first, to teach the house of Israel about God's works, covenants, and prophecies, and second, to testify of Jesus as the Christ. As we learn of God's gift of agency and enter into and maintain a covenant relationship with Him, we receive the great blessings promised in divine prophecy. Central to our covenants is the exercise of our agency as we choose to make a commitment to Christ and as we seek to follow His path of eternal life to become united with Him and the Father.

The Book of Mormon explains that our freedom to choose is a wonderful gift from God, associated with marvelous opportunities and responsibility. The promises associated with agency are, however, double-sided: the positive use of agency results in joy and liberty culminating in the kind of peace that only Christ and righteousness can bring; the negative use of agency results in misery and captivity degenerating into the perpetual warfare that only Satan and wickedness can bring. Wickedly applied agency carries us on a satanic path toward selfish conflict and misery, while wisely applied agency follows the Master's path toward shared peace and joy. Agency, as understood and practiced in righteousness, will bring us nearer to God.

Just as Laman and Lemuel made significant choices during challenging and difficult times, we often face unpleasant circumstances where we must make difficult decisions. Like Laman and Lemuel, we may even feel as if we have been forced onto a certain path in our life and have reaped consequences we did not deserve. Although Laman and Lemuel used their agency in a way that fostered hatred and wars, we can use our agency to build understanding and peace. Their choices affected the race, culture, and history of the Book of Mormon peoples in America. Our choices will extend beyond our lifetime and affect many others, especially our posterity.

Agency is our choice! But, considering the opposing consequences highlighted in the Book of Mormon—to exercise our agency in righteousness is our only wise choice.

## NOTES

1. *Webster's New Twentieth Century Dictionary of the English Dictionary,* unabridged (William Collins Publishers, 1979), s.v. "agency."

2. Corel WordPerfect 11 Dictionary, s.v. "agency."

3. Agency appears only six times in the standard works: four times in the Doctrine and Covenants (29:36; 64:18; 93:31; 101:78) and twice in the Pearl of Great Price (Moses 4:3; 7:32). Passages about being free or moral "agents" are also found six times in the same works of scripture: Doctrine and Covenants 29:35, 39; 58:28; 64:29; 104:17 and Moses 6:56.

4. Fewer listings are in the other standard works: thirteen are in the Doctrine and Covenants, twelve in the Bible, and seven in the Pearl of Great Price.

5. In the Topical Guide, the word "will" (or "wills," "wilt") appears five times; "choose" is shown nine times; "free" (or "freely") is listed eight times; and "act" (or "do," "doest") is found seven times.

6. See C. Terry Warner, "Agency," in *Encyclopedia of Mormonism,* ed. Daniel H. Ludlow (New York: Macmillan, 1992), 1:26–27.

7. Fewer references were cited in the other standard works with six from the Doctrine and Covenants, two from the Bible, and one from the Pearl of Great Price (see *Encyclopedia of Mormonism,* 1:26–27).

8. This covenant relationship of baptism was the culminating element of agency that King Benjamin desired of his people; see Mosiah 2–5.

# 7

# LAMAN AND LEMUEL: A CASE STUDY IN "NOT BECOMING"

## Michael A. Goodman

We can easily see Laman and Lemuel as being lost from the start. Almost like stock characters in a novel, they may appear to have little depth or complexity. This simplistic view makes it hard to identify the reasons behind, as well as the consequences of, Laman and Lemuel's behavior. Consequently, if we do not look for deeper meaning in Laman and Lemuel's story, we may fail to identify the necessary precepts to avoid the pitfalls they fell into and to which we are vulnerable today.

Through a more contextual view of Laman and Lemuel's lives, we are provided with a set of precepts to help us thrive spiritually in our day. As President Spencer W. Kimball taught, to be "forewarned is [to be] forearmed."[1] Ultimately, Laman and Lemuel's lack of faith in and incorrect understanding of God led to their failure to become the righteous sons of God they were intended to be.

The Book of Mormon often teaches principles by contrast, or through opposites.[2] Readers learn the value of freedom as they view the consequences of captivity. They learn the joy of righteousness by

---

*Michael A. Goodman is a part-time instructor of ancient scripture in Religious Education at Brigham Young University.*

viewing the price of wickedness. Some wonder why Mormon included so many examples of wickedness in a book meant to bring us to Christ. One reason is to warn against all things that might take us away from the Savior. Hugh Nibley noted: "To the casual reader it might seem that the Book of Mormon refers too much to evil-doing and 'all manner of iniquity.' But the reasons for this emphasis on the ways of the wicked are fully explained by the book itself. They are meant as a warning and example to that peculiarly wicked age for which the Book of Mormon message has been preserved and to which it is addressed."[3]

A careful study of Laman and Lemuel can provide great insights into our own situation. Consider the following historical narrative that selectively omits Laman and Lemuel's unrighteous behavior. Laman and Lemuel agreed to leave everything they possessed and journey into the wilderness to an unknown location at their father's request (see 1 Nephi 2:4). This involved not only leaving their material possessions but also their hopes and dreams of a future among the only people they knew. They agreed to travel a three-day journey back to Jerusalem to fulfill the request of their father and the Lord to bring back the plates (see 1 Nephi 3:9). They agreed to approach Laban and request the records, surely suspecting that the success of such a request was not likely (see 1 Nephi 3:11–14). When their first attempt failed, they agreed once again, at Nephi's suggestion, to sacrifice all their family wealth in an attempt to secure the scriptural record (see 1 Nephi 3:22). They dutifully returned to the tent of their father after successfully obtaining the plates (see 1 Nephi 4:38). Once there "they did rejoice exceedingly, and did offer sacrifice and burnt offerings unto the Lord; and they gave thanks unto the God of Israel" (1 Nephi 5:9).

They were soon commanded to return to Jerusalem again. This time they were to petition Ishmael's family to sacrifice everything and join them on their journey to a still-unknown promised land. They agreed to this without murmuring (see 1 Nephi 7:3). They returned once again to the tent of their father in the wilderness after succeeding in their mission. While there, Lehi had a dream and shared it with his children. Laman and Lemuel inquired as to the meaning of the dream (see 1 Nephi 15:2–3, 7). They were "pacified and did humble themselves before the Lord" as they began to understand the meaning of the dream

(1 Nephi 15:20). They continued to inquire about the meaning of their father's dreams (see 1 Nephi 15:21–26), and they did "humble themselves" again before the Lord (1 Nephi 16:5). They commenced building a ship that ultimately carried them beyond the hope of ever returning to their homeland again. After travailing in the wilderness for over a decade, they arrived in the promised land (see 1 Nephi 18:23). Finally, before his death, Lehi blessed them and promised them the birthright blessing on conditions of righteousness: "And he spake unto them concerning their rebellions upon the waters, and the mercies of God in sparing their lives, that they were not swallowed up in the sea. . . . But, said he, notwithstanding our afflictions, we have obtained a land of promise, a land which is choice above all other lands; a land which the Lord God hath covenanted with me should be a land for the inheritance of my seed. Yea, the Lord hath covenanted this land unto me, and to my children forever, and also all those who should be led out of other countries by the hand of the Lord" (2 Nephi 1:2, 5).

## FAILURE TO EXERCISE FAITH

Even though this account of mostly correct choices seems to apply more easily to Lehi's two younger sons, Nephi and Sam, it is in reality the beginning of Laman and Lemuel's tragic story. How could this tale of obedience and sacrifice possibly apply to Laman and Lemuel, who eventually separated from their family and became truly wicked? (see 2 Nephi 5). The answer to this question is a key to discovering, as well as applying, important precepts and principles in our own lives. As shown, righteous actions may not lead to *becoming* righteous if our faith is not centered in Jesus Christ. Understanding this removes the unrealistic façade from Laman and Lemuel and allows us to liken their experience to ourselves. It is likely that sincere Church members rarely gain much from comparing their life experiences with the oversimplified vilification of Laman and Lemuel. Most of us are not trying to murder our family members. The scriptures provide ample clues to help us more accurately understand this story and thereby apply the pertinent principles in our lives more readily.

The history of righteous actions mentioned previously does not negate or necessarily mitigate Laman and Lemuel's wickedness. As one scholar put it, Laman and Lemuel "emerge as fundamentally corrupt men."[4] Instead, the history places their unrighteousness in a context that allows lessons to be more applicable and makes their story even more tragic as we realize their potential and their failure to live worthy of receiving blessings. Lehi never gave up on his two eldest sons and even promised them the birthright blessing if they would soften their hearts and repent. Lehi did not just wish for their repentance as he was dying. Laman and Lemuel had humbled themselves and had submitted to the Lord no fewer than six times throughout their lives (see 1 Nephi 7:19–21; 15:20; 16:5, 22–24, 32; 17:53–55; 18:1–4, 20). One time they felt such remorse that they bowed down before their younger brother and pled for his forgiveness (see 1 Nephi 7:20–21). However, Laman and Lemuel ultimately refused to humble themselves and turned away from the Lord. As Elder Neal A. Maxwell explained, "Laman and Lemuel became rebels instead of leaders, resentful instead of righteous—all because of their failure to understand either the character or the purposes of God."[5] Understanding the reasons for this failure to live up to their potential provides a fruitful field from which to harvest saving principles for our lives.

## FAILURE TO OVERCOME FALLEN NATURE

Four personal weaknesses become obvious as we study the lives of Laman and Lemuel: pride, worldliness, slothfulness, and anger. These weaknesses inhibited them from developing a living faith in Christ and laid the groundwork for their complete rejection of God. Each weakness was not only a symptom of but also a reason for their failure to come unto Christ and be saved. Ultimately, it was Laman and Lemuel's failure to develop living faith in Christ that prevented them from overcoming their personal weaknesses and led to their spiritual destruction. The Savior promises to help us overcome our weaknesses and redeem us from our fallen state (see Ether 12:27). Laman and Lemuel's failure to develop faith in Christ left them to battle their weakness by themselves, ultimately a losing cause. Their refusal to "grow up in Christ"[6] left them to become "for themselves" (see 3 Nephi 1:29). Therefore, even though Laman and Lemuel *did* many good things, when left to their own merits, they failed to *become* what the Savior desired them to become.[7] To better understand how this happened, it is helpful to examine the relationship between these four weaknesses and Laman and Lemuel's lack of faith in Christ.

Pride was a fundamental problem for Laman and Lemuel. In their commentary, Reynolds and Sjodahl wrote: "The great weakness of Laman was his pride. He was a man with a strong personality, capable of impressing others as a leader. He, no doubt, had as much education as his younger brothers. He was skilled in oratory, and he had the legal advantage of being the firstborn. But with all these qualifications he was weak, because he lacked humility."[8] Laman and Lemuel's pride is evident throughout the scriptural record. They always claimed their right to rule over their siblings (see 1 Nephi 16:37; 2 Nephi 5:3). They continually chafed under the directing hand of Lehi. Even with a belief in God,[9] they regularly questioned His guidance and commandments, especially when it came through their brother or their father (see 1 Nephi 2:11; 3:31; 7:6; 17:18).

Ultimately, pride precluded the possibility of their spiritual growth. It made the requisite dose of humility unobtainable: "Humility is a concept that plays an essential role in the origins of spirituality. Naturally, there are other important considerations, but the scriptures are clear and consistent on two points regarding humility and spirituality. First, the absence of humility virtually precludes the development of spirituality. And, second, the presence of humility is essential for spiritual growth."[10]

Likewise, a materialistic orientation kept Laman and Lemuel's focus earthbound. One author stated that "Laman can be viewed as a prototype of the 'natural man.'"[11] From their first complaint at having to leave their possessions behind (see 1 Nephi 2:11) to their lament on the seashore (see 1 Nephi 17:21), Laman and Lemuel continually focused on worldly things. This focus made it hard for them to appreciate spiritual manifestations, even when those manifestations led them through the "more fertile parts of the wilderness" (see 1 Nephi 16:16). President James E. Faust taught, "As the scales of worldliness are taken from our eyes, we see more clearly who we are and what our responsibilities are concerning our divine destiny."[12] Laman and Lemuel were never able to see clearly through the lens of worldliness through which they had chosen to view life. Laman and Lemuel's worldliness decreased the pos-sibility that they would focus on the things of the Spirit. This kept them from viewing Christ as a necessary part of their lives.

In connection with Laman and Lemuel's pride and worldly focus, they were slothful and easily discouraged when faced with difficult tasks. This further complicated any effort to build a relationship with God. When they were sent back to get the plates, they complained that it was a "hard thing" Lehi required of them (see 1 Nephi 3:5). When their first attempt failed, they wanted to give up and go back (see 1 Nephi 3:14). When Laman and Lemuel didn't understand Lehi's words, they would argue among themselves and even ask Nephi about their meaning; but they refused to exercise the faith and effort neces-sary to obtain an answer from the Lord (see 1 Nephi 15:8–9). Their lament that "the Lord maketh no such thing known unto us" was not an indictment of God but of their own lack of effort.

When their bows lost their springs and Nephi's bow broke, Laman and Lemuel murmured instead of working to find a solution (see 1 Nephi 16:20). When Nephi was commanded to build a ship, they "were desirous that they might not labor" (1 Nephi 17:18). Laman and Lemuel showed a consistent pattern of slothfulness in starting tasks commanded by the Lord and were easily discouraged when those tasks proved difficult. One scholar refers to part of this problem as the "wilderness factor." He questions Laman and Lemuel's willingness to adjust to the hardships of the wilderness. "As the hardships of their journey increased, perhaps Laman and Lemuel began to lose faith in the entire venture and became defensive when Lehi and Nephi contin-ued to attribute their journeyings to the Lord's will."[13]

These examples clearly illustrate that it is impossible to sustain a relationship with God without the requisite effort and sacrifice. Hugh Nibley wrote: "We cannot enjoy optional obedience to the law of God, or place our own limits on the law of sacrifice, or mitigate the charges of righteous conduct connected with the law of the gospel. We cannot be willing to sacrifice only that which is convenient to part with, and then expect a reward. The Atonement is everything; it is not to be had 'on the cheap.'"[14]

Finally, when Laman and Lemuel refused to obey the Lord's

commandments, they were inevitably censured by Lehi, Nephi, or an angel of the Lord. Because of the hardness of their hearts, they typically refused to accept correction and chose to be offended. This further stunted their spiritual growth and reduced the possibility of a meaningful relationship with the Lord. Nephi did not even have to rebuke them to make them angry. He simply had to be an example of obedience. "Just as Abel's righteousness aroused Cain's hatred, so Nephi's righteousness aroused the hatred of Laman and Lemuel."[15]

In fact, Laman and Lemuel's most serious outbursts and wickedness flowed from uncontrolled anger at being rebuked. When Nephi rebuked them for their desire to return to Jerusalem, they became so angry that they bound him and "sought to take away my [Nephi's] life." (1 Nephi 7:16). When Nephi rebuked them for their unwillingness to help build the ship, "they were angry with me [Nephi], and were desirous to throw me into the depths of the sea" (1 Nephi 17:48). When Nephi rebuked them for their rudeness on the boat, Laman and Lemuel once again were angry with Nephi and tied him up (see 1 Nephi 18:10–11). Ultimately, their anger at Nephi's rebukes led them to seek his life. Each of their murderous attempts came because of uncontrolled anger at being rebuked.

As with each of the weaknesses reviewed previously, Laman and Lemuel's anger was not only a symptom of but also a reason for their failure to come unto Christ and be saved. In addition to the obvious wickedness engendered by their anger,[16] the anger created a wedge between Laman, Lemuel, and those who were best situated to help them. It turned their hearts cold and hard, closed to the promptings of parents, siblings, and the Holy Spirit.

## MISUNDERSTANDING THE TRUE NATURE OF GOD

According to the scriptural record, Laman and Lemuel never denied the reality of God. Unlike most mortals, they actually had angelic evidence of His existence. However, "they knew not the dealings of that God who had created them" (1 Nephi 2:12). They failed to understand the nature of their relationship with God and the nature of this probationary state. So even though God was a reality to Laman and Lemuel, He was largely irrelevant to them. They never drew upon His power to help them overcome their fallen state. They never progressed from a basic knowledge that God exists to having living faith in Him.

In many ways, Laman and Lemuel serve as a bad example of President Boyd K. Packer's dictum that "true doctrine, understood, changes attitudes and behavior."[17] Their understanding turned Jehovah into a god of convenience. For Laman and Lemuel, God was not central in their lives or in the lives of others. They wanted a god who was pleased by minimal efforts and who left life largely to them (see 1 Nephi 17:20–22). Their god was not a god of revelation. Even with the examples of a prophetic father and brother, they refused to pray to God because He "maketh no such thing known unto us" (1 Nephi 15:8–9). Clearly, the god of Laman and Lemuel's understanding is only loosely related to who God truly is. Elder Maxwell explained, "Their enormous errors [in understanding God's true nature] led to almost comical inconsistencies, such as Laman and Lemuel's believing that God could handle mighty Pharaoh and great Egypt's army at the Red Sea all right, but not a local Laban!"[18]

As a result of their misperception of God, they never developed the spiritual maturity that could have helped them overcome their weaknesses and "go on unto perfection" (see Joseph Smith Translation, Hebrews 6:3). As the scriptures make clear, Laman and Lemuel's failure to comprehend God was not due to lack of instruction. Lehi, Nephi, and angels ministered to them. It appears that through their choices and actions, they simply refused to comprehend what was being taught. Far from growing from grace to grace as the Savior did (see D&C 93:13), they never spiritually matured. Elder Richard G. Scott taught: "We are here on earth to gain experience we can obtain in no other way. We are given the opportunity to grow, to develop, and to gain spiritual maturity. To do that, we must learn to apply truth."[19] Laman and Lemuel failed to learn and apply truth.

## BECOMING SPIRITUALLY MATURE

Learning and applying truth with "real intent" leads to *becoming* spiritually mature. Elder Dallin H. Oaks taught: "It is not enough for anyone just to go through the motions. The commandments, ordinances, and covenants of the gospel are not a list of deposits required to be made in some heavenly account. The gospel of Jesus Christ is a plan that shows us how to become what our Heavenly Father desires us to become."[20] Elder Oaks went on to explain that "we are challenged to move through a process of conversion toward that status and condition called eternal life. This is achieved not just by doing what is right, but by doing it for the right reason—the pure love of Christ."[21] Though Laman and Lemuel did many things right, their lack of doing right things for the right reasons kept them from receiving blessings and experiencing growth. So it is in our day. Elder David A. Bednar has taught: "The issue is not going to church; rather, the issue is worshipping and renewing covenants as we attend church. The issue is not going to or through the temple; rather, the issue is having in our hearts the spirit, the covenants, and the ordinances of the Lord's house. The issue is not going on a mission; rather, the issue is becoming a missionary and serving through-out our entire life with all of our heart, might, mind, and strength."[22]

How could Laman and Lemuel have grown to spiritual maturity and become like Christ? What can we learn from Laman and Lemuel's failure that will help us "work out our salvation with fear and trem-bling"? (Philippians 2:12). Surely it takes a combination of righteous actions and a living faith in Jesus Christ. However, if our personal weak-nesses deter us from developing faith in Christ—and if our lack of faith in Christ keeps us from overcoming our personal weaknesses—how do we break out of this downward cycle? As Elder Oaks mentioned, the ultimate motivation leading to righteousness is a pure love of Christ. Laman and Lemuel never developed this love for the Savior. Though we clearly must continue to emphasize righteous behavior, the best way to achieve our true potential is by developing a pure love for and faith in God. By focusing on God's word and the Atonement of Jesus Christ, each of us will develop this pure love for and faith in God.

Focusing on God's word as contained in the gospel is the beginning of developing faith in and a love for Christ. Speaking of the youth of the Church, President J. Reuben Clark Jr. taught: "These students already know that they must be honest, true, chaste, benevolent, virtu-ous, and to do good to all men. . . . They should be encouraged in all proper ways to do these things which they know to be true. . . . These students fully sense the hollowness of teachings which would make the

Gospel plan a mere system of ethics, they know that Christ's teachings are in the highest degree ethical, but they also know they are more than this. . . . These students hunger and thirst, as did their fathers before them, for a testimony of the things of the spirit and of the hereafter, and knowing that you cannot rationalize eternity, they seek faith, and the knowledge which follows faith."[23] As we come to know Heavenly Father and the Savior through their words, we develop a living faith and a love for them.

This knowledge and faith is most effectively learned from God's word. President Kimball's famous statement on scripture study emphasizes this important truth: "I find that when I get casual in my relationships with divinity and when it seems that no divine ear is listening and no divine voice is speaking, that I am far, far away. If I immerse myself in the scriptures the distance narrows and the spirituality returns."[24] Though Laman and Lemuel put forth great effort to get the scriptures from Laban, they did not put that same effort into immersing themselves in them and thus never came to truly know God.

Like Laman and Lemuel, we are all susceptible to an incorrect understanding of God and His gospel. Elder Scott spoke of the power of the scriptures to overcome false traditions and doctrinal misunderstandings. Recalling his efforts to lead a group of Church leaders nearer to the Savior, he said: "I realized in my heart that all the efforts that I had expended for six years in trying to help those beloved leaders overcome the effects of false traditions and learn to apply the teachings of the Lord would have been better directed had I strongly encouraged them to ponder and apply the teachings of the Book of Mormon. The Book of Mormon contains messages that were divinely placed there to show how to correct the influence of false tradition and how to receive a fulness of life."[25] Just as Lehi and Nephi continually used the scriptures in their attempts to reach Laman and Lemuel, so must we "try the virtue of the word of God" (Alma 31:5) as we come unto Christ and invite others to do so.

Perhaps the most important thing we must emphasize in our attempt to "grow up" spiritually and come unto Christ is His infinite Atonement. President Howard W. Hunter explained that spiritual maturity is a direct result of understanding and applying the

Atonement: "Spiritual maturity comes when we understand the Atonement. . . . When we come to the point where we understand the atoning sacrifice of the Master, we are approaching a spiritual maturity. I don't think spiritual maturity ever comes to us until we understand the true significance of the atoning sacrifice of the Master by which he gave his life that we might have life everlasting. When we understand the principle, we realize this is the greatest of love—that the Master laid down his life for us, that the grave will not be the end, but that we will live again."[26] When we realize the priceless gift of love that the Savior offered through His Atonement, we experience a "mighty change" of heart (see Alma 5:12). We act out of love and gratitude, not only out of obedience and duty. This provides the motivation to overcome our personal weaknesses and also provides the divine assistance necessary for the task. Clearly, Laman and Lemuel failed to allow the Atonement to work in their lives and never developed the needed motivation and help.

In the end, like Laman and Lemuel, some people may ultimately refuse this priceless gift of love. As a result of not overcoming their fallen nature and failing to comprehend the nature of God and their relationship to Him, they may refuse to partake from the tree of life. However, understanding the possible reasons for this refusal enables each of us to more fully "come unto Christ, and be perfected in Him" (Moroni 10:32). We are then more able to help others avoid the same mistakes that ensnared Laman and Lemuel. The most powerful motivation to attain spiritual maturity and come unto Christ is to comprehend and understand all that the Savior has done for us. As we begin to understand and believe, we are motivated to repent (see Helaman 14:13; 3 Nephi 5:1–3). Through our repentance, the Atonement of Jesus Christ begins to cleanse and transform us into the "stature of the fulness of Christ" (Ephesians 4:13).

---

NOTES

1. Spencer W. Kimball, *Faith Precedes the Miracle* (Salt Lake City: Bookcraft, 1972), 161.

2. See Byron R. Merrill, *Elijah: Yesterday, Today, and Tomorrow* (Salt Lake City: Bookcraft, 1997), 31.

3. Hugh Nibley, *An Approach to the Book of Mormon* (Salt Lake City: Deseret Book, 1988), 378.

4. Rodney Turner, in *The Book of Mormon: First Nephi, The Doctrinal Foundation,* ed. Monte Nyman and Charles D. Tate Jr. (Salt Lake City: Bookcraft, 1988), 82.

5. Neal A. Maxwell, in Conference Report, October 1999, 7; or *Ensign,* November 1999, 8.

6. Erastus Snow and Benjamin Winchester, *Times and Seasons,* November 15, 1841, 578.

7. For further insights into this concept, see Dallin H. Oaks, in Conference Report, October 2000, 40; or *Ensign,* November 2000, 32

8. George Reynolds and Janne M. Sjodahl, *Commentary on the Book of Mormon,* ed. Philip C. Reynolds (Salt Lake City: Deseret Book, 1955–61), 1:239.

9. Even though they lacked true faith in God, they nevertheless acknowledged His reality throughout the scriptural record (see 1 Nephi 3:29; 7:21; 15:8–9; 17:20–22).

10. Richard L. Bednar and Scott R. Peterson, *Spirituality and Self-Esteem: Developing the Inner Self* (Salt Lake City: Deseret Book, 1990), 27.

11. See "Laman," in *Book of Mormon Reference Companion,* ed. Dennis L. Largey (Salt Lake City: Deseret Book, 2003), 492–93.

12. James E. Faust, in Conference Report, October 2000, 74; or *Ensign,* November 2000, 59

13. Douglas E. Brinley, *Doctrines of the Book of Mormon,* ed. Bruce A. Van Orden and Brent L. Top (Salt Lake City: Deseret Book, 1992), 38.

14. Hugh Nibley, in *Approaching Zion,* ed. Don E. Norton (Salt Lake City: Deseret Book, 1989), 590.

15. Allen E. Bergin, in *The Book of Mormon: It Begins with Family* (Salt Lake City: Deseret Book, 1983), 34.

16. For further insights into this concept, see David A. Bednar, in Conference Report, October 2006, 94–98; or *Ensign,* November 2006, 89–92; or Lynn G. Robbins, in Conference Report, April 1998, 105–6; or *Ensign,* May 1998, 80–81.

17. Boyd K. Packer, in Conference Report, April 2004, 80; or *Ensign,* May 2004, 79.

18. Neal A. Maxwell, in Conference Report, October 1999, 6; or *Ensign,* November 1999, 7.

19. Richard G. Scott, in Conference Report, October 1989, 38; or *Ensign,* November 1989, 30.

20. Dallin H. Oaks, in Conference Report, October 2000, 40–41; or *Ensign,* November 2000, 32.

21. Dallin H. Oaks, *Ensign,* November 2000, 34; see also Moroni 7:6–9.

22. David A. Bednar, in Conference Report, October 2005, 47; or *Ensign,* November 2005, 45.

23. *Messages of the First Presidency of The Church of Jesus Christ of Latter-day Saints* (Salt Lake City: Bookcraft, 1965–75), 6:49–50.

24. *Teachings of Presidents of the Church: Spencer W. Kimball* (2006), 67.

25. Richard G. Scott, in Conference Report, October 1988, 89; or *Ensign*, November 1988, 76.

26. *The Teachings of Howard W. Hunter,* ed. Clyde J. Williams (Salt Lake City: Bookcraft, 1997), 8.

# 8

# "WE ARE NOT CUT OFF": SEPARATION AND RECONCILIATION THROUGH SACRED COVENANTS

## Daniel L. Belnap

Perhaps no theme in the Book of Mormon resonates so powerfully to modern readers as that of separation from and reconciliation with God. The sense of being cut off, isolated, or driven out is attested throughout the book. Similarly, messages from the Book of Mormon prophets of hope, reconciliation, and communion with God seek to alleviate the fears and depression that arise from loneliness or abandonment.

This theme is particularly evident in Jacob's great speech recorded in 2 Nephi 6–10 and the two "last" speeches from Moroni in Mormon 8 and Moroni 10. Jacob and Moroni both address separation from and reconciliation with God, providing a template for the reader to understand their own experiences. In particular, these prophets quote the words of Isaiah to teach how sacred covenants reconcile us to God.

## SEPARATION IN JACOB'S SPEECH

Jacob's speech, recorded in 2 Nephi 6–10, can be divided into two sections, the first being the Isaiah chapters quoted in chapters 6–8, and

---

*Daniel L. Belnap is a part-time instructor of ancient scripture at Brigham Young University.*

the second being Jacob's commentary on the passages quoted. Though the record does not state when the speech was given or the specific circumstances leading to the speech, we do know that it was delivered in the land of Nephi, probably at the temple. More importantly, the reason for the speech is given both in 2 Nephi 9:1 and 10:22, where Jacob explains that he quoted the scriptures from Isaiah so his people "might know concerning the covenants of the Lord" (9:1) and how, through those covenants, "the Lord remembereth all them who have been broken off, wherefore he remembereth us also" (10:22). These two references suggest that the Nephites did not understand their covenant relationship with God. They likely believed that because they were "broken off," the covenant itself had been broken. This sense of being broken off from the covenant arises from their loss of land, as Jacob states: "We have been driven out of the land of our inheritance" (10:20).

The Nephite concern of being driven out of the lands of inheritance would have been understood to have covenantal implications as the promise of lands of inheritance are found in the covenant between God and Abraham and later reestablished with Israel in Sinai. Beginning in Genesis 13:14–15, Abraham is promised "all the land which thou seest" (v. 15). This promise is then given to his descendants as well: "To thee will I give it, and to thy seed forever" (v. 15). The promise is reiterated in Genesis 15:18: "Unto thy seed have I given this land," and in Genesis 17:8: "And I will give unto thee, and to thy seed after thee, the land . . . for an everlasting possession." Thus, tied in to the promises of posterity and priesthood is the granting of lands of inheritance to Abraham and his seed. Generations later, when Israel was delivered from Egypt, God reiterates these promises with those who were to enter the promised land (see Exodus 12:25; Deuteronomy 6:3; 19:8; 27:3; Joshua 23:5).

This promise of land was contingent on Israel's personal righteousness. On Mount Nebo, immediately prior to Israel's entering of the promised land, Moses warns the people of the curses that would be placed on Israel if they were disobedient. These curses conclude with God's warning that Israel would "be removed into all the kingdoms of the earth" (Deuteronomy 28:25) and that "the Lord shall bring thee . . .

unto a nation which neither thou nor thy fathers have known" (v. 36). Finally, the curse was directly connected to the Abrahamic covenant: "And ye shall be left few in number, whereas ye were as the stars of heaven for multitude. . . . And ye shall be plucked from off the land whither thou goest to possess it. And the Lord shall scatter thee among all people, from the one end of the earth even unto the other. . . . And among these nations shalt thou find no ease. . . . And the Lord shall bring thee into Egypt again" (vv. 62–68). In these references, Israel's unrighteousness is the cause of their being forced out from the lands of inheritance. Thus, the loss of the promised land during the exile would be understood as being "cut off" from the covenant and Israel's relationship with God.[1] Yet being "cut off" had other implications as well. The term is also used elsewhere in the Old Testament to refer to death.[2] Indeed, being cut off from the land of inheritance would have been viewed as a form of death.[3]

The Nephites, like their Israelite counterparts, were in exile from their homelands, having been driven out not once, but twice, first from Jerusalem and second from the land of first inheritance in the New World. Though Jacob's reference to the term *cut off* does not mean death, he does describe his people as a "lonesome and a solemn people, wanderers, cast out from Jerusalem, born in tribulation, in a wilderness, and hated of [their] brethren," and they "did mourn out [their] days" (Jacob 7:26).[4] Clearly, the Nephites felt abandoned, lost, and without a homeland. This passage describes a people who feel that they do not belong anywhere, that they do not have a place to provide identity or meaning. Being Israelites, the lack of a land to call their own would have been especially painful since their identity as God's chosen people specifically includes a promised land of inheritance. It would seem then that the loss of land led the Nephites to a sense of having a broken covenant relationship with God. Thus, they experience a sense of being lost, abandoned, and "cut off."[5]

## SEPARATION IN MORONI'S INITIAL "LAST" SPEECH

This same sense of abandonment and separation can be found in the account of Moroni following the destruction of Nephite society. These feelings are recorded in Moroni's "last" speech delivered at the end of his father's record, chapters 8 and 9 of Mormon. Though these chapters are not, in fact, Moroni's last words, it appears that Moroni believed they would be such. In the first few verses of Mormon 8, Moroni writes: "The Nephites who had escaped into the country southward were hunted by the Lamanites, until they were all destroyed. And my father also was killed by them, and I even remain alone" (vv. 2–3). He reiterates this loneliness a few verses later: "I am alone. My father hath been slain in battle, and all my kinsfolk, and I have not friends nor whither to go" (v. 5). At this point, it is clear that Moroni is completely isolated, having no one to turn to or to provide companionship.

Though Mormon expresses that he does not know "whither to go," in both verses 4 and 5, the context in which this expression appears in verse 4 is significant. In verse 4, the clause "whither I go it mattereth not" means that not only is there no place for Moroni to go but there is no reason to go anywhere. It no longer matters. This lack of caring for his well-being reveals the extent of his sense of loss.[6] In verse 7, he writes, "And behold, the Lamanites have hunted my people, the Nephites, down from city to city and from place to place, even until they are no more." It is hard to imagine an existence like this. Not only is Moroni lacking a home, but he is also hunted from place to place. Thus, there is no closure for Moroni. He cannot stay long enough to mourn for his dead, but instead he must constantly move to avoid capture. The added stress of having to always look over his shoulder in fear would have only heightened his sense of loneliness and abandonment.

Yet though his description of the loss of family and land is moving, the implication of being cut off from God is perhaps even more poignant. Mentioned twice in verses 3 and 5 are his statements that he does not know God's will.[7] Certainly this lack of knowledge does not come from his own personal unrighteousness, nor does it suggest that he has not asked God for support. Nevertheless, the fact that he has not received revelation suggests that his prayers have gone temporarily unanswered.

Significantly, throughout this speech Moroni feels it necessary to continually make mention of his own failings. For instance, in verse 12 he speaks of the imperfections that may exist in the record. In verse 17, he speaks again of the faults that may be in the record, but now relates them to his own faults: "And if there be faults they be the faults of a man." Finally in Mormon 9:31, these faults are made explicitly personal: "Condemn me not because of mine imperfection, neither my father, because his imperfection, neither them who have written before him; but rather give thanks unto God that he hath made manifest unto you our imperfections, that ye may learn to be more wise than we have been."

This context sets the scene for the last two chapters. These are not happy messages; instead Moroni focuses on the negative consequences that he sees unfolding in latter days. Though he admits that he knows of the "great and marvelous things" that will happen, his words are filled with warning and condemnation. For instance, chapter 8 ends with the warning that the sword of vengeance hangs over our heads and is ready to fall. While the warnings and exhortations are true and should be heeded, they also demonstrate the sense of loss that Moroni is experiencing. Moroni warns a later covenant people that, like his own people, their actions will lead to their being cut off from God.[8]

Moroni's sense of being cast out also reveals itself in his words concerning the covenant. In 8:23, after stating that he has no room to write any Isaiah passages, he adds: "Yea, behold I say unto you, that those saints who have gone before me, who have possessed this land, shall cry, yea, even from the dust will they cry unto the Lord; and as the Lord liveth he will remember the covenant which he hath made with them."

While it is true that the Book of Mormon literally emerged from the dust, the association of broken covenants and death provides added meaning to this statement by Moroni. In chapter 9, verse 30, he repeats the concept for himself: "Behold, I speak unto you as though I spake from the dead." Though he is addressing an audience who will read these things after his death, it also affirms the sense found elsewhere that, having lost all, he is as being dead.

Finally, the entire speech ends with the plea: "May God the Father remember the covenant which he hath made with the house of Israel" (Mormon 9:31), suggesting that, for the time, the covenant is not in force because of unworthiness by the Nephites, with Moroni feeling all the effects of the broken covenant, being left utterly alone and bereft of purpose.

## RECONCILIATION IN JACOB'S SPEECH

But all is not lost. As powerful as the theme of separation and abandonment may be in the Book of Mormon, even more powerful is the theme of reconciliation, that the sense of loss and of being cut off can be overcome. This is certainly the case in Jacob's speech as he sought to convey a sense of hope to those who felt cut off and forgotten by God. While acknowledging that the Nephites had been driven out, Jacob goes on to say: "Let us remember him, and lay aside our sins, and not hang down our heads, for we are not cast off" (2 Nephi 10:20). Jacob makes an important distinction here that is lacking in the Old Testament explanations of being cut off. Though the Nephites had been physically separated from their lands of inheritance, this did not necessarily mean that they were cast off from God.

This message is reinforced throughout the Isaiah passages quoted by Jacob. Using the imagery of God as warrior, Jacob emphasizes God's ability and character as Israel's deliverer. In 2 Nephi 6:17 we read, "For the Mighty God shall deliver his covenant people.[9] For thus saith the Lord: I will contend with them that contendeth with thee." In chapter 7, Isaiah states, "Yea, for thus saith the Lord: Have I put thee away, or have I cast thee off forever? . . . And the Lord is near, and he justifieth me. . . . For the Lord God will help me" (vv. 1, 8–9). Chapter 8 is replete with promises of God's deliverance, including verse 12: "I am he; yea, I am he that comforteth you."

Jacob begins his own discourse in chapter 9 by stating that he offered the passages from Isaiah so that "ye might know concerning the covenants of the Lord that he has covenanted with all the house of Israel, . . . that they shall be restored to the true church and fold of God; when they shall be gathered home to the lands of their inheritance, and shall be established in all their lands of promise" (vv. 1–2). Thus, Jacob's message was one of hope and eventual return, that the covenants were still, somehow, in effect. As he states in verse 3: "My beloved brethren, I speak unto you these things that ye may rejoice, and lift up your heads forever." Central to his message is the role of Jesus as the Christ, the one anointed to deliver them. As pointed out, being cut off was associated with death; thus Jacob begins to emphasize the role of Christ as one who must be cut off from the Father in order to provide us with life: "For it behooveth the great Creator that he suffereth himself to become subject unto man in the flesh, and die for all men . . . to fulfil the merciful plan of the great Creator" (vv. 5–6).

This understanding of Christ as our deliverer from death and abandonment is also found in Alma's words to the people of Gideon. Like Jacob, he speaks of Christ's ability to care for us: "And he shall go forth, suffering pains and afflictions, and temptations of every kind. . . . And he will take upon him death" (Alma 7:11–12). Though we often ponder Christ's physical suffering and death, too often we forget His spiritual suffering, particularly on the cross. Though the physical pain was tremendous, it is his cry, "Eli, Eli lama sabachthani? My God, my God, why hast thou forsaken me?" that demonstrates a completely different level of suffering. There, on the cross, Christ experienced something so unique and alien to Him that He cried out in anguish. For the first time in His mortality, Christ was forsaken by His Father—cut off from God. His cry suggests His surprise and shock at experiencing this ultimate abandonment.[10]

Back in Alma 7 we are told that Christ experienced these things, "that he may know . . . how to succor his people." The word *succor* means "to run to."[11] Thus, Christ experienced all things so He would know how to succor His people, or, in other words, know how to run to them and be able to get to them, no matter how lost, abandoned, or cut off they are. He performed the Atonement, both in the garden and on the cross, to gain the power and knowledge necessary to be able to succor. It is Christ's succoring that is Jacob's message of hope.

Moreover, as Jacob points out, the true land of inheritance promised in the covenants was not an earthly possession but a heavenly one, made possible through Christ: "Behold, the righteous, the saints of the Holy One of Israel, they who have believed in the Holy One of Israel, . . . they shall inherit the kingdom of God, which was prepared for them from the foundation of the world" (2 Nephi 9:18). This is reinforced at the end of his speech: "Wherefore, may God raise you from death . . . that ye may be received into the eternal kingdom of God" (2 Nephi 10:25). This is the true land of inheritance, not some earthly land that can be lost. Regardless of physical land, covenantal worthiness brings upon one the blessings of a place in the eternal kingdom of God. With this as his message, Jacob exhorts: "And now behold, the Lord remembereth all them who have been broken off, wherefore he remembereth us also. Therefore, cheer up your hearts" (2 Nephi 10:22–23).[12]

## RECONCILIATION IN MORONI'S FINAL WORDS

Moroni's true last speech in Moroni 10 expresses a similar hope in the reconciliation with God made possible through Christ's Atonement. Mormon chapters 8–9 emphasize Moroni's loneliness and separation; his abandonment and forsaken state from his family, people, and God; and provides warnings for us about similar states based on unworthiness. Moroni 10, however, stresses the reconciliation made possible through Christ.

Not surprisingly, Moroni demonstrates this reconciliation through the writings of Isaiah. In fact, Moroni uses the same passage from Isaiah that Jacob ends with: "And awake, and arise from the dust, O Jerusalem; yea, and put on thy beautiful garments, O daughter of Zion" (Moroni 10:31). This is then followed by another passage from Isaiah: "And strengthen thy stakes and enlarge thy borders forever" (v. 31). These two verses from Isaiah 52 and 54 refer to the eventual return of the tribes of Israel to their lands of inheritance and are used by both Christ and Jacob to emphasize that Israel is not cut off if her people will come unto Christ.[13] Importantly, both suggest that it is Israel who determines the outcome. It is Israel who, though driven out, can still stand up and strengthen her stakes. By doing these things, "the covenants of the Eternal Father which he hath made unto thee, O house of Israel, may be fulfilled" (v.31), which is exactly what he pled for at the end of the earlier "last" speech.

In Moroni 10:32, he once again exhorts Israel to "come unto Christ, and be perfected in him." Like Jacob, Moroni points out that the true covenant is not necessarily about land possession but about coming to the Father: "And again, if ye by the grace of God are perfect in Christ, . . . then are ye sanctified in Christ by the grace of God, through the shedding of the blood of Christ, which is in the covenant of the Father, . . . that ye may become holy" (v. 33). In fact, this is the context of the entire chapter: by seeking personal revelation one can be reconciled with God. Nothing has changed physically for Moroni since the events described in Mormon 8. He is still alone and wandering, but the sense of abandonment and loss is missing in this chapter. Instead of warning us of being cut off from God, he encourages us to come unto Christ. Instead of a sword of vengeance bringing judgment and separation, he looks forward to uniting with us before the "pleasing bar" of God (see Moroni 10:34).

## "THAT THEY MAY KNOW"

While we are separated by the events described within the Book of Mormon by hundreds, even thousands of years, this does not mean that its writers do not speak to us. The Nephite concerns of abandonment, loss, and feeling cut off are not unique experiences but are all too common emotions experienced today. As Moroni rightly points out, the sense of isolation and loneliness and of being cast out is characteristic of our time.[14] Whether through our own errors or the mistakes and sins of others, we will all experience the trials and tribulations of being cut off like the ancient Israelites. The Book of Mormon's message resonates within all of us when we too cry out to our Heavenly Father in times of need.

Yet the Book of Mormon's messages of hope and reconciliation are just as applicable as the negative experiences mentioned above. Through the words of the ancient prophets, we learn that it is our covenant relationship with God that allows us to have both communion with Him and an eternal inheritance. Though we may be experiencing isolation and loneliness, even being cast away from those we care about, we are not cut off—thanks to the covenants made possible through the Atonement of Christ. His power to succor us as demonstrated in the Book of Mormon means that we need never feel cut off or alone. Thus, the necessity of the Book of Mormon is revealed as it demonstrates the true power of our covenants and of the Atonement of Christ. Moroni's explanation of the purpose of the book, that we "may know the covenants of the Lord, that [we] are not cast off forever" (Book of Mormon title page), whispers to us still, providing peace and reconciliation with God and promising that our true inheritance, eternal life with Him, has not been forgotten.

## NOTES

1. In 1 Kings 9:6–7, the Lord, speaking to Solomon, promises that He would be with Solomon as long as he remained obedient but then warns: "But if ye shall at all turn from following me . . . and will not keep my commandments and my statutes, . . . then will I cut off Israel out of the land which I have given them; and this house, which I have hallowed for my name, will I cast out of my sight." Similarly in the Psalms, the righteous are promised an earthly inheritance, while the wicked are cursed with being cut off (see Psalm 37:22, 34). "Adversity—drought, famine, epidemic, defeat, or whatever—could be accounted for by reference to a violation of covenant obligations. Conversely, the prosperity and tranquility of either the past or the coming age could be seen as a consequence of faithful partnership with God" (Jon D. Levenson, *Sinai and Zion: An Entry into the Jewish Bible* [New York: Harper Collins, 1986], 55); see also Stephen L. Cook, *The Social Roots of Biblical Yahwism,* Studies in Biblical Literature 8 (Atlanta: Society of Biblical Literature, 2004).

2. See Isaiah 53:8: "For he was cut off out of the land of the living," and Psalm 88:4–5: "I am like . . . the slain that lie in the grave, whom thou rememberest no more: and they are cut off from thy hand"; see also Saul M. Olyan, "'We Are Utterly Cut Off': Some Possible Nuances of נגזרנו לנו in Ezek 37:11," *Catholic Biblical Quarterly* (2003), 43–51.

3. The connection between the dead and the lands of inheritance is also intriguing since the family burial grounds would have been on the family's land of inheritance: "An ancestral tomb, whether located on inherited land or in the village cemetery, served as a physical, perpetual claim to the patrimony. . . . Interment in the family tomb guaranteed a continuous claim to the *naḥ⁽la* or patrimony, and propitiatory post-mortem care for the ancestors with its consequent benefits for the living" (Elizabeth Bloch-Smith, *Judahite Burial Practices and Beliefs about the Dead* [Sheffield, England: Sheffield Academic Press, 1992], 146, 150).

4. The imagery of being in the wilderness was often used in the scriptures to describe separation from family and God. "Wilderness imagery does not express beauty, success, or security. It crystallizes abject fear, destruction, and desolation" (Shemaryahu Talmon, "The 'Desert Motif' in the Bible and in Qumran Literature," *Biblical Motifs: Origins and Transformations,* ed. Alexander Altmann [Cambridge, MA: Harvard University Press, 1966], 45); see also Robert Barry Leal, *Wilderness in the Bible: Toward a Theology of Wilderness,* Studies in Biblical Literature 72 [New York: Peter Lang, 2004]).

5. This same sense of loss is also addressed by Nephi in 1 Nephi 19:24, immediately preceding a quote from Isaiah: "Hear ye the words of the prophet, ye who are a remnant of the house of Israel, a branch who have been broken off; hear ye the words of the prophet . . . that ye may have hope as well as your brethren from whom ye have been broken off." Unfortunately, the land of Nephi does not remain their land of inheritance since they are driven out again because of unrighteousness

into the land of Zarahemla, a land already inhabited. Unlike the Canaanites in the Old Testament, the descendants of Mulek are allowed to remain. That at least some Nephites continue to feel driven out can be seen in the Nephite expedition to reclaim the land of Nephi recorded in Mosiah 9–24. Later, Captain Moroni also reveals the Nephite sense of loss when writing to Ammoron. Captain Moroni declares: "I will arm my women and my children, and I will come against you, and I will follow you even into your own land, which is the land of *our* first inheritance" (Alma 54:12; emphasis added). He repeats this later in verse 13: "Behold, if ye seek to destroy us more . . . we will seek *our* land, the land of *our* first inheritance" (emphasis added). Since Ammoron is residing in the land of Nephi, it is probably this particular land to which Captain Moroni is referring.

6. A lack of caring for one's own well-being is a symptom of depression. Though Moroni may not be suffering from a full case of depression, having witnessed not only the destruction of his civilization, but also the continuing destruction of Lamanite civilization, it would not be surprising to see Moroni exhibit some characteristics of depression.

7. Mormon 8:3: "Whether they will slay me, I know not;" 8:5: "How long the Lord will suffer that I may live I know not."

8. In Mormon 8:21, he warns those who work against the covenant that they are in danger of being cast into the fire. In Mormon 9:3–4, he speaks of being unable to be in the presence of God. In 9:26, he states that those who despise the works of the Lord "shall wonder and perish." Finally, in 9:29, he proclaims, that we must be baptized worthily, partake of the sacrament worthily, and do all things in the name of Christ to keep from being "cast out."

9. Interestingly, this clause is not found in the biblical Isaiah, nor in the same quoted passage in 1 Nephi 21:24, suggesting that it was added by Jacob to emphasize the meaning of the original Isaiah.

10. James E. Talmage, *Jesus the Christ* (Salt Lake City: Deseret Book, 1954), 660–61: "At the ninth hour, or about three in the afternoon, a loud voice, surpassing the most anguished cry of physical suffering issued from the central cross, rending the dreadful darkness. It was the voice of Christ: '*Eloi, Eloi, lama sabachthani? which is, being interpreted, My God, my God, why hast thou forsaken me?*' What mind of man can fathom the significance of that awful cry? It seems, that in addition to the fearful suffering incident to crucifixion, the agony of Gethsemane had recurred, intensified beyond human power to endure. In that bitterest hour the dying Christ was alone, alone in most terrible reality."

11. The word *succor* literally means "to run towards," from the Latin prefix *suc/sub* (toward) and the verb *currere* (to run).

12. This understanding for the promise of land is also recognized by Abraham himself. In Hebrews 11, Paul states that the patriarchs Abraham, Isaac, and Jacob "all died in faith, not having received the promises, but having seen them afar off, . . . and confessed that they were strangers and pilgrims on the earth. . . . They desire a better country, that is, an heavenly: wherefore God is not ashamed to be called their God: for he hath prepared for them a city" (vv. 13, 16).

13. In 3 Nephi 20:36–37, Christ quotes Isaiah 52:1–2 in reference to Israel being restored to their lands of inheritance. Importantly, the restoration of lands of inheritance is then associated not necessarily with physical land, but with salvation or redemption, and the fulfillment of covenants: "Then will the Father gather them together again, and give unto them Jerusalem for the land of their inheritance. Then shall they break forth into joy—Sing together, ye waste places of Jerusalem; for the Father hath comforted his people, he hath redeemed Jerusalem. . . . Verily, verily, I say unto you, all these things shall surely come, even as the Father hath commanded me. Then shall this covenant which the Father hath covenanted with his people be fulfilled" (3 Nephi 20:33–34, 46). The relationship between God's comfort and the fulfillment of His covenant is also expressed in 2 Nephi 8:12, where the Lord states that He will comfort His people by delivering them.

14. A similar experience can be found in Doctrine and Covenants 121:1. After five months of extreme persecution and suffering of the Church, Joseph Smith pleaded that God reveal Himself. Like Moroni, Joseph had earlier prayed for alleviation of the Saints' suffering.

# 9

# WRITING THE THINGS OF GOD

## Terry Szink

Latter-day Saints are a record-keeping people. We keep institutional records such as sacrament meeting attendance, home and visiting teaching percentages, and priesthood ordinations. Leaders have also encouraged us to keep journals and write personal histories. For example, President Spencer W. Kimball urged, "We renew our appeal for the keeping of individual histories and accounts of sacred experiences."[1]

Likewise, the Book of Mormon provides ample evidence of the importance of writing and reading records. From Nephi to Moroni, the prophets of the Book of Mormon viewed the keeping of records as a sacred commandment. It also contains examples of the consequences of not abiding by this commandment. This chapter will demonstrate the importance the Book of Mormon places on record keeping and journal writing, using several examples that demonstrate principles of personal record keeping.

*Terry Szink is an assistant professor of ancient scripture at Brigham Young University.*

## WRITING IN THE BOOK OF MORMON

More than any other volume of scripture, the Book of Mormon is concerned with writing. Various forms of the word *write* occur 344 times in the Book of Mormon, compared to 258 in the Old Testament, 214 in the New Testament, and 110 in the Doctrine and Covenants and Pearl of Great Price. When we expand the search to include words like *engrave* or *plates,* which describe specific ways the records were kept, the Book of Mormon emphasis on writing is even more pronounced.[2] Furthermore, the Book of Mormon contains several instances in which writers are specifically commanded by God to write (see 1 Nephi 9:5; 19:1; 2 Nephi 33:11; 3 Nephi 16:4; 23:13; 24:1; 26:12; 30:1; Ether 4:1; 4:5; 5:1).

The first Book of Mormon prophet to receive this command was Nephi. God first instructed Nephi to make plates that would contain the complete record of the Nephite people (see 1 Nephi 19:1–2). Those plates contained genealogies, accounts of wars, history, and information regarding the reign of the kings as well as the complete prophecies of Lehi, Nephi, and presumably other Nephite prophets. This record, which Nephi called the "first plates" (1 Nephi 19:2) and Jacob called the "larger plates" (Jacob 3:13), was handed down from king to king, beginning with Nephi and ending with King Mosiah II (see Words of Mormon 1:10–11). Mosiah, the last king of the Nephites, turned the plates over to Alma the Younger, who became the chief judge upon Mosiah's death. We can perhaps consider these plates to be a kind of public record.

God also commanded Nephi to make a second set of plates. Nephi made these plates and began writing on them thirty years after the group had left Jerusalem (see 2 Nephi 5:28–30). Nephi explained that these plates were not to be complete but that they were to contain things "pleasing unto God" (2 Nephi 5:32) and the "more plain and precious parts" of his "ministry and the prophecies." God stated that two of the purposes of these plates were "for the instruction of my people" and "for other wise purposes" (1 Nephi 19:3). In hindsight, we understand that one of these "wise purposes" was that the record on these plates was meant to take the place of the 116 pages lost by Martin Harris.[3]

## NEPHI AND JACOB AND THE THINGS OF THE SOUL

If we understand the first set of plates to be a type of public record, then the second set of plates, which Jacob described as small, is more of a private record. Perhaps this is why Nephi included "the things of [his] soul" (2 Nephi 4:15). Indeed, this record contains the type of biographical details that have made Nephi one of the most beloved figures in all scripture. The reader admires Nephi's resolve to follow God's commandments (see 1 Nephi 3:7), his anguish because of his failed relationship with his elder brothers (see 1 Nephi 17:45–47), his sincere desire to lead his people in righteousness (see 2 Nephi 33:3–4), and, most of all, his great love for Jesus Christ (see 2 Nephi 25:12–13, 25–26; 33:9–11).

Nephi's small plates are an example of what good personal histories and journal writing should be. He not only recorded events from his life but also explained how those events affected him. He wrote about what mattered in his life, not shying away from painful episodes. He bore strong personal testimony and described how he had obtained that testimony. In writing our journals and personal histories, we should follow this example and write those details of our lives that will enrich the faith of our descendants and draw them unto Christ.

This second set of plates did not pass down from king to king but went from Nephi to his brother Jacob, who seems to have become the spiritual leader of the community. Nephi made sure Jacob understood the purposes and nature of the record entrusted to him. Jacob began his portion of the plates by repeating the instructions Nephi had given him. He was to include only the things he considered "most precious" and focus on sacred preaching, great revelation, and prophesying. Jacob stated categorically that he would not write Nephite history because the other plates would contain a complete history (see Jacob 1:2). Jacob certainly followed his brother's instructions. A glance at the content of the book of Jacob reveals the text of an important talk he delivered at the temple (see Jacob 2), Zenos's prophetic allegory of the olive tree (see Jacob 5–6), and the confrontation with the anti-Christ Sherem (see Jacob 7). There is little of what we would call political history: Jacob did not even name the king who succeeded Nephi. Jacob's purpose was identical to his brother's: to help people come unto Christ. Jacob then delivered the plates to his son Enos (see Jacob 7:27).

## ENOS'S PERSONAL EXPERIENCES

Jacob stated that he had relayed Nephi's instructions regarding the plates to his son Enos (see Jacob 7:27). Although Enos did not describe his contribution as "precious" as his father Jacob (see Jacob 1:2) and his uncle Nephi did (see 1 Nephi 19:3), his decisions regarding what to include in the record indicate understanding of the nature and purpose of the plates.

He began his story telling of his long prayer to God, which he described as a "wrestling" (see Enos 1:2). The account of Enos's prayer can teach us important things. God promised Enos three things: (1) his sins were forgiven, (2) the Nephites would be preserved in their land according to their obedience to His commandments, and (3) the Lamanites would not be destroyed and a record of the Nephites would be preserved and brought to them so that they might someday believe and be saved. Note that in answering Enos's prayers, God did not reveal anything new. He had already made the promise numerous times that the Nephites would be protected in the land if they kept the commandments (see 1 Nephi 13:30; 2 Nephi 1:7, 4:4). He had also previously promised that a remnant of the Lamanites would survive and that the Nephite record would someday come forth unto them (see 1 Nephi 13:31–40; 2 Nephi 27:6–20). What makes the account of Enos's prayer memorable is how his encounter with the divine changed him. Notice how his concerns shifted as he prayed. At first, he was worried about his own welfare. He cried "unto [God] in mighty prayer and supplication for [his] own soul" (Enos 1:4). After his first prayer was answered and he was assured that his sins were forgiven, he continued to pray, but his thoughts were now for "the welfare of [his] brethren, the Nephites" (Enos 1:9). Upon hearing the Lord's promise to them, Enos's circle of concern widened to include "[his] brethren, the Lamanites" (Enos 1:11). As Enos prayed, his soul expanded to include even those who might previously have been considered enemies.

Enos's account illustrates another principle of good personal record keeping—personal history and journal entries do not need to contain new revelations from God to be useful and interesting to our posterity. The facts of the gospel do not change, but they can and should change us, and that is why we need to record our relationship with these truths.

## JAROM'S MISUNDERSTANDING

Enos's son Jarom seems to have not understood the nature or purpose of the record to be kept upon the plates. He began his portion, stating, "Now behold, I, Jarom, write a few words according to the commandment of my father, Enos, that our genealogy may be kept" (Jarom 1:1). As noted, Nephi made the small plates to write the things "pleasing to God." He intended that the genealogy and history be written on the first set of plates. Jarom continued, "I shall not write the things of my prophesying, nor of my revelations" (Jarom 1:2). Again, this is at variance with the original purpose of the record.

We should not think Jarom an evil man. He stated that he did have prophecies and revelations but decided not to include them because his fathers had already revealed the plan of salvation and "this sufficeth [him]" (Jarom 1:2). Instead of prophecy or revelations, Jarom wrote a general evaluation of the Nephites, a little about their culture, and the fact that they were in a state of apostasy. I believe that Jarom made a mistake in not writing his prophecies and revelations because the information he gave is, for the most part, forgettable. It does not have the impact Jacob's preaching or Enos's prayer have, and it does nothing to help bring us to Christ. In fact, Jarom does not so much as mention the name of Jesus Christ in his book. Jarom may have gone against Nephi's commandment that his seed "not occupy these plates with things which are not of worth unto the children of men" (1 Nephi 6:6). Jarom's book teaches us to make our histories and journals personal. Simply writing about the general events of the day is not enough. We need to inject ourselves into what we write if we are to have an impact upon those who read our words. President Joseph Fielding Smith commented on this: "Some people keep a daily record; about like this: 'Got up in the morning, made the beds, washed the dishes, went to the picture show, came home, went to bed'; and so it goes. That means nothing. If you have accomplished *something worth while* during the day, put it down; it may be of use to posterity."[4] Certainly every one of us has accomplished something worthwhile in our lives. We should commit these accomplishments to paper for our posterity.

## PERSONAL PROBLEMS IN PERSONAL RECORDS

Omni continued his father's misunderstanding about the purpose of the plates. He also wrote that the plates were to preserve genealogy. Omni also stated that he was "a wicked man" who had "not kept the statutes and the commandments of the Lord as [he] ought to have done" (Omni 1:2). However, we should not be too quick to condemn Omni. We might ask ourselves, Who among us has kept the statutes and commandments of the Lord as he or she ought to have done? The fact that Omni admits that he was a wicked man is at least evidence of humility. Wicked people do not normally acknowledge the fact that they are wicked. A clue to Omni's personality may be found in his reporting that he "fought much with the sword to preserve [his] people, the Nephites, from falling into the hands of their enemies, the Lamanites" (Omni 1:2) and that there were "many seasons of serious war and bloodshed" (Omni 1:3). Omni may have been a victim of what has been called "soldier's heart," "shellshock," and, most recently, "combat stress reaction." Often those called upon to defend themselves and their families and country in war are affected negatively by their military service.

Omni's contribution to the book that bears his name raises the issue of what not to include in our journals and personal histories. Certainly we should not gloss over our problems or personal failings, but we should not dwell upon our sins or weakness, nor should we write too explicitly about them. Our posterity do not need to read about the exact nature of our shortcomings but rather on how we battled and overcame them.

## THE DANGER OF PROCRASTINATION

Omni passed the plates on to his son Amaron. We can perhaps best understand his short contribution by examining the one verse his brother Chemish wrote: "Now I, Chemish, write what few things I write, in the same book with my brother; for behold, I saw the last which he wrote, that he wrote it with his own hand; and he wrote it in the day that he delivered them unto me. And after this manner we keep the records, for it is according to the commandments of our fathers. And I make an end" (Omni 1:9). One possibility is that Amaron was a procrastinator. His father had given him the responsibility to maintain the record, but he may have put this off until he delivered the plates to his brother, writing a brief passage on the very day he gave them up. Certainly there are other possible scenarios which may explain why Amaron's contribution was so brief.[5] Amaron, however, does appear to be a righteous individual. He wrote that the "the more wicked part of the Nephites were destroyed" (Omni 1:5) in accordance with the words of the Lord.

Without question, procrastination is an enemy of good journal keeping and personal history writing. The advantage writing has over memory is that it does not change with time. A Chinese proverb states, "The palest ink is better than the best memory." The more time that passes between an event and an account of it, the greater chance that details will be changed or lost.

Chemish's son Abinadom wrote two scant verses, reporting that warfare between the Nephites and the Lamanites continued. He also wrote, "I know of no revelation save that which has been written, neither prophecy; wherefore, that which is sufficient is written. And I make an end" (Omni 1:11). It may not always be necessary to write about new revelations or prophecies. Personal responses to the gospel are often some of the most interesting parts of journals and personal histories.

## AMALEKI'S RETURN TO GOOD RECORD KEEPING

This brings us to Abinadom's son Amaleki, the most significant writer in the book of Omni.[6] Not only did Amaleki write almost two-thirds of this small book, but he was the first writer in the small plates of Nephi after Enos who mentioned Christ. Amaleki wrote: "And now, my beloved brethren, I would that ye should come unto Christ, who is the Holy One of Israel, and partake of his salvation, and the power of his redemption. Yea, come unto him, and offer your whole souls as an offering unto him, and continue in fasting and praying, and endure to the end; and as the Lord liveth ye will be saved" (Omni 1:26). He clearly understood the purpose of the plates that had been handed down from Nephi. As Dennis L. Largey has written, "Amaleki's writing is consistent with the commandment given by his ancestor Nephi that the small plates were to persuade readers to 'come unto' Christ."[7]

Amaleki also provided important historical information. He explained that God had commanded the Nephites to leave the land of Nephi. Those who followed King Mosiah escaped destruction and discovered the people of Zarahemla. These people descended from a group that had left the Old World at the time of the destruction of Jerusalem and included Mulek, who was a son of Zedekiah (see Omni 14–19; Helaman 6:10; 8:21). Amaleki's description of the people of Zarahemla included the fact that because they brought no records from the Old World, their language had become corrupted. Perhaps this may have been the cause of their serious contentions and their loss of religious faith, as Amaleki mentioned. He explained that the Nephites taught the people of Zarahemla their language and that Mosiah became the king of the united people.

Throughout the rest of the history of this united people, the Nephites appeared to have dominated politically and culturally though the people of Zarahemla were numerically superior.[8] All the kings, high priests, and chief judges of the Nephite people were descendants of Nephi rather than descendants of the people of Zarahemla. Perhaps this is because the Nephites had a culture of record keeping. Pete Carril, the great basketball coach of Princeton University, relates a truth he learned from his father: "In this life . . . the big, strong guys are always taking from the smaller, weaker guys, but . . . the smart take from the strong."[9]

Certainly keeping and reading records makes one smart. The book of Mosiah offers an example of the power of writing. The Lamanites appointed Amulon, leader of the apostate priests of King Noah, as a teacher. Although they did not teach about God, Amulon and his priests "taught them that they should keep their record, and that they might write one to another. And thus the Lamanites began to increase in riches, and began to trade one with another and wax great, and began to be a cunning and a wise people, as to the wisdom of the world" (Mosiah 24: 6–7). President Gordon B. Hinckley has mentioned the educational value of record keeping: "To you women of today, who are old or young, may I suggest that you write, that you keep journals, that you express your thoughts on paper. Writing is a great discipline. It is a tremendous educational effort. It will assist you in various ways, and you will bless the lives of many—your families and others—now and in the years to come, as you put on paper some of your experiences and some of your musings."[10] As writers record the events, accomplishments, and feelings of their lives, their ability to express themselves will grow.

## BENJAMIN TEACHES HIS SONS

Wise Benjamin, in preparing his sons to take his place as king, emphasized the importance of writing and reading, especially sacred texts, in preserving civilization. Mormon explained that Benjamin taught his sons the language of the plates "that thereby they might become men of understanding; and that they might know concerning the prophecies which had been spoken by the mouths of their fathers, which were delivered them by the hand of the Lord" (Mosiah 1:2). He explained it would be impossible to remember all the commandments. He further pointed out that without the written records, the Nephites would have dwindled in unbelief as the Lamanites had. Benjamin understood that writing is one of the greatest tools mankind possesses. Through written records, we can read the wisdom and folly of previous generations. As King Benjamin pointed out to his sons, the tool of writing means that we can pass on the accumulated knowledge of mankind to future generations. The collective knowledge of a culture is as large as the written records that exist in that culture. Alma understood this too. While handing over the sacred plates to his son, he said that the written records had "enlarged the memory" of the people (Alma 37:8).

## PRESERVING THE RECORD

We can learn one final lesson about journal and personal history writing from the authors of the Book of Mormon. Jacob wrote, "Whatsoever things we write upon anything save it be upon plates must perish and vanish away; but we can write a few words upon plates, which will give our children, and also our beloved brethren, a small degree of knowledge concerning us, or concerning their fathers" (Jacob 4:2). He understood the importance of not only writing records but also preserving them so future generations could read them. As we record our lives for our posterity, we should take care to do so in a way that our records will be preserved. We must first use an appropriate medium. We may be tempted by the ease of recording our thoughts in the latest technology. However, we should remember that the very speed with which technology advances may threaten the records kept by it. Documents can become inaccessible as the word-processing programs used to produce them become obsolete. Records stored on floppy disks may no longer be read as computer manufacturers replace the floppy drives with Zip drives and subsequently with flash memory. Certainly important records should not be left only on hard drives, which can crash, destroying all the information they contain. Printed copies on acid-free paper should be produced and stored in safe places. Perhaps we should take a lesson from the ancients. Some of the oldest writing has been preserved by very low technology—incised on rocks, or written on baked clay tablets. Joseph was able to read the record of the Nephites because it had been engraved on gold plates, a "low-tech" method of preservation.

Once produced, records can best be preserved by making multiple copies and distributing them far and wide. Single copies of records can be destroyed in fires, floods, or other natural disasters. Multiple copies ensure that if one copy is lost, others will survive.

## CONCLUSION

The Book of Mormon not only demonstrates the importance of record keeping but also gives examples of how good records should be kept. We have seen that personal records should record the personal feelings and accomplishments of the record keeper without dwelling excessively on sins and personal problems. Furthermore, the Book of Mormon has shown that one need not write about visions or new revelations to produce a record that will be interesting and important to future readers. One wonders if some authors knew the future of their writings. Did Enos know that millions would be uplifted by the account of his great prayer? This should inspire us in our writing. Future generations may well look upon our efforts in the same way we view Nephi's writing, as scripture.

––––––––––––––

## NOTES

1. Spencer W. Kimball, *The Teachings of Spencer W. Kimball,* ed. Edward L. Kimball (Salt Lake City: Bookcraft, 1982), 349.

2. Versions of the word *engrave* appear 46 times in the Book of Mormon, compared to 11 times in the Bible. There are 147 instances of the word *plates* in the Book of Mormon, compared to 11 in the Bible. Kent Jackson has noted that the Book of Mormon is a "thoroughly self-conscious book" that is replete with references to it own writing (see "Joseph Smith and the Historicity of the Book of Mormon," in *Historicity and the Latter-day Saint Scriptures,* ed. Paul Y. Hoskisson [Provo, UT: Religious Studies Center, Brigham Young University, 2001], 125–26).

3. See D&C 3; 10:1–46; and Joseph Smith, *History of the Church of Jesus Christ of Latter-day Saints,* ed. B. H. Roberts, 2nd ed. rev. (Salt Lake City: Deseret Book, 1957), 1:20–31.

4. Joseph Fielding Smith Jr., *Doctrines of Salvation* (Salt Lake City: Bookcraft, 1955), 2:204.

5. Jarom mentioned that the plates were "small" (Jarom 1:2, 14), which may explain why he and the authors of the book of Omni did not write much. Amaleki reported at the end of his portion of the book of Omni that the plates were "full" (Omni 1:30). However, one wonders that if this were the problem why did they not simply make additional plates.

6. Victor L. Ludlow has suggested that this book be named for Amaleki, who wrote almost two-thirds of it ("Scribes and Scriptures," in *Studies in Scripture, Vol. 7: 1 Nephi to Alma 29,* ed. Kent P. Jackson [Salt Lake City: Deseret Book, 1987], 201).

7. Dennis L. Largey, "Amaleki," in *Book of Mormon Reference Companion,* ed. Dennis L. Largey (Salt Lake City: Deseret Book, 2003), 44.

8. Mormon explained, "There were not so many of the children of Nephi, or so many of those who were descendants of Nephi, as there were of the people of Zarahemla" (Mosiah 25:2).

9. Pete Carril with Dan White, *The Smart Take from the Strong* (New York: Simon and Schuster, 1997), 17.

10. Gordon B. Hinckley, in Conference Report, October 1984, 111.

## 10

# ABINADI ON THE FATHER AND THE SON: INTERPRETATION AND APPLICATION

## *Jared T. Parker*

An important part of drawing nearer to God is coming to know and understand Him through the scriptures He has given us (see John 5:39; Jacob 4:8)—especially the Book of Mormon, since it contains many plain and precious truths missing from our current Bible. Although most Book of Mormon passages are easy to understand, some are more difficult, such as Abinadi's teachings about the Father and the Son in Mosiah 15:2–5. Yet Mormon's inclusion of these words in his abridgment suggests that the Lord wants us to have these teachings and wants us to understand them.[1] Accordingly, many have written about *what* Abinadi taught—that Jesus Christ is the Father and the Son—and have provided valuable insights and explanations.[2] In these discussions, however, a satisfactory explanation of *why* Abinadi spoke this way appears to be unaddressed.[3] Abinadi's teachings can help us know God better and thereby draw nearer to Him if we (1) correctly interpret the *why* and *what* of his message and (2) apply his teachings in our study of the scriptures.

*Jared T. Parker has a PhD in chemical engineering from Brigham Young University and is a medical device specialist in Flagstaff, Arizona.*

## INTERPRETATION: WHY AND WHAT

Abinadi was brought before King Noah because he had prophesied of the Nephites' forthcoming bondage and destruction (see Mosiah 11:20–25; 12:1–9). After some initial questioning, King Noah ordered his priests to slay Abinadi (see Mosiah 12:18–13:1), but he was protected by divine power and spoke "with power and authority from God" (Mosiah 13:6). In this setting, Abinadi taught the true meaning of the law of Moses, quoted Isaiah 53, and then spoke about the Father and the Son.

Abinadi taught about Jesus Christ as the Father and the Son immediately after quoting the entire chapter of Isaiah 53 (see Mosiah 14). This sequence is significant. Abinadi declared that Moses prophesied "concerning the coming of the Messiah, and that God should redeem his people" and that "even all the prophets . . . [have] spoken more or less concerning these things" (Mosiah 13:33). Furthermore, he stated, "Have [the prophets] not said that God himself should come down among the children of men, and take upon him the form of man, and go forth in mighty power upon the face of the earth? Yea, and have they not said also that he should bring to pass the resurrection of the dead, and that he, himself, should be oppressed and afflicted?" (Mosiah 13:34–35).

Abinadi, on trial for his life, then turned to Isaiah 53 to prove his words (see Mosiah 14:1). Isaiah 53 declares that the Messiah would be "despised and rejected of men" (v. 3) and "wounded for our transgressions" (v. 5), and even though He would be "cut off out of the land of the living" (v. 8), He would "prolong his days" (v. 10). Certainly, quoting Isaiah was a powerful defense and second witness of Abinadi's assertions that the Messiah would be oppressed and afflicted and would bring about the Resurrection. Yet what about Abinadi's statement that God Himself would come down among men as the Messiah? Does Isaiah 53 support this doctrine? Let us turn to the Hebrew behind Isaiah's prophecy to answer this important question and uncover why Abinadi next spoke of Jesus Christ as the Father and the Son.

The King James Version (KJV) of the Bible regularly reads "the LORD" or "GOD" (small caps) where the Hebrew reads "Jehovah."[4] If we identify Jehovah and the Messiah in Isaiah 53 where indicated by the Hebrew or the appropriate pronoun, we find that "the LORD [Jehovah] hath laid on him [the Messiah] the iniquities of us all" (v. 6), that "it pleased the LORD [Jehovah] to bruise him [the Messiah]," that "he [Jehovah] hath put him [the Messiah] to grief," and that "the pleasure of the LORD [Jehovah] shall prosper in his [the Messiah's] hand" (v. 10).

In light of the context and the meaning of the words in Hebrew, these verses actually appear to contradict Abinadi's statement that God Himself, the great Jehovah, will come down to redeem His people. The text reads as if Jehovah and the Messiah are two different individuals—as if Jehovah will *send* the Messiah but not that He will *be* the Messiah.[5]

This apparent contradiction is the key to understanding Abinadi's subsequent teachings.[6] Immediately after quoting Isaiah 53, Abinadi declares again that "God himself shall come down among the children of men" (Mosiah 15:1), evidently to ensure his audience understands that Jehovah Himself will come down as the Messiah. In fact, it appears that Abinadi specifically taught about "the Father" and "the Son" after quoting Isaiah 53 to explain how Jehovah and the Messiah are actually the same person.[7]

To interpret Abinadi's teachings, we first need to review the ways Jesus Christ is properly referred to as "the Father." From an official statement by the First Presidency and the Twelve,[8] we understand that Jesus is (1) the Father as the Creator of all things, (2) the Father of mankind's spiritual rebirth, and (3) the Father when acting for Elohim[9] by divine investiture of authority. Significantly, all three of these reasons why Jesus is the Father can be identified in Abinadi's message: (1) Jesus is the Creator, "the very Eternal Father of heaven and of earth" (Mosiah 15:4); (2) Jesus is the Father of His seed, or posterity, begotten through the Atonement (see Mosiah 15:10–13); and (3) Jehovah speaks as Elohim in Isaiah 53 by divine investiture of authority (see vv. 6, 10). In addition, some have understood that Abinadi taught of Jesus as the Father in yet another way—that He inherited Elohim's attributes and capacities so He could perform the Atonement.[10]

The common theme for all of these senses in which Jesus is the Father is that they are directly tied to His status as God. It is because Jesus is God that He is the Father of heaven and earth. It is because

Jesus was God while in the flesh that He was able to perform the Atonement (see D&C 19:15–20) and become the Father of those who are spiritually reborn. It is because Jesus is God that He is the Father, representing Elohim by divine investiture of authority. Therefore, we will interpret Abinadi's teachings as an explanation that Jehovah and the Messiah are the same person because Jesus acted in His role of *Father* as Jehovah (God)[11] and in His role of *Son* as Christ (Messiah).

Abinadi begins his explanation by reinforcing his earlier statement that Jehovah will come to earth: "I would that ye should understand that God himself [Jehovah] shall come down among the children of men, and shall redeem his people" (Mosiah 15:1). Then he explains that Jehovah will subject His mortal flesh as Christ to His divine will as Jehovah. He says, "And because he [Jehovah] dwelleth in flesh he shall be called the Son of God [Christ], and having subjected the flesh [Christ] to the will of the Father [Jehovah], being the Father [Jehovah] and the Son [Christ]" (v. 2).

Next he explains that Jehovah will come to earth and maintain His status as Father, or God, because He will be begotten by Elohim, but He will also be Christ, or Son, because of the mortal flesh He will inherit from Mary. Therefore, Jesus is "the Father [Jehovah], because he was conceived by the power of God [Elohim]; and the Son [Christ], because of the flesh [mortality inherited from Mary]; thus becoming the Father and the Son [Jehovah and Christ]—And they [Jehovah the Father and Christ the Son] are one God [Jehovah-Christ], yea, the very Eternal Father of heaven and earth" (vv. 3–4).

Now Abinadi returns to the idea that Jesus will subject His mortal flesh to His divine spirit: "And thus the flesh [Christ] becoming subject to the Spirit [Jehovah], or the Son [Christ] to the Father [Jehovah], being one God [Jehovah-Christ], suffereth temptation, and yieldeth not to temptation, but suffereth himself to be mocked, and scourged, and cast out, and disowned by his own people" (v. 5).

Abinadi emphatically finishes his message about Jesus as the Father and the Son by declaring that Isaiah's prophecy of the Atonement will be fulfilled: "After working many mighty miracles among the children of men, he [Jehovah-Christ] shall be led, yea, even as Isaiah said, as a sheep before the shearer is dumb, so he opened not his mouth. Yea, even so he shall be led, crucified, and slain, the flesh [Christ] becoming subject even unto death, the will of the Son [Christ] being swallowed up in the will of the Father [Jehovah]. And thus God [Jehovah] breaketh the bands of death, having gained the victory over death; giving the Son [Christ] power to make intercession for the children of men" (Mosiah 15:6–8).[12] Truly, Abinadi's teachings are both profound and powerful, and they directly support one of the major purposes of the Book of Mormon—to convince all that Jesus is "the CHRIST, the ETERNAL GOD" (title page), or in other words, both Jehovah and the Messiah.

## APPLICATION: OUR SCRIPTURE STUDY

Now that we have explored an interpretation of Abinadi's teachings, how can we benefit from understanding and applying it in our study of the scriptures? First, Abinadi's teachings can strengthen our faith in God. Scripture study should build faith, leading us to eternal life by increasing our knowledge of God (see John 17:3). Instead of being confused or troubled, we can identify when the scriptures are speaking of Jesus's dual roles as the Father and the Son. Second, making the effort to apply Abinadi's teachings to other scriptures can deepen our comprehension of the doctrine he taught.

### Similar Old Testament Passages

In addition to clarifying the meaning of Isaiah 53, Abinadi gave us a necessary key to interpret many other potentially confusing Old Testament passages. The table below contains a few examples of applying Abinadi's teachings, focusing on instances where cross-references in the New Testament or latter-day scripture make it appear that Jehovah and Christ are two different persons.[13]

| OLD TESTAMENT PASSAGE | CROSS-REFERENCE |
| --- | --- |
| The LORD thy God [Jehovah the Father] will raise up unto thee a Prophet [Christ the Son] from the midst of thee, of thy brethren, like | Behold, I [Jesus] am he of whom Moses spake, saying: A prophet [Christ] shall the Lord your God [Jehovah] raise up unto you of your |

| OLD TESTAMENT PASSAGE | CROSS-REFERENCE |
|---|---|
| unto me [Moses]; unto him ye shall hearken. (Deuteronomy 18:15) | brethren, like unto me [Moses]; him shall ye hear in all things whatsoever he shall say unto you. (3 Nephi 20:23) |
| I will declare the decree: the LORD [Jehovah the Father] hath said unto me [Christ the Son], Thou [Christ the Son] art my [Jehovah the Father's] Son; this day have I [Jehovah the Father] begotten thee [Christ the Son]. (Psalm 2:7) | And we declare . . . that the promise which was made unto the fathers, God [Elohim] hath fulfilled the same unto us their children, in that he hath raised up Jesus again; as it is also written in the second psalm, Thou [Christ] are my [Elohim's] Son, this day have I [Elohim] begotten thee [Christ]. (Acts 13:32–33) |
| The LORD [Jehovah the Father] said unto my Lord [Christ the Son], Sit thou at my right hand, until I [Jehovah the Father] make thine [Christ the Son's] enemies thy foot-stool. (Psalm 110:1) | For David . . . saith himself, The LORD said unto my Lord, Sit thou on my right hand, until I make thy foes thy footstool. Therefore let all the house of Israel know assuredly, that God [Elohim] hath made that same Jesus, whom ye have crucified, both Lord and Christ. (Acts 2:34–36) |
| The LORD [Jehovah the Father] hath sworn, and will not repent, Thou [Christ the Son] art a priest for ever after the order of Melchizedek. (Psalm 110:4) | So also Christ glorified not him-self to be made an high priest; but he [Elohim] that said unto him, Thou art my Son, to day have I begotten thee. As he [Elohim] saith also in another place, Thou [Christ] art a priest for ever after the order of Melchisedec. (Hebrews 5:5–6) |
| And the spirit of the LORD [Jehovah the Father] shall rest upon him [Christ the Son] . . . the spirit of knowledge and of the fear of the LORD [Jehovah the Father]; and shall make him [Christ the Son] of quick understanding in the fear of the LORD [Jehovah the Father]. (Isaiah 11:2–3) | Who is the Stem of Jesse spoken of in the 1st, 2d, 3d, 4th, and 5th verses of the 11th chapter of Isaiah? Verily thus saith the Lord: It is Christ. (D&C 113:1–2) |

| OLD TESTAMENT PASSAGE | CROSS-REFERENCE |
|---|---|
| The Spirit of the Lord GOD [Jehovah the Father] is upon me [Christ the Son]; because the LORD [Jehovah the Father] hath anointed me [Christ the Son] to preach good tidings unto the meek; he [Jehovah the Father] hath sent me [Christ the Son] to bind up the brokenhearted. (Isaiah 61:1) | And when he [Jesus] had opened the book, he found the place where it was written, [Isaiah 61:1–2a quoted]. . . . And he began to say unto them, This day is this scripture fulfilled in your ears. (Luke 4:17, 21) |

### Jesus Teaches during His Mortal Ministry

Two fascinating comparisons to Abinadi's teachings are found in the New Testament. The first example is the King James Version record of Jesus saying that "no man knoweth who the Son is, but the Father; and who the Father is, but the Son, and he to whom the Son will reveal him" (Luke 10:22). Interestingly, the Joseph Smith Translation (JST) of this verse reads, "No man knoweth that the Son is the Father, and the Father is the Son, but him to whom the Son will reveal it." It is as if the JST reveals the doctrine hinted at in the KJV. In at least one sense, "the Son is the Father, and the Father is the Son" because Jesus is both Jehovah and Christ. Truly, no one knows that Jesus is the Father and the Son except by revelation, the kind of revelation received and taught by Abinadi.

The second New Testament example comes from the setting of the Last Supper. Jesus said to His Apostles, "If ye had known me, ye should have known my Father also: and from henceforth ye know him, and have seen him" (John 14:7). Philip then asked to be shown the Father, and Jesus responded, "He that hath seen me hath seen the Father" (John 14:9). Here "the Father" could refer to Elohim, but it may also refer to Jehovah. To see Jesus is to see the Father because He is Jehovah the Father, acting for and representing Elohim.

### The Brother of Jared Sees Jehovah

The brother of Jared saw God in a way others previously had not (see Ether 3:15). In this setting, Jehovah revealed Himself by saying,

"Behold, I am Jesus Christ. I am the Father and the Son" (Ether 3:14). Here "the Father" is understood to mean Jesus as the Father of mankind's spiritual rebirth since He next said that those who believe "shall become my sons and my daughters" (v. 14). Even so, Jesus may also be identifying Himself as both Jehovah and Christ. Jehovah's name is "I am" (see Exodus 3:14), and this phrase is found three times in verse 14. Significantly, "I am" is emphasized in connection with Jesus being the Father in a revelation referring to the experience of the brother of Jared. Jesus says, "I am the same that leadeth men to all good; he that will not believe my words will not believe me—that I am [Jehovah]; and he that will not believe me will not believe the Father who sent me. For behold, I am the Father [Jehovah], I am the light, and the life, and the truth of the world" (Ether 4:12). Certainly "the Father" who sent Christ is Elohim, but in light of Abinadi's teachings, Jesus may also be referring to Himself as Jehovah who sent Christ.

## Nephi Sees the Condescension of God

When the angel asks Nephi if he knows the "condescension of God" (1 Nephi 11:16), it is generally assumed that "God" here refers to Elohim because we read that the virgin whom Nephi saw was "the mother of the Son of God" (1 Nephi 11:18). Consequently, verses 16–25 are traditionally interpreted as referring to the condescension of God the Father and verses 26–33 as referring to the condescension of God the Son.[14] Another possibility is that Nephi's vision was focused on the condescension of Jehovah. This is suggested by three important readings, all found in the original manuscript, the unedited printer's manuscript, and the 1830 edition of the Book of Mormon. In these texts, we read that the angel called Mary "the mother of God" (instead of "the mother of the Son of God"; v. 18), that the angel called Jesus "the Eternal Father" (instead of "the Son of the Eternal Father"; v. 21), and that Nephi saw Jesus as "the Everlasting God" (instead of "the Son of the everlasting God"; v. 32) being judged by the world.[15] The manuscripts and 1830 edition speak of Jesus as both Jehovah ("God," "Eternal Father," "Everlasting God") and Christ ("Son of the Most High God," "Son of God," "Lamb of God"), similar to and consistent with the teachings of Abinadi and the angel who visited King Benjamin.[16] Thus, it is possible that the "condescension of God" Nephi was shown was actually the condescension of Jehovah.

## Nephi Receives Revelation the Night before Jesus's Birth

The words of Jehovah came to Nephi the night before His birth, saying, "Behold, I come unto my own, to fulfill all things which I have made known unto the children of men from the foundation of the world, and to do the will, both of the Father and of the Son—of the Father because of me, and of the Son because of my flesh" (3 Nephi 1:14). At first this revelation may seem confusing, but when we apply Abinadi's teachings, it becomes clear and takes on added meaning: "Behold, I [Jehovah] come unto my own, to fulfill all things which I [Jehovah] have made known unto the children of men from the foundation of the world, and to do the will, both of the Father [Jehovah] and of the Son [Christ]—of the Father because of me [Jehovah], and of the Son because of my flesh [Christ]." While the two occurrences of "the Father" in this verse can be interpreted as references to Elohim, the wording "of the Father because of me, and of the Son because of my flesh" suggests Jesus was identifying His roles as Jehovah the Father and Christ the Son, using language very similar to Abinadi's.

## Jesus Teaches the Nephites

An examination of how Jesus quoted the Old Testament when He visited the Nephites also yields insights related to Abinadi's teachings. To see this, two verses from Isaiah that Jesus quoted twice are compared in the following table:

| OLD TESTAMENT | JESUS'S FIRST QUOTATION | JESUS'S SECOND QUOTATION |
|---|---|---|
| Break forth into joy, sing together, ye waste places of Jerusalem: for the LORD [Jehovah] hath comforted his people, he hath redeemed Jerusalem. The LORD [Jehovah] | Break forth into joy, sing together, ye waste places of Jerusalem: for the Lord [Jehovah] hath comforted his people, he hath redeemed Jerusalem. The Lord [Jehovah] hath made | Then shall they break forth into joy— Sing together, ye waste places of Jerusalem; for the Father hath comforted his people, he hath redeemed Jerusalem. The Father |

| | | |
|---|---|---|
| hath made bare his holy arm in the eyes of all the nations; and all the ends of the earth shall see the salvation of our God. (Isaiah 52:9–10) | bare his holy arm in the eyes of all the nations; and all the ends of the earth shall see the salvation of God. (3 Nephi 16:19–20) | hath made bare his holy arm in the eyes of all the nations; and all the ends of the earth shall see the salvation of the Father; and the Father and I are one. (3 Nephi 20:34–35) |

Analysis of the table reveals that the first time Jesus quoted Isaiah, the verses were essentially the same as found in our current Old Testament, suggesting that our current Hebrew text is accurate. However, the second time that Jesus quoted Isaiah He substituted "the Father" where the Hebrew identifies "Jehovah." This is also true for some other Old Testament passages that Jesus quoted,[17] and we find that He described Jehovah's revelation to Malachi as having come from "the Father" (3 Nephi 24:1). It appears that Jesus wanted His listeners to understand why He substituted "the Father" for "Jehovah" because after doing so, He added the profound statement, "And the Father and I are one" (3 Nephi 20:35).

We can interpret Jesus's declaration to mean "the Father [Elohim] and I [Jehovah] are one [because I am Jehovah the Father, acting for and representing Elohim]." In addition, since Jesus specifically equated "Jehovah" with "the Father," another meaning could be "the Father [Jehovah] and I [Christ] are one [the same person]" (see also D&C 93:3–4 and associated discussion below for more support of this).

### Revelation to Joseph Smith

In a profound revelation to the Prophet Joseph Smith, Jesus promised that "every soul" who complies with certain conditions "shall see my face and know that I am" (D&C 93:1; see also D&C 67:10). Here again is emphasis on Jehovah's name "I am," and we read that whoever sees Him will know "that I am in the Father, and the Father in me, and the Father and I are one" (D&C 93:3). While "the Father" here is understood to mean Elohim, there also appears to be reference to Jehovah, as evidenced by the wording of the next verse: "The Father because he gave me of his fulness, and the Son because I was in the world and made flesh my tabernacle" (D&C 93:4). Here "the Father" refers to Jesus and is similar to what Abinadi taught. Jesus is the Father because "he [Elohim] gave me [Jehovah] of his fulness" and the Son because "I [Jehovah] was in the world and made flesh my tabernacle [as Christ]." Significantly, this revelation expands on Abinadi's teachings by explaining that Jesus is the Father *because* He and His Father are one. In fact, the concepts that Jesus is the Father and that Jesus is one with His Father are really two expressions of the same doctrine.

## CONCLUSION

Abinadi's teachings concerning the Father and the Son in Mosiah 15:2–5 can best be understood when interpreted in their context. Abinadi quoted Isaiah 53, but it seems to contradict his own statement that God Himself, the great Jehovah, would come to earth as the Messiah. It appears that Abinadi's purpose for explaining how Jesus is both the Father and the Son was to show that Jehovah and Christ are the same person. Application of this doctrine can help us understand potentially confusing scriptures, such as those that represent Jehovah and the Messiah as two different persons. In addition, we can discover insights into other scriptures that speak of Jesus's dual roles as the Father and the Son. By correctly interpreting Abinadi's teachings and applying them in our study of the scriptures, we can better understand God and His word, thereby drawing nearer to Him.

---

NOTES

1. "The Holy Scriptures—all of them, both ancient and modern—speak of many things that are hard to understand without an over-all knowledge of the plan of salvation and without the enlightening power of the Holy Ghost. . . . We cannot brush [these teachings] aside as though they were an unnecessary part of revealed writ. The mere fact that the Lord has preserved them for us in the scriptures is a sufficient witness that he expects us to ponder their deep and hidden meanings so that we shall be as fully informed about his eternal laws as were the saints of old" (Bruce R. McConkie, *The Promised Messiah: The First Coming of Christ* [Salt Lake City: Deseret Book, 1978], 6, 8).

2. For example, see George Reynolds and Janne M. Sjodahl, *Commentary on the Book of Mormon*, ed. Philip C. Reynolds (Salt Lake City: Deseret Book, 1955–61), 2:164–71; Joseph Fielding Smith, *Doctrines of Salvation*, comp. Bruce R. McConkie (Salt Lake City: Bookcraft, 1954–56), 1:29; Joseph Fielding Smith, *Answers to Gospel*

*Questions* (Salt Lake City: Deseret Book, 1957–66), 4:177–80; Hyrum L. Andrus, *Doctrinal Commentary on the Pearl of Great Price* (Salt Lake City: Deseret Book, 1967), 92–95; Sidney B. Sperry, *Book of Mormon Compendium* (Salt Lake City: Bookcraft, 1968), 301–9, 528–30; Hyrum L. Andrus, *God, Man, and the Universe* (Salt Lake City: Bookcraft, 1968), 227–28; Daniel H. Ludlow, *A Companion to Your Study of the Book of Mormon* (Salt Lake City: Deseret Book, 1976), 183–86; McConkie, *Promised Messiah*, 369–73; Monte S. Nyman, *Great Are the Words of Isaiah* (Salt Lake City: Bookcraft, 1980), 207–8; Rodney Turner, "Two Prophets: Abinadi and Alma," in *Studies in Scripture: Volume Seven, 1 Nephi to Alma 29*, ed. Kent P. Jackson (Salt Lake City: Deseret Book, 1987), 240–60; Joseph F. McConkie, Robert L. Millet, and Brent L. Top, *Doctrinal Commentary on the Book of Mormon* (Salt Lake City: Bookcraft, 1987–92), 2:225–30; Robert L. Millet, "The Ministry of the Father and the Son," in *The Book of Mormon: The Keystone Scripture,* ed. Paul R. Cheesman (Provo, UT: Religious Studies Center, Brigham Young University, 1988), 44–72; Monte S. Nyman, "Abinadi's Commentary on Isaiah," in *Mosiah: Salvation Only through Christ,* ed. Monte S. Nyman and Charles D. Tate Jr. (Provo, UT: Religious Studies Center, Brigham Young University, 1991), 161–86; John W. Welch, "Ten Testimonies of Jesus Christ from the Book of Mormon," in *Doctrines of the Book of Mormon: 1991 Sperry Symposium on the Book of Mormon* (Salt Lake City: Deseret Book, 1992), 230–31; Daniel H. Ludlow, ed., *Encyclopedia of Mormonism* (New York: Macmillan, 1992), s.v. "Jesus Christ, Fatherhood and Sonship of"; Jeffrey R. Holland, *Christ and the New Covenant: The Messianic Message of the Book of Mormon* (Salt Lake City: Deseret Book, 1997), 179–93; Paul Y. Hoskisson, "The Fatherhood of Christ and the Atonement," *Religious Educator* 1 (Spring 2000): 71–80; Andrew C. Skinner, "Jesus Christ as the Father in the Book of Mormon," in *The Fulness of the Gospel: Foundational Teachings from the Book of Mormon* (Salt Lake City: Deseret Book, 2003), 144–46; Dennis L. Largey, ed., *Book of Mormon Reference Companion* (Salt Lake City: Deseret Book, 2003), s.v. "Jesus Christ, role of, as Father and Son."

3. The Prophet Joseph Smith's comment concerning one of Jesus's parables applies here: "I have a key by which I understand the scriptures. I enquire, what was the question which drew out the answer, or caused Jesus to utter the parable? . . . To ascertain its meaning, we must dig up the root and ascertain what it was that drew the saying out of Jesus" (*Teachings of the Prophet Joseph Smith,* comp. Joseph Fielding Smith [Salt Lake City: Deseret Book, 1976], 276–77).

4. The Hebrew actually reads *YHWH,* which is the proper name of the God of Israel. Thought to have been pronounced "Yahweh" anciently, the Jews would not speak this sacred name aloud but would substitute the Hebrew word *'Adonai,* a plural first person possessive form understood to mean "Lord." When vowels were added to the Hebrew text during the eighth and ninth centuries A.D., *YHWH* was given the vowels of *'Adonai* to remind the reader of the necessary substitution, but this also produced an impossible Hebrew word (see J. Weingreen, *A Practical Grammar for Classical Hebrew,* 2nd ed. [Oxford: Oxford University Press, 1959], 23). The English pronunciation "Jehovah" comes from *YHWH* with the vowels of *'Adonai* and was apparently first introduced in A.D. 1520, although it was disputed as grammatically and historically incorrect (see Francis Brown, Stephen R. Driver,

and Charles A. Briggs, *The Brown-Driver-Briggs Hebrew and English Lexicon: With an Appendix Containing the Biblical Aramaic* [Peabody, MA: Hendrickson Publishers, 2000], 218). Even so, "Jehovah" is the way *YHWH* was rendered by the KJV translators, and it became the common English way to pronounce the name of the God of Israel. Evidently, this usage is acceptable to the Lord since "Jehovah" is found in all the standard works, the Joseph Smith Translation, and the teachings of latter-day prophets. Therefore, "Jehovah" is the rendering used in this paper for the Hebrew *YHWH*.

5.    The English "Messiah" (from the Hebrew *mashiach*) and "Christ" (from the Greek *christos*) are synonyms, both meaning "anointed one." "In the preserved Hebrew Bible (Old Testament), however, the noun *mashiach* is never explicitly used as a title for Jehovah (the premortal Jesus). . . . Because the term *mashiach* is not clearly preserved as a title for Jehovah in the Hebrew Bible nor in the minimal corpus of Israelite inscriptions, it is not possible to determine how many Israelites in Jerusalem at the time of Jeremiah and Lehi (about 600 B.C.) knew or believed that Jehovah himself would come to earth as the anointed Son of God, the Messiah" (Largey, *Book of Mormon Reference Companion*, s.v. "Messiah").

6.    While almost all the scriptures and teachings of latter-day prophets identify Jehovah as Jesus Christ, some may take the position that Jehovah also refers to Jesus's Father. This subject is beyond the scope of this paper, but it is important to note that if references to Jehovah in Isaiah 53 were to Jesus's Father, this would actually add to the apparent contradiction between Abinadi's statement and Isaiah's prophecy. In this paper it is assumed that Jehovah refers exclusively to Jesus Christ.

It may be that the legal allegation brought against Abinadi was that he contradicted the scriptures in declaring that Jehovah would come down to earth as the Messiah. King Noah said, "Abinadi, we have found an accusation against thee, and thou art worthy of death. For thou hast said that God himself should come down among the children of men; and now, for this cause thou shalt be put to death" (Mosiah 17:7–8; see also Mosiah 7:27–28).

7.    The approach taken here assumes that Abinadi knew Isaiah's writings spoke of Jehovah and the Messiah as if they are two different individuals and that he anticipated this same understanding by his audience. While this assumption cannot be proven, it is consistent with the text. We know there was a written copy of at least some of the information on the brass plates among Noah's people and that this was available to both Noah's priests and Abinadi (see Mosiah 12:20–24, 27–28; 13:11). Since the brass plates were written in the "language of the Egyptians" (Mosiah 1:4), the texts available to Noah's people may have been written in some form of Egyptian or translated and written in some form of Hebrew, or perhaps something else. In any case, the representation of Jehovah and the Messiah as two different persons in Isaiah 53 is evident to the careful reader, regardless of the language of the text. In addition, since the translation of the Book of Mormon follows the customs of the KJV, it is reasonable to assume that the content of the Isaiah text Abinadi quoted was essentially equivalent to our current Hebrew text where the wording of Mosiah 14 agrees with KJV Isaiah 53.

Therefore, the lack of information about the language of the written texts available to Abinadi and the priests does not detract from an appeal to the Hebrew where Jehovah is clearly identified in Isaiah's writings.

8.  See the doctrinal exposition on "The Father and the Son," in James R. Clark, comp., *Messages of the First Presidency of the Church of Jesus Christ of Latter-day Saints* (Salt Lake City: Bookcraft, 1965–75), 5:24–34.

9.  Following the current practice in the Church, "Elohim" is used in this paper exclusively to refer to God the Father, meaning the Father of Jesus Christ. It is important to note that *'Elohim,* a plural Hebrew form, is used in several ways in our current Hebrew Bible (see Brown, Driver, and Briggs, *Hebrew and English Lexicon,* 43–44). These uses include: (1) as a generic title for God, most often referring to Jehovah as God (for example, replace "God" with "Elohim" and "the LORD" with "Jehovah" in Exodus 3:4–14); (2) in reference to false "gods" (see Exodus 12:12); (3) in combination with *YHWH* (the English phrase "the LORD God" is "Jehovah Elohim" in Hebrew); and (4) rarely to refer to mortals (see Psalm 82:6) or judges who represent God (see Exodus 21:6; 22:8–9).

10.  See Millet, "The Ministry of the Father and the Son," 62–65; McConkie, Millet, and Top, *Doctrinal Commentary on the Book of Mormon,* 2:229; Hoskisson, "The Fatherhood of Christ and the Atonement," 71–80; Skinner, "Jesus Christ as the Father in the Book of Mormon," 144–46; Largey, *Book of Mormon Reference Companion,* s.v. "Jesus Christ, role of, as Father and Son."

11.  For scriptures that describe Jehovah as Father, see Exodus 4:22–23; 1 Chronicles 29:10; Isaiah 9:6; 63:16; Jeremiah 31:9.

12.  "Begotten of an immortal Father and a mortal mother, Jesus possessed *two natures* (one divine, one human) and, therefore, *two wills* (that of the Father, and that of the Son). . . . Abinadi described Jesus' submission as 'the will of the Son being swallowed up in the will of the Father.' (Mosiah 15:7; see also Luke 22:42; 3 Nephi 11:11.) In a sense, it was not the Son *as* Son, but the Father *in* the Son who atoned. That is, Jesus not only did the will of his Father *in heaven,* but the will of the Father *in himself.* The Father and the Son—being 'one God'—came to earth in the person of Jesus of Nazareth. 'God himself'—in perfect unity—atoned for the sins of the world" (Turner, "Two Prophets: Abinadi and Alma," 245–46).

The interpretation of "God," "Father," and "Spirit" in Mosiah 15:6–8 as identifications of Jehovah is not intended to be restrictive. Since Jesus as the Father represents Elohim in all things, it is also correct to associate certain occurrences of "Father" in these verses with Elohim.

13.  There is no revealed explanation as to why various Old Testament scriptures speak of Jehovah and Christ as two different individuals. However, we do know that at Mount Sinai, the Israelites rejected the higher priesthood and law (see Joseph Smith Translation; Exodus 34:1–2; D&C 84:19–25), and specifically asked that God not speak directly to them (see Exodus 20:18–19). Jehovah agreed to this request and said He would raise up a prophet among them instead (see Deuteronomy 18:15–19). Since Israel did not want to hear directly from Jehovah, apparently He chose to come among them disguised as the Messiah. Perhaps this is part of the "plainness" God took away from His "stiffnecked people" (Jacob

4:14) but that He revealed to those who held the higher priesthood, such as the righteous in the Americas (see Largey, *Book of Mormon Reference Companion,* s.v. "Priesthood among the Nephites").

Abinadi's teachings also help us to understand the many instances where New Testament or latter-day scriptures speak of Elohim the way the Old Testament speaks of Jehovah (compare Exodus 3:15 to Acts 3:13; Exodus 20:2–3 to 1 Corinthians 8:5–6; Deuteronomy 4:35 to John 17:3; Deuteronomy 6:4–5 to D&C 59:5; and Psalm 16:8–10 to Acts 13:35–37).

14. For example, see Bruce R. McConkie, *Mormon Doctrine,* 2nd ed. (Salt Lake City: Bookcraft, 1966), 155; McConkie, Millet, and Top, *Doctrinal Commentary on the Book of Mormon,* 1:77–85; Largey, *Book of Mormon Reference Companion,* s.v. "Condescension of God."

15. Joseph Smith made these changes when he revised the printer's manuscript for the second (1837) edition of the Book of Mormon. The most probable explanation is that the original readings are an accurate account of the angel's words and Nephi's understanding of what he saw but that the Prophet changed the text to avoid a misinterpretation. If this is correct, the additions of "the Son of" can be thought of as clarifications rather than the primary readings (see Royal Skousen, *Analysis of Textual Variants of the Book of Mormon, Part 1* [Provo, UT: FARMS, Brigham Young University, 2004], 4:230–33).

16. Assuming "the Lord" is equivalent to "Jehovah," the angel who visited King Benjamin specifically identified Jehovah as Christ at least five times (see Mosiah 3:5–8, 12, 17, 18, 19).

17. Compare Micah 5:10 to 3 Nephi 21:14–16 and Isaiah 52:12 to 3 Nephi 21:29.

## 11

# ALMA THE YOUNGER: A DISCIPLE'S QUEST TO BECOME

## Jerome M. Perkins

Those who lack an eternal perspective of life can yield to cynicism when reviewing the purpose of our existence, just as Macbeth pessimistically summarized the value of life upon hearing of Lady Macbeth's death:

> Tomorrow, and tomorrow, and tomorrow,
> Creeps in this petty pace from day to day,
> To the last syllable of recorded time;
> And all our yesterdays have lighted fools
> The way to dusty death. Out, out, brief candle,
> Life's but a walking shadow, a poor player
> That struts and frets his hour upon the stage,
> And then is heard no more. It is a tale
> Told by an idiot, full of sound and fury
> Signifying nothing.[1]

Yet a gracious God cuts through this cynicism with statements regarding the purpose of life: "And those who overcome [the natural

*Jerome M. Perkins is an associate professor of Church history and doctrine at Brigham Young University.*

man] by faith, . . . it is written, they are gods, even the sons [and daughters] of God" (D&C 76:53, 58). "Therefore I would that ye should be perfect even as I, or your Father who is in heaven is perfect" (3 Nephi 12:48). Thus, in the restored gospel of Jesus Christ, our existence is seen neither as brief nor as "signifying nothing," as Macbeth declared. Resonating in the teachings of the gospel of Christ is our eternal destiny to become like God.

Indeed, one of the key messages of the Book of Mormon is that the human soul must change, must progress, must become. The Book of Mormon is, in effect, a handbook of change, with the Lord seeking to motivate mighty change within us by using the lives and teachings of the Book of Mormon protagonists as the means to teach us how to become. At the heart of the Book of Mormon, in the books of Mosiah and Alma, Alma the Younger makes the subject of change, progression, and becoming the very essence of his life and sermons, and thus Alma the Younger becomes a quintessential standard of how to become like God.

## EXAMPLE OF ALMA THE YOUNGER

Alma the Younger provides a powerful example of the change that disciples must experience to realize their eternal destinies. First, Alma was awakened to the understanding that life is more than rebellion and selfishness. Second, he learned that God wants us all to be "born again" and to become "sons and daughters . . . new creatures" (Mosiah 27:25–26). In his teachings and sermons, Alma the Younger pleads with us that we must come to those same realizations. We know that Mormon selected the stories and doctrines of the Book of Mormon specifically for us in the latter days (see Mormon 8:35), so when Alma repeatedly bears testimony to his people of his conversion, he is really bearing his testimony to us. When Alma the Younger intimately teaches of the mighty change that occurred in his own life, and how he became more and more blessed by God, he is, in reality, teaching us to follow his example; we are to understand our spiritual standing before God and become aware that we have the capacity to become like God.

Alma bore witness to his first awakening: "My soul hath been redeemed from the gall of bitterness and bonds of iniquity. I was in the darkest abyss; . . . I rejected my Redeemer, and denied that which had been spoken of by our fathers" (Mosiah 27:29). He later testified: "I saw that I had rebelled against my God, and that I had not kept his holy commandments. . . . I had murdered many of his children, or rather led them away unto destruction" (Alma 36:13–14). His life had become so futile that he desired to "be banished and become extinct both soul and body, that [he] might not be brought to stand in the presence of God, to be judged of [his] deeds" (Alma 36:15).

However, at this crossroad, Alma the Younger was also awakened to the real meaning of life. The first sermon that he preached after his three-day experience of change was replete with his newfound wisdom regarding the purpose of life: "And the Lord said unto me: Marvel not that all mankind . . . must be born again; yea, born of God, changed from their carnal and fallen state, to a state of righteousness, being redeemed of God, becoming his sons and daughters; and thus they become new creatures; and unless they do this, they can in nowise inherit the kingdom of God" (Mosiah 27:25–26). Notice Alma's emphasis upon becoming—"born again," "born of God," "changed from a fallen state to a state of righteousness," "being redeemed of God," "becoming sons and daughters." Doctrine and Covenants section 76 explains more regarding the meaning of becoming sons and daughters of God. It teaches that to become sons and daughters of God means to become gods, to receive the nature and character of God to the point of becoming joint heirs with Jesus Christ and receiving all things that God has (see D&C 76:54–59). Alma came to these two significant understandings: first, his life had been fruitless until this defining moment, and second, the rest of his life was to be dedicated to becoming like God and helping others do the same.

## ALMA'S AWAKENING

### Awakened to the Reality of Who He Had Become

Before Alma could comprehend anything regarding eternal progression, the Lord had to awaken him to the truth that he had become an enemy to God. Alma emphasized this awakening: "I was struck with such great fear and amazement lest perhaps I should be destroyed, that

I fell to the earth and I did hear no more. . . . I was racked with eternal torment. . . . I did remember all my sins and iniquities, for which I was tormented with the pains of hell; . . . I had rebelled against my God. . . . I had murdered many of his children, or rather led them away unto destruction" (Alma 36:11–14). Alma was awakened to what he had become, and this revelation horrified him.

For individuals to embark upon the quest of becoming like God, they must first be awakened to the reality of their present lives, what they have already become. Chauncey C. Riddle stated: "As any person comes to spiritual self-consciousness, he will realize that his mind, his desires, his habits, his manners, and his politics have all been shaped by the people [and the culture] in his physical environment. What he hitherto thought to be himself he now sees as the encrustations of the world upon his true self."[2]

Elder Bruce C. Hafen told a story of a university student who had unknowingly allowed worldly influences to encrust "his true self." This bright student spoke of an earlier time of innocence and faith, when as a boy he had pled with God to save a dying calf. He cried out to the Lord for help, and "before long the little animal began breathing again. He knew his prayer had been heard. After relating this story, the tears welled up in his eyes and he said, '. . . I tell you that story because I don't think I would do now what I did then.'" He spoke of how he had become "older, less naive, and more experienced." Then he concluded: "I don't understand what has happened to me since that time, but I sense that something has gone wrong."[3]

If we are not aware, if we are not at times shaken and awakened, our lives can go terribly wrong, and we won't even notice the change. That is why, in the process of becoming, Alma the Younger stands as the example that each of us needs to be awakened to who we have really become. The Lord does this awakening all throughout scripture, especially in the chapters revolving around the life of Alma the Younger. The Savior uses many different means to help us grasp the gravity of those times when we have become less than what we and God desire. In Alma 4:3, Alma writes regarding his people: "And so great were their afflictions, . . . they were awakened to a remembrance of their duty."

In Alma 5, Alma reminds the people of Zarahemla how their fathers were brought into bondage by the hands of the Lamanites and how through that bondage, the Lord "changed their hearts; yea, he awakened them out of a deep sleep, and they awoke unto God. . . . Their souls were illuminated by the light of the everlasting word" (v. 7).

To the people of Gideon, Alma noted: "I have said these things unto you that I might awaken you to a sense of your duty to God, that you may walk blameless before him" (Alma 7:22).

Amulek realized that although he was wealthy, popular, and powerful, he had hardened his heart against God. He realized he had been called many times to serve yet would not hear the call (see Alma 10:4–10).

Zeezrom was awakened by the words of a prophet, and he cried out, "I am guilty" (Alma 14:7; see also vv. 6–11).

The Zoramites were despised because of their poverty, but Alma was overjoyed because this poverty had awakened them to their need for God and His gospel (see Alma 32:3–8).

Corianton was awakened to the peril he faced, because a loving father taught him principles of the gospel: "And now behold, my son, do not risk one more offense against your God upon those points of doctrine, which ye have hitherto risked to commit sin. Do not suppose . . . that ye shall be restored from sin to happiness. Behold, I say unto you, wickedness never was happiness" (Alma 41:9–10).

Elder Dallin H. Oaks spoke of how God uses tribulation: "Our needed conversions are often achieved more readily by suffering and adversity than by comfort and tranquility,"[4] and in looking at the way the Lord awakened Alma, Amulek, Zeezrom, the Zoramites, and so many others, this theme of suffering to awaken man is oft repeated. We as disciples also receive these wake-up calls.

As it did to the Zoramites (see Alma 32), poverty makes us desire happiness when we don't have the world's definitions of it. Poverty makes us humble, dependent upon God, sensitive to the whisperings of the Spirit. When we are poor in finances, popularity, security, strength, intellect, prestige, or any other worldly definition of success, the pain of that poverty can become a magnificent impetus to motivate us to search for something better.

Zeezrom was humbled when his powerful intellect was overwhelmed by the pure testimony of Amulek and Alma the Younger. Zeezrom had depended on his cunning, his wits, his smooth delivery to survive and thrive his entire life, but he was totally astonished when he stood indicted and convicted before these humble servants of God. Like Zeezrom, we also realize that our intellects and theories are shallow and insufficient when we strive to explain or make sense of the nuances of life. Like Zeezrom, we cry out that we are guilty of living a worthless life, of wasting our living on lies and deceptions and destruction (see Alma 14:6–7). Like Zeezrom, we become ill—emotionally, spiritually, and physically—as we deeply ponder the failures of our lives, and we also cry out to the Master, "Heal me" (see Alma 15:5).

Alma the Younger similarly realized his nothingness in his three-day ordeal of compelled introspection. He realized he had received no answers from the sorrows of life he had embraced. How immature was Alma's resolution of his life's convoluted predicament: "Oh, thought I, that I could be banished and become extinct both soul and body, that I might not be brought to stand in the presence of my God, to be judged of my deeds" (Alma 36:15). He wished that he never existed. He was so overwhelmed by life, this was his only solution.

If needed, God will bring us to our knees as He did Alma. As we face life's convoluted predicaments, we also, without God's guidance, will invent immature solutions. However, these dilemmas become motivating in the hands of our loving God. The goal of these overwhelming predicaments is to bring us to our omnipotent and omniscient God, just as Alma was brought to God: "While I was harrowed up by the memory of my many sins, behold, I remembered also to have heard my father prophesy unto the people concerning the coming of one Jesus Christ, a Son of God, to atone for the sins of the world. Now as my mind caught hold upon this thought, I cried within my heart: O Jesus, thou Son of God, have mercy on me. . . . And now, behold, when I thought this, I could remember my pains no more. . . . My soul was filled with joy" (Alma 36:17–20).

In our lives, we must not only come to an awakening of what we have become, but also to an awakening to the "Son of God, [sent] to atone for the sins of the world" (Alma 36:17), and we must cry out, "O Jesus, have mercy on me." Then joy becomes ours.

Although Elder Oaks emphasized that "our needed conversions are often achieved more readily by suffering and adversity than by comfort and tranquility," the wisest disciple will seek, on his own, an awakening to the reality of what he has become. Elder Neal A. Maxwell gently counseled: "Meek introspection may yield bold insights."[5] In the story told by Elder Hafen, the college student remembered when he had the faith to heal the calf through the mercy of God, yet he could no longer feel that faith, and he said, "I don't understand what has happened to me . . . , but I sense that something has gone wrong." Throughout his sermons, Alma the Younger consistently asked the Nephites, and more importantly each one of us, "Has something gone wrong in your lives, or do you still feel the redeeming love of Christ" in statements such as these: "Have you sufficiently retained in remembrance the captivity of your fathers? Yea, and have you sufficiently retained in remembrance [God's] mercy and longsuffering towards them?" (Alma 5:6). It is the judicious disciple who consistently seeks honest answers to Alma the Younger's questions: "I ask of you . . . have ye spiritually been born of God? Have ye received his image in your countenances? Have ye experienced this mighty change in your hearts," and "if ye have experienced a change of heart . . . can ye feel so now?" (Alma 5:14, 26).

Alma stressed that if needed, the Lord will compel the child to be humble and repent, yet the real disciple is humble because of his understanding of and love for the Master of mercy: "And now, as I said unto you, that because ye were compelled to be humble ye were blessed, do ye not suppose that they are more blessed who truly humble themselves because of the word? Yea, he that truly humbleth himself, and repenteth of his sins, and endureth to the end, the same shall be blessed— yea, much more blessed than they who are compelled to be humble because of their exceeding poverty" (Alma 32:14–15). Uncompelled humility leads the disciple to consistently answer, "I have experienced a change of heart, and I can still feel it now."

### Awakened to the Reality of Who He Could Become

Alma had experienced that mighty change of heart. When he cried out, "O Jesus, thou Son of God, have mercy on me," the Savior eliminated the pain of Alma's horrendous past and established the pathway of Alma's future. Alma felt exquisite joy that filled his whole soul. He beheld the light of eternal truth, and he said that there was nothing so sweet. And he was awakened to his destiny: "I saw . . . God sitting upon his throne, . . . and my soul did long to be there" (Alma 36:22; see also Alma 36:18–21). Alma ached to return and be with this God who had rescued him. He testified of this destiny: "God has delivered me from prison . . . and from death; yea, and I do put my trust in him, and he will still deliver me. And I know that he will raise me up at the last day, to dwell with him in glory; yea and I will praise him forever" (Alma 36:27–28). Alma knew that he would return to God because of his conversion. Now his task was to assist his beloved people to do the same. So he spent the rest of his life teaching his people the gospel.

Alma consistently emphasized that there were barriers to this eternal destiny. He asked the people in Zarahemla if they, being wicked, would be able to enter the kingdom of God and sit down with Abraham, Isaac, and Jacob. He is asking us the very same question which he forcefully answered with a direct, "Nay" (see Alma 5:21–25). He taught all of us that if we are in a state of filthiness, that awful state will condemn us (see Alma 12:13), and that if we are filthy in this life, we will be filthy in the next life and no unclean thing can enter into the kingdom of God (see Alma 7:21). Alma was aware of the doctrine that the "same spirit which doth possess your bodies at the time that ye go out of this life, that same spirit will have power to possess your body in that eternal world" (Alma 34:34), and this doctrine impelled Alma to command his people and us to make sure our earthly spirit, or who we had really become, would qualify us for entrance into the kingdom of God. He taught the Nephites and us that men will be judged regarding entrance to the kingdom of God not only by their works but by the desires of their hearts, the state of their being, and the intrinsic nature of who they have become. He stressed that if our desires, states of being, and intrinsic natures are good, we will receive good in the world to come; if evil, evil in the world to come. Alma asked very basic and logical questions that when carefully considered, change the focus of our lives: Can sin lead to happiness? Can you find joy when your nature is contrary to joy? Can you become like God, when your nature is contrary to God? (see Alma 41:3–15).

Alma the Younger spoke of the "state" of our being as the significant criterion for our judgment: "For our words will condemn us, yea our works will condemn us; we shall not be found spotless; and our thoughts will also condemn us; and in this awful state we will not dare to look up to our God" (Alma 12:14). Notice how Alma the Younger combines words, works, and thoughts into a composite whole he calls our "state." The definition of the word *state* indicates that our entrance into the kingdom of God will not be based on what we show to the world—our actions, works, deeds, words, and promises—but will be based upon who we have intrinsically become.[6] Alma taught that we must be changed from a carnal and fallen state to a state of righteousness (see Mosiah 27:25) or that we must change from being intrinsically carnal to intrinsically righteous.

Elder Oaks stated: "From such teachings we conclude that the Final Judgment is not just an evaluation of the sum total of good and evil acts—what we have *done*. It is an acknowledgment of the final effect of our acts and thoughts [upon us]—what we have *become*."[7] In his sermon to the people of Zarahemla, Alma the Younger captured the essence of what we are to become when he asked one basic question: "Have ye received his image in your countenances?" (Alma 5:14). In other words, he asked, when people see you, do they see Jesus the Christ? Have you become such a representative disciple of Christ that when you are present the Spirit of Christ is there? These questions awaken all disciples to the fact that we must consider the essence of our existence; we are here to become like Christ. Ephesians 4:13 testifies that we are here to attain "the measure of the stature of the fulness of Christ." Alma had been awakened to the reality of what he could become, and he then called for his people to have a similar awakening. That call is also to us, to all disciples of Christ. Regarding the importance of being a disciple who becomes, Chauncey Riddle taught: "The word *disciple* comes from the Latin *discipulus,* a learner. A disciple of Christ is one who is learning to be like Christ—learning to think, to feel, and to act as he does. To be a true disciple, to fulfill that learning task, is the most demanding regimen known to man. No other discipline compares with it in either requirements or rewards. It involves *the total transformation* of a person from a *state* of the natural man to that of the saint, one who loves the Lord and serves with all his heart, might, mind, and strength."[8]

Elder Oaks testified that this total transformation is achievable:

> This process requires far more than acquiring knowledge. It is not even enough for us to be *convinced* of the gospel; we must act and think so that we are *converted* by it. In contrast to the institutions of the world, which teach us to *know* something, the gospel of Jesus Christ challenges us to *become* something. . . .
>
> It is not enough for anyone just to go through the motions. The commandments, ordinances, and covenants of the gospel are not a list of deposits required to be made in some heavenly account. The gospel of Jesus Christ is a plan that shows us how to become what our Heavenly Father desires us to become. . . .
>
> The gospel of Jesus Christ is the plan by which we can become what children of God are supposed to become. This spotless and perfected state will result from a steady succession of covenants, ordinances, and actions, an accumulation of right choices and from continuing repentance.[9]

## CONCLUSION

Alma's change, his conversion, was so spiritually profound, he was impelled to teach this conversion process and this imperative goal of becoming to all during his entire earthly ministry. Alma testified:

> Nevertheless, after wading through much tribulation, repenting nigh unto death, the Lord in mercy hath seen fit to snatch me out of an everlasting burning, and I am born of God. . . .
>
> And now it came to pass that Alma began from this time forward to teach the people, and those who were with Alma at the time the angel appeared unto them, . . . preaching the word of God. . . .
>
> And thus they were instruments in the hands of God in bringing many to the knowledge of the truth, yea, to the knowledge of their Redeemer.

And how blessed are they! For they did publish peace; they did publish good tidings of good; and they did declare unto the people that the Lord reigneth. (Mosiah 27:28, 32, 36, 37)

Alma spent the rest of his life sharing this message that man must change, become, and progress to be like God and Christ. He relinquished earthly power and prestige when he resigned as chief judge, yet "he retained the office of high priest unto himself . . . that he might preach the word of God unto them" (Alma 4:18–19). Alma "confined himself wholly to the high priesthood, . . . to the testimony of the word" (Alma 4:20), because he knew "the preaching of the word had a great tendency to lead the people to do that which was just—yea, it had had more powerful effect upon the minds of the people than the sword, or anything else" (Alma 31:5). Alma lovingly explained that he was called to the priesthood order "to preach unto my beloved brethren, yea, and every one that dwelleth in the land; yea to preach unto all, . . . to cry unto them that they must repent and be born again" (Alma 5:49). In this verse, one can see Alma's charge to also teach us.

In his teaching of God's word, Alma was motivated by Christlike ideals: "I do not glory of myself, but I glory in that which the Lord hath commanded me; yea, and this is my glory, that perhaps I may be an instrument in the hands of God to bring some soul to repentance; and this is my joy" (Alma 29:9). He taught that each of us must awaken to the dangers of a sinful life. We must accept and depend wholly upon Christ, and through Him we can progress, change, and become like the Master whom Alma loved so much. Alma the Younger spoke of these principles to his beloved son Shiblon: "And now, my son, I have told you this that ye may learn wisdom, that ye may learn of me that there is no other way or means whereby man can be saved, only in and through Christ. Behold, he is the life and the light of the world. Behold, he is the word of truth and righteousness" (Alma 38:9).

And at the conclusion of his life, Alma had not lost the burning desire to teach of his Savior and the mighty change the Master had fostered in his own heart and could foster in the hearts of all mankind: "The sons of Alma did go forth among the people, to declare the word unto them. And Alma, also, himself, *could not rest,* and he also went forth.

. . . They preached the word, and the truth, according to the spirit of prophecy and revelation" (Alma 43:1–2; emphasis added). Christ reached into Alma's life and saved this rebellious son of a prophet, rescued him from himself, and gave him a vision of the eternal life that could be his. Alma was mightily changed. He progressed and became like his Master, and the process was so fantastic and marvelous, so imperative and essential to all, that Alma shared this message valiantly and passionately his entire life.

---

## NOTES

1. William Shakespeare, *Macbeth* 5.5.21–30 (New York: Macmillan, 1978), 78.

2. Chauncey C. Riddle, "Becoming a Disciple," *Ensign,* September 1974, 81.

3. Bruce C. Hafen, "Is Yours a Believing Heart?" *Ensign,* September 1974, 52–53.

4. Dallin H. Oaks, "The Challenge to Become," *Ensign,* November 2000, 33.

5. Neal A. Maxwell, "Swallowed Up in the Will of the Father," *Ensign,* November 1995, 24.

6. The word *state* is defined as "the set of attributes characterizing a person's being; one's emotional, mental, or psychological condition; the way someone is, intrinsically" (*Merriam-Webster's Third New International Dictionary,* s.v. "state").

7. Oaks, "The Challenge to Become," 32.

8. Riddle, "Becoming a Disciple," 81.

9. Oaks, "The Challenge to Become," 33; emphasis added.

## 12

# CHOOSING REDEMPTION

## *Jennifer C. Lane*

The Prophet Joseph Smith taught, "If you wish to go where God is, you must be like God."[1] When we accept that we must become more godly to be in God's presence, we can better appreciate the promise that a "man would get nearer to God by abiding by [the Book of Mormon's] precepts, than by any other book."[2] The Book of Mormon teaches us how to get nearer to God, in part because it shows the distance between us and God. Once we understand the reality of our condition, we might be tempted to despair. But the Book of Mormon teaches us that Christ has power to redeem us and that as we choose to receive that power our natures are changed. The Book of Mormon also helps us understand that this redemptive change comes through the process of having faith in our Savior and repenting of our sins. Repentance and sanctification become redemption as we are delivered from the bondage of sin and the natural man. Through the Book of Mormon, we learn how to get nearer to God because we learn how to become more like Him.

---

*Jennifer C. Lane is an assistant professor of Religious Education at Brigham Young University–Hawaii.*

## THE NEED TO BE REDEEMED: THE FALL

The Book of Mormon testifies of our fallen state and need for a Redeemer.[3] While this message has not always been well received and is certainly not a popular theme today, understanding our need for redemption and divine help is absolutely essential to allow us to draw nearer to God. The condition of human nature when separated from God is powerfully conveyed in the words of Abinadi, Amulek, and King Benjamin, among others.

Abinadi speaks to King Noah and his priests, who are all intent on believing that they can be acceptable to God without faith and repentance. They want to believe that the good news sent by the Lord's messengers is that we can save ourselves without redemption (see Mosiah 12:9–32). A central part of Abinadi's witness of the redemption of Christ is his witness of our fallen state: "For they are carnal and devilish, and the devil has power over them; yea, even that old serpent that did beguile our first parents, which was the cause of their fall; which was the cause of all mankind becoming carnal, sensual, devilish, knowing evil from good, subjecting themselves to the devil. Thus all mankind were lost; and behold, they would have been endlessly lost were it not that God redeemed his people from their lost and fallen state" (Mosiah 16:3–4). This testimony of the reality of our condition without a Redeemer was the main reason Abinadi was killed.

A similar testimony of our fallen state can be found in Amulek's witness to the Zoramites, who were, like the people of King Noah, confident in their ability to please God without a Redeemer (see Alma 31:16–17). After Alma's testimony of how to plant the seed of faith in Christ's Atonement (see Alma 32–33), Amulek continued to explain how important it is to recognize our complete reliance on the power of the Redeemer: "It is expedient that an atonement should be made; for according to the great plan of the Eternal God there must be an atonement made, or else all mankind must unavoidably perish; yea, all are hardened; yea, all are fallen and are lost, and must perish except it be through the atonement which it is expedient should be made" (Alma 34:9). Like Abinadi, Amulek makes it clear that this is a universal condition: "*All* are hardened; yea, *all* are fallen and are lost" (emphasis added). Accepting the reality of our lost and fallen state requires a tremendous amount of humility, especially when we would rather look at ourselves as being "religious," as did the priests of King Noah and the Zoramites.

The message of our nature as "carnal, sensual, devilish" and of our state as fallen and lost does not immediately seem like good news or like a positive message. Like the priests of King Noah, we might ask why we are being given such discouraging news. Why does the Book of Mormon teach this? It is not to make us despair, however, but to make us humble and recognize our need for a Redeemer. When we start to learn of and believe in the existence of spiritual captivity as taught in the Book of Mormon, we begin to see the reality of our spiritual condition. We are then prepared to choose the redemptive power of Christ to change our natures.

King Benjamin preached the same message as Abinadi and Amulek but was more successful because he had an especially receptive audience. The message of the Fall and the Redemption did not remain an abstract principle for them; they allowed it to change their hearts and minds. Closely studying and pondering these messages and the impact they had can allow the same change to take place in our lives. King Benjamin clearly taught both the problem of and the solution to our spiritual state: "For the natural man is an enemy to God, and has been from the fall of Adam, and will be, forever and ever, unless he yields to the enticings of the Holy Spirit, and putteth off the natural man and becometh a saint through the atonement of Christ the Lord, and becometh as a child, submissive, meek, humble, patient, full of love, willing to submit to all things which the Lord seeth fit to inflict upon him, even as a child doth submit to his father" (Mosiah 3:19).

Learning how to read and apply these kinds of teachings is comparable to going to the doctor when we have a serious health condition or going to a financial consultant when we are deeply in debt. When we lie to ourselves and insist that we don't have a problem, nothing that we are told about how to get better will make any difference. It is a natural human tendency to want to preserve our sense that everything is okay and that we don't need to make changes. The repeated message of the Lord's prophets in the Book of Mormon is that things are not okay. We are not okay. All are fallen. All are lost. Through the Fall of Adam and Eve, we have all become subject to the devil and are in bondage to him.

When I am willing to see the reality of my natural state as an enemy to God, I begin to see my own pride, impatience, and resentment as opposites of the character of a saint, who is "submissive, meek, humble, patient, full of love" (Mosiah 3:19). When we are willing to start seeing the reality of our condition and accept the diagnosis of our problems, we can then begin to really listen to the solution that is being offered. When I acknowledge that it is *my* nature and heart that are so often an enemy to God, I can also appreciate that *I* am the one who needs to "[yield] to the enticings of the Holy Spirit" (Mosiah 3:19). When we are told the reality of our spiritual condition and are actually willing to accept the diagnosis, we are then in a condition to actually follow through with the remedy prescribed. When I read scriptural descriptions of weaknesses and apply them to other people rather than myself, I am not able to hear and follow the help being offered me.

When we are willing to face the "bad news" without evading it or lying to ourselves, then we are really prepared for the "good news"—the gospel of Jesus Christ. When we recognize our individual need to be changed, then we can learn about the power of redemption. King Benjamin's explanation of the "good news" of how the power of the redemption works in our lives directly followed the "bad news" of the natural man's being an enemy to God. That state is real, but the way out of that condition is just as real. King Benjamin explains that we do not need to stay in bondage to the power of the evil one. We can choose redemption. "For the natural man is an enemy to God, and has been from the fall of Adam, and will be, forever and ever, *unless* he yields to the enticings of the Holy Spirit, and putteth off the natural man and becometh a saint through the atonement of Christ the Lord" (Mosiah 3:19; emphasis added). We can choose to yield "to the enticings of the Holy Spirit." We can choose to put off our natural state, which keeps us in bondage, becoming Saints "through the atonement of Christ the Lord."

This joint explanation of our spiritual captivity and the potential for redemption through Christ is the Book of Mormon's message of how we can draw nearer to God. It is a message explained more clearly in this book than in any other source.[4] Spiritual bondage and sin are real, but so is redemption through the Atonement of Christ the Lord, and we have a constant invitation to choose to apply that redemptive power in our lives.

Summing up his teachings to King Noah and his priests, Abinadi focuses on the choice provided us to leave our carnal natures through Christ's Redemption. He explains both the bad news of our spiritual captivity and the good news that we do not need to be trapped forever: "Thus all mankind were lost; and behold, they would have been endlessly lost were it not that God redeemed his people from their lost and fallen state" (Mosiah 16:4). The potential for redemption is real because of Christ's Atonement, but Abinadi makes it clear that we must choose to apply that power in our lives: "But remember that he that persists in his own carnal nature, and goes on in the ways of sin and rebellion against God, remaineth in his fallen state and the devil hath all power over him. Therefore he is as though there was no redemption made, being an enemy to God; and also is the devil an enemy to God" (Mosiah 16:5).

This echoes King Benjamin's point about the certainty of remaining an enemy to God *unless* he yields to the enticings of the Holy Spirit" (Mosiah 3:19; emphasis added). Abinadi warns that "he that persists in his own carnal nature, and goes on in the ways of sin and rebellion against God, remaineth in his fallen state and the devil hath all power over him" (Mosiah 16:5). If we do not choose to be changed through Christ and leave our natural and carnal state behind, then we do not choose to accept the power of redemption in our lives. We are choosing to stay far away from God because we were not willing to give away our sins to know Him (see Alma 22:18).

Satan is very flexible in his efforts to keep us away from God. At times he uses the approach of the priests of King Noah: "What great evil hast thou done, or what great sins have thy people committed, that we should be condemned of God or judged of this man?" (Mosiah 12:13). But while he would have us believe that there are no barriers between us and God, that we are just fine the way we are and have no need to make changes, he is perfectly capable of changing his tune when necessary. When we start to see the reality of our fallen nature and our spiritual weaknesses, quiet, subtle messages come to us trying to convince us that this is just the way we are. Rather than giving us unrealistic hope, he gives us unrealistic despair. He wants us to believe that nothing can remove us from the captivity of our weaknesses.

## THE POWER TO BE REDEEMED: THE ATONEMENT

Unlike the messages of the world that either deny or excuse ungodliness, the precepts of the Book of Mormon repeatedly insist both that we are unclean and that no unclean thing can dwell in the presence of God (see 1 Nephi 10:21; Alma 11:37; Alma 40:26; 3 Nephi 27:19). But the good news of the Book of Mormon is that there is a way to be cleansed and redeemed from sin and our fallen nature. The Book of Mormon testifies that the price of redemption has been paid through the atoning sacrifice of Jesus Christ and that we can choose to accept the power of redemption in our lives.

The invitation to accept Christ's offer of cleansing and redemption is repeated throughout the Book of Mormon. Moroni ends the Book of Mormon with the invitation to "come unto Christ, and be perfected in him, and deny yourselves of all ungodliness" (Moroni 10:32). A much earlier version of this final invitation is found in the final words of Amaleki, who concluded the small plates of Nephi. Amaleki, like Moroni, focuses both on what we need to do and what Christ will do for us that is beyond our own power: "And now, my beloved brethren, I would that ye should come unto Christ, who is the Holy One of Israel, and partake of his salvation, and the power of his redemption. Yea, come unto him, and offer your whole souls as an offering unto him, and continue in fasting and praying, and endure to the end; and as the Lord liveth ye will be saved" (Omni 1:26). We cannot redeem ourselves. Only Christ has power to do that. But we can choose to "partake of . . . the power of his redemption." We make that choice step by step as we "offer [our] whole souls as offering unto him." With each choice to give up our sins, the power of redemption is able to become operative in our lives. Our faith and repentance enable us to be redeemed.

Christ has the power of His Redemption to offer us, and we offer Him our whole souls to be redeemed. This parallels King Benjamin's invitation to put off the natural man. The choice to put off the natural man is not painless. Each step of the process can be difficult, especially to the extent that we think that our weaknesses define us. As we recognize even one aspect of ourselves or our behavior as ungodly we are tempted to feel as though that is just the way we are. We can't change that much. We can't let that go. But letting go is precisely what the Lord requires to redeem us. He asks us to give away part of ourselves: to "offer our whole souls as offering unto him" (Omni 1:26).

The willingness to make this offering is beautifully illustrated by the fearsome king of the Lamanities, the father of King Lamoni. After Ammon's generosity of spirit humbled the king of the Lamanites, he allowed Ammon's brother Aaron to preach the gospel to him. Aaron's plain teaching included a no-illusions message of the Fall and the Atonement. Aaron explained "how God created man after his own image, and that God gave him commandments, and that because of transgression, man had fallen. And Aaron did expound unto him the scriptures from the creation of Adam, laying the fall of man before him, and their carnal state and also the plan of redemption, which was prepared from the foundation of the world, through Christ, for all whosoever would believe on his name. And since man had fallen he could not merit anything of himself; but the sufferings and death of Christ atone for their sins, through faith and repentance, and so forth" (Alma 22:12–14).

Having clearly been taught that he was fallen and "could not merit anything of himself" King Lamoni's father was brought down in the depths of humility. He knew that only faith and repentance could allow the "sufferings and death of Christ [to] atone for [his] sins," and so he prayed mightily: "I will give away all my sins to know thee, and that I may be raised from the dead, and be saved at the last day" (Alma 22:18). This heartfelt prayer is a perfect articulation of his willingness to give up the way he thought about himself and his old way of living. It is this godly sorrow, genuine remorse, and penitence that we must cultivate in order to want to change badly enough to be willing to give away our sins and receive Christ's Redemption.

In our day, Elder Neal A. Maxwell offered an eloquent description of this internal condition. He observed, "So it is that real, personal sacrifice never was placing an animal on the altar. Instead, it is a willingness to put the animal in us upon the altar and letting it be consumed!"[5] We sacrifice ourselves by denying ourselves all ungodliness—even, and especially, that which lies deep within our own hearts. His comments further illuminate Amaleki's exhortation to "offer your whole souls as an offering unto him" (Omni 1:26).

As we accept Christ's command to give away our sins, we also choose to accept the power of His Redemption. The power to become different people is found through opening ourselves to the power of Christ's Redemption. Moroni's closing invitation of the Book of Mormon, referred to earlier, clarifies the choices we must make to receive redemption. He exhorts us: "Yea, come unto Christ, and be perfected in him, and deny yourselves of all ungodliness; and if ye shall deny yourselves of all ungodliness, and love God with all your might, mind and strength, then is his grace sufficient for you, that by his grace ye may be perfect in Christ" (Moroni 10:32).

Redemption is in Christ. It is "by his grace ye may be perfect in Christ." This can include the justification that comes from sincere repentance and the ordinances of baptism and the sacrament. This justification means that we are forgiven for the things that we have done wrong, and they are no longer held against us because Christ's Atonement pays the price.[6] But there is an even more powerful message here. Christ's Redemption is not merely to forgive the past—it is to sanctify as well as to justify. Moroni here clarifies the choices that we can make that allow the power of Christ's Atonement to change our natures. We must deny ourselves of all ungodliness and love God with all our might, mind, and strength (see also D&C 20:30–31). As we do this and "deny not his power, then are ye sanctified in Christ by the grace of God, through the shedding of the blood of Christ, which is in the covenant of the Father unto the remission of your sins, that ye become holy, without spot" (Moroni 10:33). As we become "holy, without spot" redemption has taken place in our lives.

The Lord's prophets and apostles today continually urge us to follow this pattern and accept the power of redemption and sanctification. Elder David A. Bednar explained how the choice to deny ourselves of all ungodliness is also a choice to invite the sanctifying Spirit of the Lord to be in our lives. He warns us about the daily choices we make that open up, or close off, the potential for redemption, saying:

> We should attend to and learn from the choices and influences that separate us from the Holy Spirit. The standard is clear. If something we think, see, hear, or do distances us from the Holy Ghost, then we should stop thinking, seeing, hearing, or doing that thing. If that which is intended to entertain, for example, alienates us from the Holy Spirit, then certainly that type of entertainment is not for us. Because the Spirit cannot abide that which is vulgar, crude, or immodest, then clearly such things are not for us. Because we estrange the Spirit of the Lord when we engage in activities we know we should shun, then such things definitely are not for us.[7]

As we choose to draw nearer to God, He will help us identify things that could keep us far away from Him. As we live worthy of the gift of the Holy Ghost, we open ourselves up for the sanctifying power of the Atonement to redeem us and change us.

The good news of the gospel testifies that Christ's power can change our very natures. He does not impose that power upon us without our will, but when we want Him and His righteousness more than we want to keep our sins, we feel His redeeming power.

Significantly, the Book of Mormon testifies that Christ came to redeem us *from* our sins, not *in* our sins (see Helaman 5:10). This statement comes in a powerful set of statements by the prophet Helaman to his sons, Nephi and Lehi, in which he encapsulates the most critical doctrinal precepts of the Book of Mormon. First he reminds them that King Benjamin taught "that there is no other way nor means whereby man can be saved, only through the atoning blood of Jesus Christ, who shall come; yea, remember that he cometh to redeem the world" (Helaman 5:9). Then he reminds them of "the words which Amulek spake unto Zeezrom, in the city of Ammonihah; for he said unto him that the Lord surely should come to redeem his people, but that he should not come to redeem them in their sins, but to redeem them from their sins" (Helaman 5:10). Accepting these two points about redemption is essential if we wish to draw closer to God. We must recognize that "there is no other way" than through Christ's atoning blood and also recognize that this redemption demands that we leave our sins behind. Christ has the power to redeem us from our sins. We alone have the power to stop Him.

We choose to invite the power of His Redemption to be with us when we choose to invite the Spirit of the Lord into our lives. King Benjamin explains how choosing to invite the Spirit and "yielding to its enticings" is choosing to be redeemed. When we follow the Spirit's enticings to do good we "[*become* saints] through the atonement of Christ the Lord" (Mosiah 3:19; emphasis added). A further explanation of the process of redemption is given by Alma, who pleads with the people to allow Christ to change them: "But that ye would humble yourselves before the Lord, and call on his holy name, and watch and pray continually, that ye may not be tempted above that which ye can bear, and thus be led by the Holy Spirit, *becoming* humble, meek, submissive, patient, full of love and all long-suffering" (Alma 13:28; emphasis added). This passage further expands on how the influence of the Holy Ghost allows the redemptive process of sanctification and transformation to occur. Like King Benjamin, Alma notes that as we choose to place ourselves under the influence of the Holy Ghost we *become* Saints. It is not a one-time event but a lifelong process. As we continually choose to follow this process of faith, repentance, and obedience, we choose to be redeemed.

## CHOOSING REDEMPTION: OUR AGENCY

Even though Christ has worked out our redemption, we must want to be redeemed. It is as though we are individually in dark prison cells, bound in the chains of our sins, weaknesses, and fears. The Savior stands at the door, pleading with us to come to Him, assuring us that the chains and the prison will not hold us fast because He has paid our ransom price—He has redeemed us. The choice to believe His voice and to act in faith is the choice to be redeemed. The price has been paid, and we truly are free to leave the prison of our fallen state through the power of the Atonement. But redemption is not complete until we exercise our faith and repentance and come unto Him.

As we recognize that we must choose to accept the Lord's

invitation to "partake of . . . the power of his redemption" (Omni 1:26), we realize that our spiritual state is in our own hands. The responsibility of our agency should not, however, be mistaken for redeeming or saving ourselves. The Book of Mormon teachings about the relationship of the Fall and the Redemption make this abundantly clear. Remembering that our sins and weaknesses are truly a captivity and bondage is essential to remembering that redemption is "only through the atoning blood of Jesus Christ" (Helaman 5:9). The Book of Mormon consistently teaches that hope for deliverance from spiritual captivity comes only from faith in the Lord Jesus Christ, our Redeemer. It also, significantly, explains how our faith in Christ will lead us to repent and obey (see Helaman 13:14; Alma 34:15–17).[8] Choosing faith in Christ is choosing redemption. As we trust in His promise that He has power to redeem us, we will repent of all our sins. Our repentance delivers us from the prison of our sinful state. This redemption occurs, however, only to the extent that we trust in and obey His voice pleading with us to come unto Him and "be perfected in Him" (Moroni 10:32).

If we choose not to listen to His voice, the Book of Mormon prophets warn us that someday we will acknowledge that only we are accountable for our state. Alma explains that "if we have hardened our hearts against the word" then at some day "we must come forth and stand before him in his glory, and in his power" and "acknowledge to our everlasting shame" that He is just, merciful, and "has all power to save every man that believeth on his name and bringeth forth fruit meet for repentance" (Alma 12:13, 15). The power of redemption is available. It is essential that we know that Christ "has all power to save every man" because Satan wants so badly for us to feel unredeemable. It is also essential that we know what this redemption means. It is not to be redeemed in our sins, but from them, and that is why it is only available to those who "[believe] on his name and [bring] forth fruit meet for repentance."

The Lord Himself testified that we must individually choose redemption. He told Alma that at the Judgment Day there will be those that shall "know that I am the Lord their God, that I am their Redeemer; but they *would not* be redeemed" (Mosiah 26:26; emphasis added). If we are not willing to receive the redemption of having our natures sanctified, then it will be as if there was no redemption made. The hope for each of us is in realizing that the Redemption has been made, the price has been paid, and the power is available. Satan wants us to think that our fallen state is just the way we are. Christ's witness in the Book of Mormon is that we can be redeemed from our carnal state. We do not have to stay in the prison of our sins and weaknesses, but we can move forward with confidence in His power to redeem.

---

## NOTES

1. Joseph Smith, *Teachings of the Prophet Joseph Smith,* comp. Joseph Fielding Smith (Salt Lake City: Deseret Book, 1976), 216.

2. Joseph Smith, *History of the Church of Jesus Christ of Latter-day Saints,* ed. B. H. Roberts, 2nd ed. rev. (Salt Lake City: Deseret Book), 4:461.

3. In the ancient Near East, a redeemer was someone who paid a ransom price to buy another out of slavery. The image of the Lord as the Redeemer of Israel has a very developed role in the Old Testament. Here we see that the Lord's ability to act as the kinsman-redeemer of Israel is tied to His family relationship to Israel created by adoptive covenant. This background clearly informs the way that redemption is discussed in the Book of Mormon. What the Book of Mormon adds to the biblical framework is a clearer understanding of the sense to which this individual redemption is from the bondage of sin and that it comes as people choose to apply the Atonement in their lives. For an overview of the Old Testament foundation for the Book of Mormon imagery, see Jennifer C. Lane, "The Lord Will Redeem His People: Adoptive Covenant and Redemption in the Old Testament," in *Sperry Symposium Classics: The Old Testament,* ed. Paul Y. Hoskisson (Provo, UT: Religious Studies Center, Brigham Young University; Salt Lake City: Deseret Book, 2005), 298–310. In addition to the clearly Christ-centered explanation of spiritual redemption in the Book of Mormon, the explanation of Christ's atoning sacrifice as the price of redemption is also found in the New Testament (see Jennifer C. Lane, "Hebrew Concepts of Adoption and Redemption in the Writings of Paul," in *The Apostle Paul: His Life and His Testimony,* ed. Paul Y. Hossikson [Salt Lake City: Deseret Book, 1994], 80–95). I develop the idea of how covenant redemption can be understood in an individual's life in "The Redemption of Abraham," in *The Book of Abraham: Astronomy, Papyrus, and Covenant,* ed. John Gee and Brian M. Hauglid, Studies in the Book of Abraham, vol. 3 (Provo, UT: ISPART, 2005), 167–74.

4. On this subject, President Ezra Taft Benson observed that "just as a man does not really desire food until he is hungry, so he does not desire the salvation of Christ until he knows why he needs Christ. No one adequately and properly knows why he needs Christ until he understands and accepts the doctrine of the

Fall and its effect upon all mankind. And no other book in the world explains this vital doctrine nearly as well as the Book of Mormon" ("Gospel Classics: The Book of Mormon and the Doctrine and Covenants," *Ensign*, January 2005, 27). While there is no question that the doctrines of the Fall and Christ's Redemption are also clearly and emphatically taught in the New Testament, I believe it is in the Book of Mormon that the explanation of the relationship between the Fall and the Redemption has a clarity and consistency that is unmatched in any other book of scripture. While this paper can only examine highlights from the discussion of prophets in the Book of Mormon, I hope that it can give a sense of the depth and consistency with which these topics are both taught and illustrated.

5. Neal A. Maxwell, "'Deny Yourselves of All Ungodliness,'" *Ensign*, May 1995, 68.

6. A helpful discussion of justification and sanctification can be found in Elder D. Todd Christofferson's article "Justification and Sanctification," *Ensign*, June 2001, 18–25.

7. David A. Bednar, "That We May Always Have His Spirit to Be with Us," *Ensign*, May 2006, 30.

8. For a more complete development of the relationship of faith and repentance in the Book of Mormon, see my discussion in "Faith unto Repentance: The Fulness of the Simple Way," in *The Fulness of the Gospel: Foundational Teachings from the Book of Mormon* (Salt Lake City: Deseret Book, 2003), 181–93.

## 13

# RESTORATION, REDEMPTION, AND RESURRECTION: THREE *R'S* OF THE BOOK OF MORMON

## *Richard O. Cowan*

We have long heard of the "three R's" of elementary education—reading, 'riting, and 'rithmetic. Similarly, a set of interrelated doctrines might be referred to as the three R's of the Book of Mormon—restoration, redemption, and resurrection. In fact, we might add a fourth R, repentance, which is essential for the first two to function.

Material for this chapter is drawn primarily from two experiences recorded in the book of Alma. First, Alma and Amulek confronted a group of antagonistic lawyers in the wicked city of Ammonihah. Amulek's response to Zeezrom's hostile questioning is recorded in chapter 11. Then, as Alma the Younger neared the end of his life, he took time to give instructions to his three sons. Notice how he spent the most time with, and gave particularly profound teachings to, his wayward son Corianton—recorded in chapters 39–42. Apparently Alma agreed with the principle President Boyd K. Packer later enunciated—that "the study of the doctrines of the gospel will improve behavior quicker than a study of behavior will improve behavior."[1]

---

*Richard O. Cowan is a professor of Church history and doctrine at Brigham Young University.*

## THE DOCTRINE OF RESTORATION

The doctrine of restoration found in the book of Alma is closely related to the specifically announced mission of the Book of Mormon—"the convincing of the Jew and Gentile that Jesus is the Christ" (title page). It is His Atonement that makes restoration possible. When Latter-day Saints hear the term *restoration,* they typically think of the renewed revelation of the gospel and reestablishment of the Church on earth following an era of apostasy. However, *restoration* as taught in the Book of Mormon refers to different concepts.

To fully understand what restoration involves, we must realize that the scriptures speak of two kinds of death. Spiritual death, an alienation from God, is caused by sin. Physical or temporal death is the separation of the body from the spirit, introduced into the world by Adam's transgression. We shall see how restoration overcomes both spiritual death, through the process of redemption, and physical death, through resurrection. This chapter will also show how repentance is the key to achieving the maximum blessings through both redemption and resurrection.

## THE GIFT OF REDEMPTION

Zeezrom, a leader among the antagonistic lawyers in Ammonihah, asked a series of questions calculated to entrap Amulek. An obviously loaded question was, "Shall [God] save his people *in* their sins?" Amulek explained that this would be impossible because "no unclean thing can inherit the kingdom of heaven" (Alma 11:34, 37; emphasis added). He later explained, "That same spirit [of the Lord or of the devil] which doth possess your bodies at the time that ye go out of this life . . . will have power to possess your body in that eternal world" (Alma 34:34). Furthermore, Alma emphasized to Corianton that the principle of restoration definitely would not place persons who are carnal, evil, or devilish in a state opposite to their nature (see Alma 41:11–13). This agrees with the affirmation made by Jacob centuries earlier that following the Resurrection and Judgment, "they who are righteous shall be righteous still, and they who are filthy shall be filthy still" (2 Nephi 9:16).

A system of divine law explains why these teachings are true. Where a law is given, we have the choice to obey or disobey, to be righteous or wicked. An oft-quoted latter-day revelation affirms that we can obtain a blessing only "by obedience to that law upon which it is predicated" (D&C 130:21). The opposite consequence, resulting from disobedience, is not mentioned as often. Nevertheless, Alma warned his disobedient son that "there is a law given and a punishment affixed" and that "the law inflicteth the punishment" on those who do not obey (Alma 42:22). Blessings bring happiness or joy, while punishments create sorrow or pain. Hence, Alma's frequently cited affirmation is true—that "wickedness never was [nor can produce] happiness" (Alma 41:10). The following chart illustrates the effects of either obeying or disobeying God's laws.

Thus, according to the principle of justice, punishment is the inevitable consequence of breaking the law. According to the companion principle of mercy, however, another person may pay the penalties

## GOD'S LAWS

| Obey | Disobey |
|---|---|
| Righteousness | Wickedness |
| Blessings | Punishment |
| Happiness, joy | Sorrow, pain |
| Liberty | Captivity |
| Eternal life | Second death |
| Exaltation | Damnation |

resulting from our sins if he is willing and able. Of course, Jesus Christ is that person. Not only God the Father loved the world, but the Son also loved us enough that He was willing to take upon Himself the punishments of all mankind (compare John 3:16 with D&C 34:3). He was able to do so for at least two reasons. His sinlessness gave Him power over spiritual death. Notice how He mentions this as He is pleading our cause: "Father, behold the sufferings and death of him who did no sin, in whom thou wast well pleased" (D&C 45:4). Also, because He was born of an immortal Father, He had power over physical death. Following His statement about "other sheep," Jesus added the following: "Therefore doth my Father love me, because I lay down my life, that I might take it again. No man taketh it from me, but I lay it down of myself. I have power to lay it down, and I have power to take it again" (John 10:17–18). Thus, He was completely qualified to redeem us from both kinds of death.

The Bible Dictionary describes *redemption* as "the sacrificial work of Jesus Christ and our deliverance from sin" (Bible Dictionary, "Redemption," 760). The biblical concept translated as *redemption* refers to the practice of purchasing a slave in order to free him from slavery. In this sense, Christ has purchased us through His atoning blood and frees us from our bondage to sin (see 1 Peter 1:18–19). Another definition of redemption might be "to repurchase something previously possessed and subsequently lost. . . . Redemption is thus God's way of reclaiming his children from the fall of man by sacrificing Christ's redeeming blood as reparation for their repossession."[2]

There are two important aspects of redemption. First, it unconditionally frees us from the binding or limiting consequences of the Fall. Second, it provides the means by which we can overcome the penalties from our own sins. Speaking of the Fall, Lehi declared: "Adam fell that men might be; and men are, that they might have joy." Lehi then testified that the Messiah would redeem us from the Fall and added, "Because that they are redeemed from the fall they have become free forever. . . . And they are free to choose liberty and eternal life, through the great Mediator of all men, or to choose captivity and death, according to the captivity and power of the devil" (2 Nephi 2:25–27).

Because we are free to choose, redemption from the effects of our own sins must come with conditions attached. Alma explained: "And now, there was no means to reclaim men from this fallen state, which man had brought upon himself because of his own disobedience; therefore, according to justice, the plan of redemption could not be brought about, only on conditions of repentance of men in this probationary state, yea, this preparatory state; for except it were for these conditions, mercy could not take effect except it should destroy the work of justice.

Now the work of justice could not be destroyed; if so, God would cease to be God" (Alma 42:12–13).

Alma then explained that because "all mankind were fallen," they were "in the grasp of justice," which "consigned them forever to be cut off from [God's] presence." He therefore concluded that the Atonement was necessary "to appease the demands of justice, that God might be a perfect, just God, and a merciful God also" (Alma 42:14–15). Still, Alma felt the need to ask his wayward son if mercy could rob justice. "Nay; not one whit," he responded emphatically to his own question (Alma 42:25).

Amulek had similarly testified that the Atonement would "bring about the bowels of mercy, which overpowereth justice, and bringeth about means unto men that they may have faith unto repentance. And thus mercy can satisfy the demands of justice, and encircles them in the arms of safety, while he that exercises no faith unto repentance is exposed to the whole law of the demands of justice" (Alma 34:15–16).

In his response to Zeezrom, Amulek had insisted that Christ would "come into the world to redeem his people" and to "take upon him the transgressions of those who believe on his name; and these are they that shall have eternal life, and salvation cometh to none else." Because we are free to choose whether we will obey God's commandments, "the wicked remain as though there had been no redemption made, except it be the loosing of the bands of death; for behold, the day cometh that all shall rise from the dead and stand before God, and be judged according to their works." Amulek reminded us that on that occasion we would "have a bright recollection of all our guilt" (Alma 11:40–43). In this same passage, Amulek clearly testified that Christ's Atonement would also bring to pass the resurrection of our physical bodies.

## THE REMARKABLE RESURRECTION

Physical death is overcome specifically through the wonderful blessing of the Resurrection. The Bible bears witness of this promise. Ezekiel's vision of the "dry bones" that would live again suggests a very literal physical resurrection (see Ezekiel 37:1–14). The New Testament witnesses that Jesus was physically resurrected. He ate fish and honey in the presence of His disciples; as the Apostles handled His resurrected body, they could tell it was actually composed of "flesh and bones" (see Luke 24:36–43). In his great chapter on the Resurrection, the Apostle Paul taught: that which was "sown a natural body" will be "raised a spiritual body" (1 Corinthians 15:44).

The Book of Mormon's teachings are much clearer concerning the precise nature of the Resurrection. In his response to Zeezrom's probing questions, Alma's missionary companion Amulek testified: "The spirit and the body shall be reunited again in its perfect form; both limb and joint shall be restored to its proper frame, even as we now are at this time. . . . And even there shall not so much as a hair of their heads be lost; but every thing shall be restored to its perfect frame." He explained that "this mortal body is raised to an immortal body, that is from death, even from the first death unto life, that they can die no more; their spirits uniting with their bodies, never to be divided; thus the whole becoming spiritual and immortal, that they can no more see corruption" (Alma 11:43–45). Later, Alma bore the same testimony in almost identical language as he taught his son Corianton (see Alma 40:23).

Elder Orson Pratt pointed out, tongue in cheek, how taking these teachings too literally may result in strange conclusions:

> We are in the habit of taking knives or rasors and paring our nails every little while, so much so that we can safely say that in the course of a year we cut off or pare from our fingers and toes, as the case may be, perhaps an inch of nail, at this rate, a man who lives to be seventy-two years of age would pare off seventy-two inches of nail, which would be six feet. Now can we suppose than when a man rises from the dead that he will come forth with nails six feet long? (laughter,) I cannot conceive any such thing. . . . Then again, we are in the habit of having our hair shingled. . . . In the course of a year perhaps four or five inches of hair may be cut from the head and cast away. Now, in seventy-two years, if a man did not lose his hair altogether, he would perhaps cut off something like twenty-four feet of hair and beard. Can we suppose that in the resurrection we shall come forth with our hair and beard a rod long? I do not look for any such thing. . . . I look for a sufficient quantity of the

material once existing in the hair and beard to be restored to make one appear comely.[3]

The Book of Mormon provides another testimony of the Resurrection in an interesting and most significant way. It records that when the Savior appeared to the people gathered at the temple in ancient Bountiful, He invited them all to come forth "that ye may thrust your hands into my side, and also that ye may feel the prints of the nails in my hands and in my feet, that ye may know that I am the God of Israel, and the God of the whole earth, and have been slain for the sins of the world" (3 Nephi 11:14). Because there were 2,500 present and because they came forth "one by one" (see 3 Nephi 11:15; 17:25), this process must have taken hours, even assuming that each person had only a few seconds with the Lord. Simply seeing Him was not enough to prove the Resurrection because a spirit can look like a tangible body (see Ether 3:6–16) and a body of flesh and bone can be believed to be a spirit (see Luke 24:36–39). The Master wanted the people to know without any doubt that even though He had been "slain," He now possessed a resurrected body they could actually feel. Thus, these 2,500 witnesses make the Book of Mormon's testimony of the Resurrection certain and convincing.

President Joseph F. Smith provided an interesting perspective of the process of restoration as it applies to the Resurrection: "The body will come forth as it is laid to rest, for there is no growth or development in the grave. As it is laid down, so will it arise, and changes to perfection will come by the law of restitution." Specifically he taught that "every organ, every limb that has been maimed, every deformity caused by accident or in any other way, will be restored and put right. . . . Not that a person will always be marred by scars, wounds, deformities, defects or infirmities," he clarified, "for these will be removed in their course, in their proper time, according to the merciful providence of God. Deformity will be removed; defects will be eliminated, and men and women shall attain to the perfection of their spirits."[4]

Concerning those who die in childhood, President Smith explained, "We know our children will not be compelled to remain as a child in stature always," adding, "for it was revealed from God, the fountain of truth, through Joseph Smith the prophet, in this dispensation, that in the resurrection of the dead the child that was buried in its infancy will come up in the form of the child that it was when it was laid down; then it will begin to develop. From the day of the resurrection, the body will develop until it reaches the full measure of the stature of its spirit, whether it be male or female."[5]

Even though our resurrected bodies will be physically perfect, they will be adapted to the kingdom we qualify to inherit, although the scriptures do not specify the exact nature of these adaptations. Paul taught that there would be "celestial bodies, and bodies terrestrial, and bodies telestial" (Joseph Smith Translation, 1 Corinthians 15:40). The great latter-day revelation known as the Olive Leaf taught that our bodies will be "quickened" by the glory we are worthy to receive and that we must live the celestial law if we hope to inherit that kingdom. The Lord then made the intriguing observation that those who will enter lesser glories will qualify for that which they were "*willing* to receive, because they were not *willing* to enjoy that which they might have received" (D&C 88:32; emphasis added).

What, then, does it mean to live the celestial law? A clue may be found in Christ's teachings to the Nephites, which paralleled His well-known Sermon on the Mount. While it had been taught "thou shalt not kill," He specified that "whosoever is angry with his brother shall be in danger of [God's] judgment" (3 Nephi 12:21–22). Similarly, the prevailing standard was "thou shalt not commit adultery," but He taught that "whosoever looketh on a woman, to lust after her, hath committed adultery already in his heart" (3 Nephi 12:27–28). Since "honorable men" who will inherit the terrestrial glory (D&C 76:75) do not kill or commit adultery, Christ's prohibition of anger and lustful thoughts suggest a higher, perhaps celestial, standard. We might similarly ask ourselves what is involved in truly being celestial parents, Church workers, and so forth. Even though the Resurrection is a gift guaranteed to all through the Atonement of Christ, we need to repent if we are not living up to the standards required for obtaining a celestial body.

## REPENTANCE, THE KEY

We have seen that the Atonement of Christ redeems us unconditionally from the effects of Adam's Fall. All will be resurrected. All will be redeemed from the consequences of Adam's transgression. But to be redeemed from our own sins, we must repent because mercy cannot rob justice. Likewise, to receive the kind of resurrected body we want, we must repent and live according to the celestial law. Hence, repentance is the key to our receiving the greatest blessings of both redemption and resurrection. It is significant that each time Alma or Amulek spoke about every part of the body being restored to its perfect frame and to the spirit in the Resurrection, they also reminded us that we will be returned to the presence of God to be judged. They consistently linked the Resurrection and Judgment to the promised restoration (see, for example, Alma 11:40–45; 40:21–26; 41:2–6; 42:2–4; 42:23).

Because personal worthiness is the key to fully realizing the blessings of both redemption and resurrection, repentance could well be regarded as a fourth R of the Book of Mormon. The thrust of the teachings of both Alma and Amulek was that we must do something positive to escape the bondage of sin and qualify for the glorious restoration. For example, after Alma had warned Corianton that those who are carnal and sinful cannot be restored to a condition of happiness, he pointedly counseled: "Therefore, my son, see that you are merciful unto your brethren; deal justly, judge righteously, and do good continually; and if ye do all these things then shall ye receive your reward" (Alma 41:14). Amulek emphatically declared that "this life is the time for men to prepare to meet God"; he pleaded, "I beseech of you that ye do not procrastinate the day of your repentance until the end" (Alma 34:32–33). Notice that this is the same passage where he taught that we will be influenced by the same spirit in eternity we have chosen to follow now (v. 34).

The scriptures clearly set forth the benefits of repentance. Isaiah testified that even though our "sins be as scarlet, they shall be as white as snow" (Isaiah 1:18). Alma gratefully witnessed that when he recalled his own father's teachings about Jesus Christ and humbly turned to the Savior for help, "I could remember my pains no more; yea, I was harrowed up by the memory of my sins no more," but rather, "my soul was filled with joy as exceeding as was my pain!" He testified that exquisitely bitter pain had been replaced by exquisitely sweet joy (Alma 36:19–21). In our own day, the Lord has promised, "He that repents and does the commandments of the Lord shall be forgiven" (D&C 1:32). And again, "He who has repented of his sins, the same is forgiven, and I, the Lord, remember them no more" (D&C 58:42).

The teachings of Amulek and Alma about the principle of restoration had a positive impact. The Book of Mormon indicates that Zeezrom the lawyer was converted, healed, and then baptized. He immediately began sharing with others what he had been taught (see Alma 15:6–12). He was also listed among those whom Alma took with him to preach to the Zoramites (see Alma 31:5–6). At the conclusion of his counsel to Corianton, Alma exhorted him: "And now, O my son, ye are called of God to preach the word unto this people . . . that thou mayest bring souls unto repentance" (Alma 42:31). Mormon's abridgment continues: "And now it came to pass that the sons of Alma [not excluding Corianton] did go forth among the people, to declare the word unto them" (Alma 43:1). Two decades later, Corianton specifically was identified as assisting with the migration into the land northward (see Alma 63:10). I hope that the Book of Mormon's teachings about restoration, redemption, resurrection, and repentance will have an equally salutary impact on the lives of Saints in the latter days.

---

## NOTES

1. Boyd K. Packer, "Little Children," *Ensign,* November 1986, 17; see also Boyd K. Packer, "Washed Clean," *Ensign,* May 1997, 9; Boyd K. Packer, "Do Not Fear," *Ensign,* May 2004, 79.

2. Dennis L. Largey, ed., *Book of Mormon Reference Companion* (Salt Lake City: Deseret Book, 2003), 673, s.v. "redemption."

3. Orson Pratt, in *Journal of Discourses* (London: Latter-day Saints' Book Depot, 1854–86), 16:356.

4. Joseph F. Smith, *Teachings of Presidents of the Church: Joseph F. Smith* (Salt Lake City: Intellectual Reserve, 1998), 91–92.

5. Smith, *Teachings of Presidents of the Church,* 130.

## 14

# ALMA'S REFORM OF ZARAHEMLA: A MODEL FOR ACTIVATION

## Terry B. Ball

Certainly one of the most remarkable missionary efforts ever recorded in scripture was that of the sons of Mosiah as they labored among their Lamanite brothers to "bring them to the knowledge of the Lord their God" (Mosiah 28:2; see Alma 17–26).[1] Today we encourage our missionaries to pattern their preparation and efforts after that of the sons of Mosiah. Modern missionaries can learn much from their example.

Equally as remarkable and instructive as the labors of the sons of Mosiah among the Lamanites was another work conducted among the Nephites at the same time by their companion in conversion, Alma the Younger.[2] While the sons of Mosiah worked to convert the Lamanites, Alma labored to reconvert or activate the hardened and apostate Nephite nation in the land of Zarahemla. At that time even the Church itself had fallen into wickedness, so much so that their wickedness was a "stumbling-block" to conversion for those who had not joined (Alma

---

Terry B. Ball is a professor of ancient scripture and dean of Religious Education at Brigham Young University.

4:10). Seeing this great wickedness, Alma set out to reclaim and reform the Church (see Alma 4:6–20).[3]

Just as modern missionaries can learn much from the methods of the sons of Mosiah, we can learn much about strengthening wavering members from the example of Alma the Younger in his remarkable reform of the Nephites in Zarahemla. A careful study of Alma 4–16 shows that Alma the Younger models many important principles of activation that are helpful to us today. This study examines principles of activation derived from the account of Alma's labors among the apostate Nephites, particularly in the city of Zarahemla in Alma 4 and 5.[4]

## PRINCIPLES MODELED BY ALMA

### Build Trust

Alma began his labors by making a considerable sacrifice in order to do the work. Nine years earlier he had been appointed the first chief judge of the Nephites, the highest political office in the nation (see Mosiah 29:42). This was a demanding position that gave him great authority and prestige among the people, yet he determined that to bring the people back into righteousness, he would have to surrender his political office and devote himself full time to the effort. Accordingly "he delivered the judgment-seat unto Nephihah," a man he deemed a competent successor (Alma 4:18). Certainly that act must have sent a clear signal to the Nephites of how important the gospel and their salvation were to Alma. Considering what he gave up in order to teach the people, none could question his sincerity or the depth of his conviction. With this great sacrifice, Alma accomplished one of the most important and difficult steps in helping others regain their testimonies and commitment to the gospel. He established a relationship of trust by showing how much he genuinely cared about them and the gospel he wanted to share with them. Perhaps many who listened to him afterward did so simply to try to understand why he cared so much about them and his faith.

Today, too, our activation efforts can be enhanced by establishing a relationship of trust with those we hope to help. Unfortunately, few of us can so quickly communicate our sincerity and commitment by making a great and public sacrifice as did Alma, yet if we consistently, persistently, and sincerely fellowship, opportunities to serve and communicate our genuine faith and interest will come. As we take advantage of such opportunities, those we seek to help may eventually come to trust and appreciate our relationship. It typically takes time. I recall having been given the privilege of home teaching a man who had not been to church for decades. He was a good and friendly man, easy to like, but he had no interest in the gospel. After several months of visiting with him in his home and having made little progress, I one day simply asked him, "Why don't you come to church?" He told me that Sunday was his only day off and the only day to get his chores done at home. Seeing an opportunity to show the man that I really cared about his family and the gospel, I volunteered to come to his home early the next Sunday morning and help him get his chores done so he could go to church with me. He laughed at the idea. I don't think he believed me. The next Sunday at 7:00 A.M. I was on his doorstep in my work clothes ringing his doorbell. When he answered the door, he looked at me and gruffly said, "Go home. I'll come to church." He did. Our trust and appreciation for one another grew from there. Many months of fellowshipping and teaching followed, but eventually he became my quorum president. I witnessed the principle Alma modeled so well with his great sacrifice: those we are trying to help reclaim faith will be more responsive to our efforts if they trust and know we are genuine in our concern for them and sincere in our commitment to the gospel.

### Remember the Past

Alma began his efforts to reclaim the Nephites to the faith in the capital city of Zarahemla in the land of Zarahemla.[5] With the exception of the people in Ammonihah, those living in this city had apparently strayed more than most in the land (see Alma 7:5–6; 8:9). As Alma began teaching, he reminded them of the role God played in their forefathers' lives. He told of both the physical and spiritual captivity and bondage their forefathers endured and of their great deliverance wrought by the "mercy and power of God" (Alma 5:4). He spoke of the "mighty change" that occurred in the hearts of those ancestors and of how "they humbled themselves and put their trust in the true and living God" (Alma 5:13). He assured them that their forefathers "were saved" because "they were faithful until the end" (Alma 5:13). As he rehearsed this history, he repeatedly asked the Nephites to consider if they had "sufficiently retained in remembrance" these remarkable sacred events (Alma 5:6). In so doing, Alma modeled another helpful principle of activation. As we help those who have strayed remember the blessings, happiness, and faith that accompanied past activity in the Church, we can help them reconsider why they left and perhaps find the desire to return.

While we may not know and be able to rehearse the history and details of past church activity of those we are trying to help as Alma did the Nephites, we can help them remember and reflect on their past with questions such as, How did you come to be a member of the Church? Has there ever been a time when you were happily active in the Church? Were your parents or ancestors deeply committed to the gospel? If they were and you asked them why they were so committed, what do you think they would say? Can you identify times in your life or the lives of your loved ones or ancestors when God intervened or blessed them?

These kinds of questions can solicit honest answers from those we are trying to help and lead to a discussion of the blessings, hope, confidence, and happiness that accompany those trying to live a righteous life. Such discussions may not only help them understand and reconsider why they may have strayed in the first place but also bolster their desire to return to a life of faith.

Once that spark of desire is found, the door may be opened to further invite them back to activity. I recall another occasion serving as a home teacher to a wonderful couple that had not attempted to live the gospel for many years. I remember the first time I visited their home. They came to the door together. The two were friendly but reluctant to invite my young companion and me inside. As we visited on the doorstep, they informed us they were not interested in religion. The wife, who at the time was employed as a bartender at a local tavern, boasted to us, "We don't just break the commandments—we smash 'em!" Still, they agreed to let us come by occasionally for a visit. On the next visit, we were invited in.

Over the course of several visits, it became apparent that though they had a rough exterior, there was goodness in these two and a sweet commitment to each other. When the occasion was right, I asked them how they came to be members of the Church. In response they spoke fondly of the good people who introduced them to the gospel when they lived in Hawaii. What followed was a rather nostalgic discussion of their short but happy time in Hawaii when they were active members of the Church. As we talked, it seemed that they began to yearn for some of those former experiences and feelings. The discussion naturally led me to ask why they were not active members of the Church now. They explained that when they first came to the mainland they went to church dressed in their bright, floral-print Hawaiian attire. They told of feeling out of place in their dress and of feeling unaccepted by the congregation for it. Consequently, they determined the Church was different here and not for them. I tried to assure them that they would be welcome at our ward no matter what they were wearing, but they did not seem convinced. I ultimately volunteered to wear a Hawaiian shirt to church for a month to prove the point. They found the proposition amusing and encouraged me to try it.

Finding a Hawaiian shirt in that small desert town in Idaho was not easy. At the local thrift store, I eventually found a long-sleeved, silky-looking thing that had what appeared to be dead and dying vines printed on it. It was hideous, but it was the best I could do. After I wore it for three weeks to our Sunday meetings, I visited the couple and told them I was going to wear it only one more time, so if they wanted to see it they were going to have to come to church. They did. Needless to say, everyone in the ward had already asked why I was wearing such a ghastly shirt to church, so they were especially anxious to meet the couple who drove the local seminary teacher to do such a thing. What followed was a wonderful fellowshipping experience as they were warmly welcomed into the ward. Months later, as the couple prepared to go to the temple, the wife frequently commented, "When I walk out of the temple, I want to die in the parking lot because that will probably be the best I'll ever get!" Sadly, she did pass away within a year of their sealing in the house of the Lord, but what a blessing it was for them to have made their relationship eternal! Their experience validated for me the principle Alma modeled—that remembering and discussing the blessings, happiness, and faith that accompanied past activity in the Church may encourage those who have strayed to want to find their way back into activity.

## Evaluate the Present

After helping the Nephites reflect upon the blessings and happiness their righteous forefathers enjoyed, Alma demonstrated another principle of activation as he invited the Nephites to evaluate their own current spiritual condition: "And now behold, I ask of you, my brethren of the church, have ye spiritually been born of God? Have ye received his image in your countenances? Have ye experienced this mighty change in your hearts?" (Alma 5:14). He further invited them to evaluate how prepared they were to stand before God, should they be "called to die" at that time, and to sincerely consider if they were sufficiently pure and humble (see Alma 5:15–31). Such questions must have been sobering for an apostate people and would have caused them to ponder what they should do to better prepare for the life to come.

Today, too, helping those who have fallen into inactivity seriously evaluate their current spiritual status and preparation for the next life can help them find the desire to renew their faith. Again, sincere questions asked at the right time in a trusting relationship can facilitate this kind of evaluation. Helpful questions might include, Can you remember a time when you were striving to be righteous and active in the faith? Did you have a better relationship with God then? Were you happier? Were you better able to deal with the trials of life? How are you now? Are you happier? Is life really going better for you? Are you better prepared to meet God? Are you being blessed by Him? Could you, with confidence, call upon Him for help? Are you now a better person, spouse, or parent? If those who have let their faith and activity slip honestly consider such questions, they may come to the conclusion that life is better when they are trying to live righteously. Reaching such a conclusion can help prepare them to accept an invitation to come back.

### Extend an Invitation

Alma gives us a model for such an invitation: "Repent, repent, for the Lord God hath spoken it! Behold, he sendeth an invitation unto all men, for the arms of mercy are extended towards them, and he saith: Repent, and I will receive you. Yea, he saith: Come unto me and ye shall partake of the fruit of the tree of life; yea, ye shall eat and drink of the bread and the waters of life freely; yea, come unto me and bring forth works of righteousness" (Alma 5:32–35). If they know that there is a way back and that they would be welcomed, the decision to come back may be made easier for those who have wandered from the faith. A sincere invitation like that given by Alma may do much to help them come to the realization that they are indeed wanted, needed, welcomed, and able to come back.

### Teach the Way

Alma demonstrated another helpful principle of activation as he taught the Nephites the way they could return to righteous lives. Having once himself strayed from the faith, Alma was able to speak with the voice of experience. As he taught the people, he asked, "Do ye not suppose that I know of these things myself? Behold, I testify unto you that I do know that these things whereof I have spoken are true. And how do ye suppose that I know of their surety?" (Alma 5:45). Those familiar with Alma the Younger's history might expect that in answer to the question, he would next speak of the angel of the Lord that appeared to him and called him to repentance when he was a rebellious young man trying to destroy the Church (see Mosiah 27).

The actual answer he gave is both surprising and deeply significant: "Behold, I say unto you they are made known unto me by the Holy Spirit of God. Behold, I have fasted and prayed many days that I might know these things of myself. And now I do know of myself that they are true; for the Lord God hath made them manifest unto me by his Holy Spirit; and this is the spirit of revelation which is in me" (Alma 5:46).

Although the visit from the angel started him on the road to a righteous life, his testimony came the way it does for most of us—through the whisperings of the Holy Spirit as we sincerely seek, pray, and fast for knowledge and confirmation. Alma also made it clear that the way back to the faith for those Nephites would also require them to repent and come unto Christ through works of righteousness (see Alma 5:31–36, 50–52). The formula is not difficult to apply. Seek and pray for direction and answers. Fast sincerely. Repent of sins. Do good works by trying to live a Christlike life. This was the way to faith anciently, and it still is the way today. As we strive to assist others in finding faith, it can be helpful for us to teach the way back—by precept and example.

## Bear Testimony

Because of Alma's position as the prophet and the high priest over the Church, throughout his discourse he also testified to the people of their wickedness and warned of the misery and destruction that awaited them if they did not repent. Alma declared, "For behold, the time is at hand that whosoever bringeth forth not good fruit, or whosoever doeth not the works of righteousness, the same have cause to wail and mourn" (Alma 5:36). He further warned that "whosoever bringeth forth evil works, the same becometh a child of the devil, for he hearkeneth unto his voice, and doth follow him. And whosoever doeth this must receive his wages of him; therefore, for his wages he receiveth death, as to things pertaining unto righteousness, being dead unto all good works" (Alma 5:41–42).

While we typically will not be in a position to so warn and prophesy against the sins of those we are trying to help, we can, as Alma did, bear testimony of the love and mercy of God. Alma declared to the Nephites, "Behold, I say unto you, that the good shepherd doth call you; yea, and in his own name he doth call you, which is the name of Christ" (Alma 5:38). He further testified, "I know that Jesus Christ shall come, yea, the Son, the Only Begotten of the Father, full of grace, and mercy, and truth. And behold, it is he that cometh to take away the sins of the world, yea, the sins of every man who steadfastly believeth on his name" (Alma 5:48). As we obtain and bear similar testimony to those who struggle to maintain faith, we may provide an opportunity for the Spirit to confirm our witness in their hearts. That witness can increase their desire to return to activity.

## CONCLUSION

Not everyone we try to invite back to activity in the Church will respond to our efforts. Alma certainly learned that in Ammonihah (see Alma 9–14). That fact should not discourage us from trying. As one whose own family struggled with activity in the Church for a season, I have a great interest in activation efforts. Though I was a young boy when my family finally found its way into faith and activity in the Church, I still remember those good people who helped us. As I look at Alma's example, I have come to realize that these good people persistently, patiently, and sincerely loved and served my family, following many of the principles Alma modeled. They helped us love and trust them. They helped us remember why we joined the Church in the first place. They encouraged us to consider our spiritual status and standing before God. They showed us the way to increase our faith and commitment. They bore inspiring testimony to us through their words and actions. I will love them forever. I know that one way we can show the depth of our gratitude for all the blessings we receive from our Heavenly Father is to strengthen others, especially those who struggle, by practicing the principles so well taught and demonstrated by Alma during his remarkable mission in Zarahemla.

---

## NOTES

1. As Alma described the challenge the sons of Mosiah undertook in trying to preach the gospel to the Lamanites, he explained: "And assuredly it was great, for they had undertaken to preach the word of God to a wild and a hardened and a ferocious people" (Alma 17:14). We marvel at their faith as they endured rejection, persecutions, and prisons. We teach our prospective missionaries to pattern their preparation after that of the sons of Mosiah by being prayerful students of the gospel (see Alma 17:28). We encourage our missionaries in the field to work as the sons of Mosiah did, building relationships of trust and serving the people among whom they labor (see Alma 17–18). We challenge our missionaries to seek the Spirit in their labors that they, like the sons of Mosiah, might teach with the "power and authority of God" (Alma 17:3).

2. For an account of the conversion of Alma the Younger and the sons of Mosiah, see Mosiah 27–28, and Alma 36.

3. In some ways, Alma's task may have been more challenging than that of the sons of Mosiah, for it can be more difficult to reclaim someone who has strayed from the Church than to convert one who had never been taught the gospel. Like

the sons of Mosiah, Alma endured rejection, persecution, and prison as he labored, and like the sons of Mosiah, he enjoyed remarkable success. In the space of five years, he taught repentance not only in the city of Zarahemla but also in Gideon, Melek, Ammonihah, Sidon, and the surrounding areas. As a result of his faith and efforts, "they began to establish the order of the church in the city of Zarahemla (see Alma 6:4), Gideon (see Alma 8:1), and Sidon (see Alma 15:17), and he baptized those who "came to him throughout all the borders of the land" of Melek (Alma 8:5). He even was able to reclaim many of the exceptionally wicked Ammonihahites, who were steeped in the profession of Nehor, including Amulek and Zeezrom (see Alma 8–15). The timing of Alma's reform of the land of Zarahemla proved fortuitous for the sons of Mosiah and their converts, the Anti-Nephi-Lehies, for as they fled the wrath of their unconverted Lamanite brethren who were determined to slay them, these new converts found compassion and refuge among the recently activated Nephites. As a result of Alma's contemporary labors the Nephites' hearts were prepared not only to welcome the refugees to their land but also to give the Anti-Nephi-Lehies the land of Jershon (see Alma 27:4–28:14) and to defend their new brethren in the faith with their own lives. Likely, if Alma had not just activated the Nephites, the Anti-Nephi-Lehies' petition for refuge would have been rejected by what would have still been a hardened and apostate Nephite nation. Surely an omniscient Father in Heaven directed this work and its timing.

4. Please note the list of principles presented hereafter is intended to be illustrative rather than exhaustive. Moreover, the account recorded in Alma was not written primarily for this purpose, but the principles that can be derived from the historical record constitute a valuable secondary message.

5. Book of Mormon geography is divided into two great divisions, the land northward and the land southward, separated by a narrow neck of land. The land southward appears to have had three major subdivisions, the land of Nephi or Lehi-Nephi in the southern end, the land of Zarahemla in the middle, and the land of Bountiful in the northern portion next to the narrow neck. The land of Zarahemla itself had several subdivisions as well, such as the land of Gideon and the land of Melek. Thus, the term "land of" could refer to a large or small division. Lands typically contained a major city that bore the land's name. Therefore, the city of Zarahemla is located in the land of Zarahemla in the land southward, while the city of Melek is located in the land of Melek, in the land of Zarahemla, in the land southward.

# 15

# "ALL ARE ALIKE UNTO GOD": EQUALITY AND CHARITY IN THE BOOK OF MORMON

## Lloyd D. Newell

The very existence of the Book of Mormon is evidence that the gospel of Jesus Christ is for everyone, everywhere, not just for a chosen few. The book itself is living proof of the claim made on its own title page—that Jesus Christ, the Eternal God, manifests "himself unto all nations." After prophesying that the resurrected Christ would show Himself to the Nephite nation, not just to those in Jerusalem, Nephi taught that all people have equal potential for salvation and exaltation: "[The Lord] inviteth . . . all to come unto him and partake of his goodness; and he denieth none that come unto him, black and white, bond and free, male and female; and he remembereth the heathen; and all are alike unto God" (2 Nephi 26:33). Consequently, Book of Mormon prophets can often be found speaking boldly against those who "persist in supposing that [they] are better one than another" (Alma 5:54).

Hundreds of years later, Mormon wrote to his son, Moroni, that charity, the pure and universal love of God, is what inspires us to treat each other equally: "I am filled with charity, which is everlasting love;

---

*Lloyd D. Newell is an associate professor of Church history and doctrine at Brigham Young University.*

wherefore, all children are alike unto me; wherefore, I love little children with a prefect love; and they are all alike and partakers of salvation. For I know that God is not a partial God, neither a changeable being; but he is unchangeable from all eternity to all eternity" (Moroni 8:17–18). God is both omniloving and omniscient. He knows and loves all His children with perfect understanding and compassion.

Equality and charity are two expressions of the same principle—both require humility and meekness; both are central to the message of the Book of Mormon.[1] With distinct clarity, the Book of Mormon teaches over and over again that "all are alike unto God," and this simple truth is the antidote for many of the pride problems that keep people from coming unto Christ and from extending service and love to all of His children. Whenever an individual or a nation achieves greatness in the Book of Mormon, it is because the people are free with their substance and treat each other as equals. In contrast, the many tragic pitfalls of pride that the Book of Mormon outlines can be traced to a person or persons withholding charity and thinking they are above another. Alma's deep sorrow was because of the "great inequality among the people, some lifting themselves up with their pride, despising others, turning their backs upon the needy and the naked and those who were hungry, and those who were athirst, and those who were sick and afflicted" (Alma 4:12). In the kingdom of God, righteousness and devotion are what matter—not prestige, power, or possessions. Love, compassion, and abundance of heart characterize the real Christian, not acquisitiveness and selfishness. The Book of Mormon declares that the true Saints of God are those who put "off the natural man" (Mosiah 3:19) and become "new creatures" in Christ (Mosiah 27:26)—"submissive, meek, humble, patient, full of love" (Mosiah 3:19).

One group in the Book of Mormon who seemed to achieve this state, at least for a time, were the members of the Church during the first few years of Alma's service as chief judge. They were prosperous materially, but they "did not set their hearts upon riches." The spirit of equality and charity they exhibited to all, "whether out of the church or in the church," is a worthy example to the Saints of God today (see Alma 1:25–30).

## EQUALITY AND CHARITY IN THE CHURCH

As members of the Lord's Church, we are a congregation of equals. As in the Church in Alma's day, the teacher is no better than the learner, the leader no better than those who are served (see Alma 1:26).[2] We each have individual interests and strengths, unique talents and gifts, and we have our share of weaknesses and foibles. The purpose of the Church is to make us better, to give us opportunities to fellowship with the Saints (see Ephesians 2:19), and ultimately to bring us to Christ. In this regard, we are equal. Even when members of our Church have attained notoriety in their professional, public, or private lives, they come to church on Sunday as every other member of the congregation—in need of the Lord's grace and prepared to partake of His sacrament. An eminent professor may sit in the congregation and listen to a thirteen-year-old give a talk on faith. A corporate executive may sit in counsel with a plumber who is called to preside over him. Though an individual member may have outstanding skills and experience as an administrator or teacher, he or she can't demand more attention, garner special favors, or change a Church program. The civic leader, the schoolteacher, the prominent business person, the retail clerk, and the professional athlete are simply members of the household of faith—and all are alike.

No one is above another in the kingdom of God. We serve in callings for a season and then are released. We serve humbly in whatever calling may come through the Lord's appointed representatives. President Gordon B. Hinckley explained the importance of every calling in this way: "We are all in this great endeavor together. We are here to assist our Father in His work and His glory, 'to bring to pass the immortality and eternal life of man' (Moses 1:39). Your obligation is as serious in your sphere of responsibility as is my obligation in my sphere. No calling in this church is small or of little consequence. All of us in the pursuit of our duty touch the lives of others. To each of us in our respective responsibilities the Lord has said: 'Wherefore, be faithful; stand in the office which I have appointed unto you; succor the weak, lift up the hands which hang down, and strengthen the feeble knees' (D&C 81:5)."[3]

So we speak in Church one week and then clean the chapel or

shovel snow off the sidewalks the next week; sometimes we teach a gospel lesson, and other times we listen as others teach; we preside in council with members of our branch, ward, or stake, and when released, we sustain others who preside. All the while, we see each other's weaknesses and foibles, even in our leaders, yet we choose to love and sustain them anyway as they serve worthily and faithfully in callings. This process elevates all members of the congregation and affirms the doctrine of equality and unity. We recognize that some have more and different talents than others, but we believe everyone is capable of serving in some way.

Of course, we also know that no member of the Church is perfect. We're all on common ground as we try to overcome the world and move toward exaltation, and we're all at different places along the pathway of spiritual development. President George Albert Smith said:

> One of the beautiful things to me in the Gospel of Jesus Christ is that it brings us all to a common level. It is not necessary for a man to be a president of a stake, or a member of the Quorum of the Twelve, in order to attain a high place in the celestial kingdom. The humblest member of the Church, if he keeps the commandments of God, will obtain an exaltation just as much as any other man in the celestial kingdom. The beauty of the Gospel of Jesus Christ is that it makes us all equal in as far as we keep the commandments of the Lord. In as far as we observe to keep the laws of the Church we have equal opportunities for exaltation. As we develop faith and righteousness our light is made to shine as a guide and blessing to those with whom we mingle.[4]

The gospel teaches us that we need each other in order to become all that we're capable of becoming. We need the growth that comes from using our agency to obey and endure faithfully, to serve and sustain humbly.

Leaders and teachers who understand this will not use their callings to draw attention to themselves. When we serve as the Savior would have us serve, our focus is on loving and blessing those we serve, on helping them come unto Christ. Elder Dallin H. Oaks gave us a vivid example of what dedicated service in the Church looks like in a gospel teacher:

> A gospel teacher, like the Master we serve, will concentrate entirely on those being taught. His or her total concentration will be on the needs of the sheep—the good of the students. A gospel teacher does not focus on himself or herself. One who understands that principle will not look upon his or her calling as "giving or presenting a lesson," because that definition views teaching from the standpoint of the teacher, not the student.
>
> Focusing on the needs of the students, a gospel teacher will never obscure their view of the Master by standing in the way or by shadowing the lesson with self-promotion or self-interest. This means that a gospel teacher must never indulge in priestcrafts, which are "that men preach and set themselves up for a light unto the world, that they may get gain and praise of the world" (2 Ne. 26:29). A gospel teacher does not preach "to become popular" (Alma 1:3) or "for the sake of riches and honor" (Alma 1:16). He or she follows the marvelous Book of Mormon example in which "the preacher was no better than the hearer, neither was the teacher any better than the learner" (Alma 1:26). Both will always look to the Master.[5]

We truly are all in this together. Yet while we are all "alike unto God" (2 Nephi 26:33) (and hopefully to each other), we are not equal in authority. At any given time, we defer to the leaders who have been called by God to have stewardship over us. Our very salvation depends on our freely following the counsel of living prophets, on our being submissive to guidance from the Lord's authorized representatives. President James E. Faust has said, "To stay on the right track, we must honor and sustain those who hold the presiding priesthood keys." Ultimately, however, we are all called by the same God, and we all answer to Him for the way we fulfill our callings.

President Faust continued: "We are reminded that many are 'called, but few are chosen.' When are we chosen? We are chosen by the Lord only when we have done our best to move this holy work forward through our consecrated efforts and talents."[6] Though callings come and go, while we have them they ought to be taken seriously. At some future day, we will each hear the voice of the Lord calling us to account for our stewardships. This accounting will occur when we are called up to "stand before [the Lord] at the great and judgment day" (2 Nephi 9:22). Elder James E. Talmage put it this way: "Of every one shall be demanded a strict and personal accounting for his stewardship, a report in full of service or of neglect, of use or abuse in the administration of the trust to him committed."[7] One bishop said upon his release, "I hope I've made a difference in the lives of the members of my ward. I hope I've helped bring them to Christ. I've tried my best and learned a lot. I've loved serving. But this is not my ward—it's the Lord's. I'm now happy to take my place in the congregation and follow the counsel of our new bishop."[8] As members of the household of faith and the kingdom of God on earth, we have countless opportunities to choose to serve and sustain, to lead and to follow. We thereby reap the spiritual growth, love, and joy that come of humility and consecration—all of which brings us closer to the Savior, individually and as a Church.

## EQUALITY AND CHARITY OUTSIDE THE CHURCH

Feelings of equality and charity are not for members of the Church alone. As Church members truly cultivate these feelings, their love extends far beyond the boundaries of Church membership. True humility and meekness leads to a generosity of spirit that reaches to all of God's children—everywhere. The Saints in Alma's day "did not send away *any* who were naked, or that were hungry, or that were athirst, or that were sick, or that had not been nourished; . . . they were liberal to all, both old and young, both bond and free, both male and female, whether out of the church or in the church, having no respect to persons as to those who stood in need" (Alma 1:30; emphasis added). King Benjamin taught, "When ye are in the service of your fellow beings ye are only in the service of your God" (Mosiah 2:17). *Fellow beings* clearly means more than the believers, more than active, temple-going Saints of God. *Fellow beings* implies *all* people. Benjamin taught that when you have "come to the knowledge of the glory of God" and "have known of his goodness and have tasted of his love, and have received a remission of your sins," then "ye yourselves will succor those that stand in need of your succor; ye will administer of your substance unto him that standeth in need; and ye will not suffer that the begger putteth up his petition to you in vain, and turn him out to perish" (Mosiah 4:11, 16). Jacob similarly did not limit the charity he professed: "Be familiar with all and free with your substance" (Jacob 2:17).

As we strive to become more like Christ, we love and serve *all* of God's children without regard to their race, religion, or socioeconomic status. The Prophet Joseph Smith said, "Love is one of the chief characteristics of Deity, and ought to be manifested by those who aspire to be the sons of God. A man filled with the love of God, is not content with blessing his family alone, but ranges through the whole world, anxious to bless the whole human race."[9] Elder Dallin H. Oaks similarly explained:

> The Bible tells us how God made a covenant with Abraham and promised him that through him all "families" or "nations" of the earth would be blessed (see Genesis 12:3; 22:18). What we call the Abrahamic covenant opens the door for God's choicest blessings to all of His children everywhere. The Bible teaches that "if ye be Christ's, then are ye Abraham's seed, and heirs according to the promise" (Galatians 3:29; see also Abraham 2:10). The Book of Mormon promises that all who receive and act upon the Lord's invitation to "repent and believe in his Son" become "the covenant people of the Lord" (2 Nephi 30:2). This is a potent reminder that neither riches nor lineage nor any other privileges of birth should cause us to believe that we are "better one than another" (Alma 5:54; see also Jacob 3:9). Indeed, the Book of Mormon commands, "Ye shall not esteem one flesh above another, or one man shall not think himself above another" (Mosiah 23:7).[10]

All of God's children are alike with regard to opportunity and gospel possibilities: all will either have occasion to receive gospel truth here, or else that privilege will be granted hereafter in the spirit world. The gospel and its blessings are to go to all nations and lineages before the Second Coming of the Lord.

In the meantime, "we claim the privilege of worshiping Almighty

God according to the dictates of our own conscience, and allow all men the same privilege, let them worship how, where, or what they may" (Articles of Faith 1:11). We have been blessed with the fulness of the gospel, but this does not make us superior in any way to those who have not been, as yet, so blessed. Actually, it makes us more accountable to the Lord (see D&C 82:3). No one will be eternally disadvantaged for failing to live a truth or understand a principle of which he was ignorant. God has grander expectations of those who have received the revealed witness and who have been blessed and prospered by it. We are expected—no, required—to be true to the light we possess, to live a life worthy of what our loving Lord has bestowed upon us. But we are certainly not above the countless other sons and daughters of God spread throughout the earth.

As partakers of the precious and transcendent gift of the gospel, we realize that this knowledge is ours to share. We, like Alma and his people, should be liberal to all, gathering ourselves together often to join in fasting and prayer in behalf of those who do not know the restored gospel (see Alma 6:5–6; see also Alma 5:49). The knowledge of our blessings and responsibilities should fill us with humility and love for those who are not yet partakers of the fulness of the gospel. Instead of arrogance, we feel a deep sense of accountability; in place of conceit, we experience a mighty change of heart and feel "to sing the song of redeeming love" (Alma 5:26). More than anything, when we live the gospel of Jesus Christ, we feel of His pure love and want others to feel that love from us (see Moroni 7:47). President Howard W. Hunter spoke of our responsibility:

> We wish that men and women everywhere could understand and find the joy and peace that come from the knowledge that all people are children of God and therefore brothers and sisters—literally, actually, and in fact, regardless of race, color, language, or religious belief. . . .
>
> We are reminded as we participate in conference of the deep commitment we have to our fellowmen, our brothers and sisters throughout the world. It is a commitment to share with them a gift that has come to us and the greatest gift we could

give to them—an understanding of the fulness of the gospel. We are committed to declare to all the world that Jesus of Nazareth is the Savior of mankind, that he has paid for our sins by his atoning sacrifice, that he has risen from the dead, and that he lives today. Our responsibility is to help the people of the world understand the true nature of our Father in Heaven: that he is a personal God, a loving father, and one to whom each of us may go with our problems and concerns."

As we turn our hearts to the Savior, our hearts turn to our brothers and sisters of other faiths at the same time. We feel to extend to them the same brief but profound invitation the Master offered to two of His future disciples early in His ministry: "Come and see" (see John 1:38–39). Several years ago, Elder Alexander B. Morrison of the Seventy used these words to teach us about the abundance of heart that is manifest in those who truly come unto the Lord: "'Come and see,' and as you do so your eyes will be opened and you will *really* see, perhaps for the first time, who *you* are, and who *He* is. You will come to see yourself as a child of God, of divine parentage, possessed of infinite capacities to grow spiritually and become more like Him. You will come to understand that God 'hath made of one blood all nations of men for to dwell on all the face of the earth' (Acts 17:26) and you will see all men everywhere as your brothers and all women as your sisters, with all that implies in terms of sibling responsibility."[12]

The Lord invites *all* His beloved children to come unto Him, and so do His true followers. Elder Oaks, commenting on Nephi's declaration that "all are alike unto God" (2 Nephi 26:33), further illuminated this truth:

> "He inviteth them all." We understand "male and female." We also understand "black and white," which means all races. But what about "bond and free"? *Bond*—the opposite of free— means more than slavery. It means being bound (in bondage) to anything from which it is difficult to escape. *Bond* includes those whose freedom is restricted by physical or emotional afflictions. *Bond* includes those who are addicted to some substance or practice. *Bond* surely refers to those who are

imprisoned by sin—"encircled about" by what another teaching of the Book of Mormon calls "the chains of hell" (Alma 5:7). *Bond* includes those who are held down by traditions or customs contrary to the commandments of God (see Matthew 15:3–6; Mark 7:7–9; D&C 74:4–7; D&C 93:39). Finally, *bond* also includes those who are confined within the boundaries of other erroneous ideas. The Prophet Joseph Smith taught that we preach to "liberate the captives." [*History of the Church,* 2:229.] Our Savior "inviteth . . . all to come unto him and partake of his goodness; . . . he denieth none that come unto him . . . ; and all are alike unto God."[13]

As Church members, we should reach out to all peoples of the world with love and friendship. Some of the ways we can do this are through Church welfare and humanitarian efforts, broadcasting and media outreach, missionary and service work, family history resources, and, most important, living personal lives of charity. As members of the Church, such outreach and exemplary living are both an obligation and an opportunity. President Hinckley said, "We have an obligation to reach out beyond ourselves to help those in distress and trouble and difficulty wherever they may be, be they members of the Church or not."[14] He also explained that where much is given much is required:

How blessed we are. How fortunate we are in our knowledge of these transcendent truths.

But may I say, as I have said in the past, our membership in this Church, with eligibility for all of the blessings that flow therefrom, should never be any cause for self-righteousness, for arrogance, for denigration of others, for looking down upon others. All mankind is our neighbor. When asked which was the greatest commandment of the law, the Lord said: "Thou shalt love the Lord thy God with all thy heart, and with all thy soul, and with all thy mind. . . . [And] thou shalt love thy neighbour as thyself" (Matthew 22:37, 39).

Regardless of the color of our skin, of the shape of our eyes, of the language we speak, we all are sons and daughters of God and must reach out to one another with love and concern.

Wherever we may live we can be friendly neighbors. Our children can mingle with the children of those not of this Church and remain steadfast if they are properly taught. They can even become missionaries to their associates.[15]

## EQUALITY AND CHARITY IN OUR PERSONAL CHARACTER

Unfortunately, the equality and charity that the Saints achieved in Alma's day did not last in the Church collectively. But there is no reason these doctrines cannot become a permanent part of our personal character. As we truly understand the doctrine of equality and charity, we are changed. We draw closer to the Savior and more fully live His gospel, the doctrine taught by Jesus Christ and by His apostles and prophets. President Boyd K. Packer taught: "True doctrine, understood, changes attitudes and behavior. The study of the doctrines of the gospel will improve behavior quicker than a study of behavior will improve behavior."[16] The Savior drew upon the power of doctrinal truth to open our eyes and hearts. Alma likewise understood the power of true doctrine: "And now, as the preaching of the word had a great tendency to lead the people to do that which was just—yea, it had had more powerful effect upon the minds of the people than the sword, or anything else, which had happened unto them—therefore Alma thought it was expedient that they should try the virtue of the word of God" (Alma 31:5). The virtue of the word of God changes lives. Doctrinal verities can open minds to see spiritual things not visible to the natural eye; they can open hearts to feelings of the love of God and to a love for truth.[17]

For example, a teacher who has internalized the vital doctrines of equality and charity will treat class members like herself, not esteeming herself above her brothers and sisters in the congregation (see Jacob 2:17). A true disciple-leader will know that "none is acceptable before God, save the meek and lowly in heart" (Moroni 7:44) and will have no desire to excel over his companions in the work of the Lord (see D&C 58:40–41). Truly understanding doctrine—and living it—does not elevate us above others and invite self-righteousness; it invokes true humility and charity that leads us to love and serve others.

Love is the essence of the gospel of Jesus Christ. One of love's greatest manifestations is humility. And one of love's greatest inhibitors is pride. In the Book of Mormon—and most certainly in our individual lives—pride is an insidious, ever-encroaching, and pervasive plague. We cannot race against each other when it comes to righteousness; competition would only hinder our spiritual development. We are here to more fully come unto Christ and to help others do the same. Janette C. Hales of the Young Women general presidency wisely said: "A pattern of righteousness is worthy of duplication, yet there are those who suppose that our righteousness involves climbing some imaginary vertical ladder. We then think we hasten our progress by trying to get above or ahead of others. I believe this is pride. . . . Righteousness is reproduced horizontally, not vertically. When we establish a pattern of righteousness in our lives, we commit to our Heavenly Father to do all in our power to help others reproduce this pattern in their lives. This can happen over and over until, as it says in Isaiah, 'the inhabitants of the world will learn righteousness' (Isa. 26:9.)"[18]

President Spencer W. Kimball described the "pattern of righteousness" expected of true Christians in this way:

First is *love*. The measure of our love for our fellowman and, in a large sense, the measure of our love for the Lord, is what we do for one another and for the poor and the distressed.

"A new commandment I give unto you, That ye love one another; as I have loved you, that ye also love one another.

"By this shall all men know that ye are my disciples, if ye have love one to another." (John 13:34–35; see Moro. 7:44–48 and Luke 10:25–37; 14:12–14.)

Second is *service*. To serve is to abase oneself, to succor those in need of succor, and to impart of one's "substance to the poor and the needy, feeding the hungry, and suffering all manner of afflictions, for Christ's sake." (Al. 4:13.)

"Pure religion and undefiled before God and the Father is this, To visit the fatherless and widows in their affliction, and to keep himself unspotted from the world." (James 1:27.)[19]

This is the highest Christian command and the surest manifestation of our devotion to the Lord's ideals of living. Love is the measure of our faith and the substance of our discipleship. Our love for God is demonstrated in our actions and interactions with others. It is not that our good works save us, but our loving thoughts and deeds are an indication of what we are *becoming* because we have turned our hearts over to Christ. Those filled with this pure love also enjoy its accompanying virtues: happiness, generosity, kindness, compassion, and thankfulness.

Genuine love and humility creates in us an abundance of heart that will bless all with whom we come in contact. Elder Joseph B. Wirthlin encouraged us:

> Always be willing, even anxious, to help others. Nothing else you do will give you the same genuine satisfaction and joy within because, and I quote, "when ye are in the service of your fellow beings ye are only in the service of your God." (Mosiah 2:17.) Ignoring the needs of others is a serious sin. Think of the words of Alma to the people of the Church in Zarahemla. He asked: "Will ye . . . persist in the wearing of costly apparel and setting your hearts upon the vain things of the world, upon your riches? Yea, will ye persist in supposing that ye are better one than another; . . .
>
> "Yea, and will you persist in turning your backs upon the poor, and the needy, and in withholding your substance from them?" (Alma 5:53–55.)
>
> King Benjamin taught that we must care for those in need—the poor, hungry, naked, and sick—both spiritually and temporally if we are to receive a remission of our sins from day to day or, in other words, if we are to walk guiltless before God. (See Mosiah 18:29.)[20]

The power of love and humility to transform (both us and others) is one of life's sweetest joys. Love and humility, equality and charity, can work mighty miracles. When we are humble, we realize our dependence upon the Lord, and we have more hope. When we have charity, we are more patient, more tolerant, more forgiving, and more loving. President Hinckley said: "Love is of the very essence of life. . . . Love is the security for which children weep, the yearning of youth, the adhesive that binds marriage, and the lubricant that prevents devastating friction in the home; it is the peace of old age, the sunlight of hope shining through death. How rich are those who enjoy it in their associations with family, friends, church, and neighbors. I am one who believes that love, like faith, is a gift of God."[21]

All love comes from God. The more we seek Him, the more we will feel His love working a mighty change in our hearts, and the more we will feel love for those around us. With all our hearts, we will know that "all are alike unto God" (2 Nephi 26:33).

---

## NOTES

1. We get an additional witness of this truth in the New Testament: "For there is no difference between the Jew and the Greek: for the same Lord over all is rich unto all that call upon him. For whosoever shall call upon the name of the Lord shall be saved" (Romans 10:12–13).

2. This was in direct contrast to the religion of Nehor, which had just been introduced in the land and which taught that "every priest and teacher ought to become popular; and they ought not to labor with their hands, but that they ought to be supported by the people" (Alma 1:3).

3. Gordon B. Hinckley, "This Is the Work of the Master," *Ensign,* May 1995, 71.

4. George Albert Smith, in Conference Report, October 1933, 25.

5. Dallin H. Oaks, "Gospel Teaching," *Ensign,* November 1999, 79.

6. James E. Faust, "I Believe I Can, I Knew I Could," *Ensign,* November 2002, 51.

7. "The Honor and Dignity of Priesthood," in James R. Clark, comp., *Messages of the First Presidency of the Church of Jesus Christ of Latter-day Saints* (1965–75), 4:306.

8. Conversation with the author.

9. Joseph Smith, *History of the Church,* ed. B. H. Roberts, 2nd ed. rev. (Salt Lake City: Deseret Book, 1957), 4:227.

10. Dallin H. Oaks, "All Men Everywhere," *Ensign,* May 2006, 79.

11. Howard W. Hunter, "Conference Time," *Ensign,* November 1981, 12.

12. Alexander B. Morrison, "Come and See," *Ensign,* November 2000, 12.

13. Dallin H. Oaks, "All Men Everywhere," *Ensign,* May 2006, 77–78.

14. Gordon B. Hinckley, *Stand a Little Taller* (Salt Lake City: Deseret Book, 2001), 329.

15. Gordon B. Hinckley, "Closing Remarks," *Ensign,* May 2005, 102.

16. Boyd K. Packer, "Do Not Fear," *Ensign,* May 2004, 79.

17. See Henry B. Eyring, "The Power of Teaching Doctrine," *Ensign,* May 1999, 73–75.

18. Janette C. Hales, "A Pattern of Righteousness," *Ensign,* May 1991, 83–84.

19.  Spencer W. Kimball, "Welfare Services: The Gospel in Action," *Ensign*, November 1977, 77.

20.  Joseph B. Wirthlin, "Running Your Marathon," *Ensign*, November 1989, 74.

21.  Gordon B. Hinckley, "And the Greatest of These Is Love," *Ensign*, March 1984, 3.

# 16

# "WITH POWER AND AUTHORITY OF GOD": PRINCIPLES OF MISSIONARY SUCCESS

## C. Robert Line

The Book of Mormon contains powerful and priceless principles relating to the preaching of God's word to His children. Although various principles relating to missionary work are found throughout the Book of Mormon, nowhere is this more evident than in Alma 17 and 18. This chapter seeks to help students and teachers of the restored gospel identify and implement a few of these potent principles that can help all of us have greater success in missionary work.

### FINDING THE PRINCIPLES

Some students of the Book of Mormon are aware of these principles—these keys to success in missionary work, as it were. A few of these principles are simply worded and straightforward to detect. However, when one takes a closer look at Alma 17 and 18, a multitude of key precepts and principles becomes apparent. President Boyd K. Packer once stated: "That word *principle* in the revelation is a very important one. A principle is an enduring truth, a law, a rule you can adopt to guide you in making decisions. Generally principles are not

_____

*C. Robert Line is an instructor at the Salt Lake City Utah University Institute of Religion.*

spelled out in detail. That leaves you free to find your way with an enduring truth, a principle, as your anchor."[1] President Packer's definition of a principle is instructive in that principles are usually "not spelled out in detail."

As is often the case, students of the scriptures must struggle to extract these truths. The process, at times, can be time consuming and difficult yet highly rewarding. If we are not diligent, we may attain only the "lesser portion of the word" while bypassing "the greater portion of the word" (Alma 12:9–11). Elder Richard G. Scott taught: "As you seek spiritual knowledge, search for principles. *Carefully* separate them from the detail used to explain them. Principles are concentrated truth, packaged for application to a wide variety of circumstances. A true principle makes decisions clear even under the most confusing and compelling circumstances. *It is worth great effort to organize the truth we gather to simple statements of principle.* I have tried to do that with gaining spiritual knowledge."[2]

## PRINCIPLES OF SUCCESSFUL MISSIONARY WORK

The following is my attempt to articulate a few of those simple statements of principle found in Alma 17 and 18. In these chapters, the prophet-historian Mormon chronicles the account of Alma's reunion with the sons of Mosiah as they were returning from their fourteen-year mission to the Lamanites. In the process of explaining why the sons of Mosiah were such successful missionaries, Mormon helps us to see how we can be successful missionaries as well. The principles mentioned are both those evident as well as those not so evident.

### Search the Scriptures Diligently

In Alma 17:2, Mormon explains that the sons of Mosiah "had waxed strong in the knowledge of the truth; for they were men of a sound understanding and they had searched the scriptures diligently, that they might know the word of God." This, then, is the first key to success for any missionary. Before one can "declare [the] word," one must first "seek to obtain" the word (D&C 11:21). Diligent scripture study is one of the activities undergirding the success of any endeavor in God's kingdom. President Ezra Taft Benson wisely counseled: "Often we spend great effort in trying to increase the activity levels in our stakes. We work diligently to raise the percentages of those attending sacrament meetings. We labor to get a higher percentage of our young men on missions. We strive to improve the numbers of those marrying in the temple. All of these are commendable efforts and important to the growth of the kingdom. But when individual members and families immerse themselves in the scriptures regularly and consistently, these other areas of activity will automatically come. Testimonies will increase. Commitment will be strengthened. Families will be fortified. Personal revelation will flow."[3] The first prerequisite in preaching the gospel is to know the gospel. Paul aptly warned: "Thou therefore which teachest another, teachest thou not thyself?" (Romans 2:21).

### Pray and Fast

Mormon is quick to tell us, though, that successful missionaries do more than just study the scriptures: "But this is not all; they had given themselves to much prayer, and fasting; therefore they had the spirit of prophecy, and the spirit of revelation, and when they taught, they taught with power and authority of God" (Alma 17:3). Note the combination of both prayer and fasting in the scriptures. These two activities often are mentioned in tandem—as if they were one activity (see Matthew 17:21; Luke 2:37; Acts 14:23; Omni 1:26; Mosiah 27:22; Alma 5:46; 6:6; 45:1; Helaman 3:35; 3 Nephi 27:1; 4 Nephi 1:12; D&C 88:76).

When two elements, such as iron and carbon, are brought together through the proper process, they form an alloy, in this case steel. Iron in and of itself is strong, but when combined with carbon (and other trace elements), it forms an even stronger substance. Likewise, prayer and fasting are, in and of themselves, excellent activities to promote spiritual strength. But when brought together, they can give one even greater strength and power. Elder Delbert L. Stapley once described the extent of the power that can come through combining these two powerful principles: "The Saints by fasting and praying can sanctify the soul and elevate the spirit to Christlike perfection, and thus . . . insure spiritual strength and power to the individual. By observing fasting and prayer in its true spirit, the Latter-day Saints cannot be overpowered by Satan tempting them to evil."[4]

## Labor in the Spirit

Mormon continues his narration: "Now these are the circumstances which attended them in their journeyings, for they had many afflictions; they did suffer much, both in body and in mind, such as hunger, thirst and fatigue, and also much *labor in the spirit*" (Alma 17:5; emphasis added). President Benson often taught missionaries and prospective missionaries that the spirit of missionary work is work![5] He taught: "One of the greatest secrets of missionary work is work. If a missionary works, he will get the Spirit; if he gets the Spirit, he will teach by the Spirit; and if he teaches by the Spirit, he will touch the hearts of the people; and he will be happy. There will be no homesickness, no worrying about families, for all time, talents and interests are centered on the work of the ministry. That's the secret—work, work, work. There is no satisfactory substitute, especially in missionary work."[6]

Wise are the missionaries who understand that the preaching of the gospel is not a cultural extravaganza nor a tantalizing tourist trip. Elder Jeffrey R. Holland perceptively observed:

> Anyone who does any kind of missionary work will have occasion to ask, Why is this so hard? Why doesn't it go better? Why can't our success be more rapid? . . .
>
> You will have occasion to ask those questions. . . . I offer this as my personal feeling. I am convinced that missionary work is not easy because salvation is not a cheap experience. Salvation never was easy. How could we believe it would be easy for us when it was never, ever easy for [Christ]? It seems to me that missionaries and mission leaders have to spend at least a few moments in Gethsemane. . . .
>
> I'm not talking about anything anywhere near what Christ experienced. . . . But I believe that missionaries and investigators, to come to the truth, to come to salvation, to know something of this price that has been paid, will have to pay a token of that same price.
>
> For that reason I don't believe missionary work has ever been easy, nor that conversion is, nor that retention is, nor that

continued faithfulness is. I believe it is supposed to require some effort, something from the depths of our soul.[7]

To "labor in the spirit" is to do more than just proselyte with physical exertion. Success in missionary work cannot come by effort alone. Missionaries must labor in *the Spirit,* meaning that the Holy Ghost must attend the work that is done. "And again, the elders, priests and teachers of this church shall teach the principles of my gospel. . . . As they shall be directed by the Spirit. . . . And *if ye receive not the* Spirit *ye shall not teach*" (D&C 42:12–14). This does not mean that a missionary will somehow be prevented from going through the motions of teaching; it simply means that the power of the Holy Ghost, which makes the teaching authoritative, will not be present. "Verily I say unto you, he that is ordained of me and sent forth to preach the word of truth by the Comforter, in the Spirit of truth, doth he preach it by the Spirit of truth or some other way? And *if it be by some other way it is not of God*" (D&C 50:17–18; emphasis added). How unfortunate it is when a missionary presents discussions devoid of the Spirit. Perhaps some would be shocked to learn that this type of labor "profiteth him nothing" (Moroni 7:6).

To thus labor in the Spirit becomes a daunting task for any missionary. There is a deep and heartfelt humility that comes to the preacher of God's word when realizing that success depends on relying upon the third member of the Godhead, namely the Holy Ghost. His divine role of witnessing that Jesus is the Christ and that the gospel is true is a responsibility that cannot be duplicated by the efforts of any missionary, no matter how strenuous or creative those efforts may be. Accordingly, it is imperative for missionaries to remember that, although they labor in the Spirit, they need not try to generate a "spiritual" mood for their investigators. Robert L. Millet perceptively observed: "The word of God is sufficiently powerful that gospel teachers or preachers do not need to assume the burden of converting their listeners. There is sufficient for the gospel teacher to do by way of reading, studying, preparing, praying, organizing, and presenting that he or she need not feel an obligation to 'create' a spiritual experience. . . . [We] need not usurp the role of the Holy Ghost. Ultimately, he is the teacher. He is the converter.

He is the member of the eternal Godhead charged with carrying the word of truth into the hearts and minds of the children of men. He is the agent of the new birth, the one who sanctifies and empowers human beings."[8]

### Postpone Other Worthy Opportunities

Mormon informs us that Mosiah was anxious to empower his sons with the mantle of leadership; however, they chose instead to serve missions, "having refused the kingdom which their father was desirous to confer upon them" (Alma 17:6). Not only did Mosiah desire that his sons take positions of governance, but so did the citizens of the land. Obviously Mosiah was a righteous man. If his sons stayed home to serve in civic capacities, their actions would have been acceptable to Mosiah and the rest of his people.

The principle here is that successful missionaries relinquish worldly concerns and the motives of materialism in order to fully serve God and thus build His kingdom. President Benson gave this counsel and challenge: "The Lord wants every young man to serve a full-time mission. Presently only a third of the eligible young men in the Church are serving missions. This is not pleasing to the Lord. We can do better. We must do better. Not only should a mission be regarded as a priesthood duty, but every young man should look forward to this experience with great joy and anticipation. A young man can do nothing more important. School can wait. Scholarships can be deferred. Occupational goals can be postponed. Yes, even temple marriage should wait until after a young man has served an honorable full-time mission for the Lord."[9]

To be a successful missionary, one must be willing to lay aside even those endeavors that are good in favor of that which is eternal. "Now you young men, . . . a mission has been emphasized as a priesthood responsibility," said Elder Robert E. Wells, "of such priority that again today we stress, your mission comes before marriage, education, professional opportunities, scholarships, sports, cars, or girls."[10]

### Provide for Yourself

Continuing his narration, Mormon observes another critical aspect that can contribute to success in missionary work: "Nevertheless they departed out of the land of Zarahemla, and took their swords, and their spears, and their bows, and their arrows, and their slings; and this they did that they might provide food for themselves while in the wilderness" (Alma 17:7). No, the point here is not to arm our missionary force with tanks and guns! To see the modern principle, we must bridge the cultural gap. Anecdotal evidence suggests that those missionaries who provide at least part or all of the cost for their mission tend to be more committed to their mission.[11] Although not always possible, it is valuable for missionaries to work for the funds for their own missions. By so doing, a missionary comes to understand the principles of frugality and sacrifice; they are more able to recognize the sacred nature of the resources needed while in the service of the Lord.

## Be an Example of Patience

The Lord's admonition to the sons of Mosiah in Alma 17:11 is applicable to missionaries in any age: "Go forth among the Lamanites, thy brethren, and establish my word; yet ye shall be *patient in long-suffering and afflictions, that ye may show forth good examples unto them in me, and I will make an instrument of thee in my hands unto the salvation of many souls*" (emphasis added). How sad it is when missionaries are bad examples! Alma rebuked his son Corianton for his bad example and lamented the devastating effects that it had upon the work (see Alma 39). Elder Holland's observation is instructive:

> Above all else we can live the gospel. Surely there is no more powerful missionary message we can send to this world than the example of a loving and happy Latter-day Saint life. The manner and bearing, the smile and kindness of a faithful member of the Church brings a warmth and an outreach that no missionary tract or videotape can convey. People do not join the Church because of what they know. They join because of what they feel, what they see and want spiritually. Our spirit of testimony and happiness in that regard will come through to others if we let it. . . . Asking every member to be a missionary is not nearly as crucial as asking every member to be a member![12]

It is purported that St. Francis of Assisi once admonished, "Preach the gospel. And if necessary, use words."[13] People will often learn more from our actions than they will from what we say. This is a great key to successful missionary work.

### Separate Yourself from Distractions

Another key to success in missionary work can be found in Alma 17:13: "When they had arrived in the borders of the land of the Lamanites, that they separated themselves and departed one from another." Although this reference is specifically highlighting geographical separation from other missionaries, with a little imagination we can see a great application: successful missionaries know the importance of appropriate emotional separation from girlfriends, family, and so forth. It is one thing to leave scholarships and school behind—these are inanimate objects; but it is quite another thing to detach oneself from relationships that can hamper and negatively affect the service that one gives. Some missionaries go on a mission, yet they never leave home. Or, to put it another way, their hearts are not in the right place because they are focused on a relationship that for the time being just cannot be.

### Get a Vision of the Work

It is vital that missionaries have a correct vision of the work, or an understanding "that great [is] the work" (Alma 17:13). Part of having the correct vision of missionary work consists in knowing why we do missionary work. In verse 16 we learn the reason: "Therefore, this was the cause for which the sons of Mosiah had undertaken the work, that perhaps they might bring them unto repentance; that perhaps they might bring them to know of the plan of redemption." In other words, missionaries are not just to baptize, not just to have cultural experiences, not just to teach many discussions, and not just to get investigators to read the Book of Mormon. All these endeavors are commendable, but they are only peripheral aspects of missionary work. As stated by Mormon, the core reason for doing missionary work is to bring people to repentance! Elder Holland's words are instructive:

Probably there are very few missionaries, if any, who do not know the centrality of this doctrine [of repentance]. But I have been surprised to regularly be with the missionaries and discover that this is not something that readily comes forward in a discussion of missionary work. . . .

Almost never do the missionaries get around to identifying the two most fundamental things we want investigators to do prior to baptism: have faith in the Lord Jesus Christ and repent of their sins. Yet "we believe that the first principles and ordinances of the Gospel are: first, Faith in the Lord Jesus Christ; second, Repentance; [then] third, Baptism by immersion *for the remission of sins;* fourth, Laying on of hands for the gift of the Holy Ghost."[14]

Successful missionaries do not get caught up in the thick of thin things. They know that their mission is ultimately about bringing people to Christ, not just being amiable ambassadors of another well-oiled Church program. It is difficult at times to keep focused, especially with all the wonderful handbooks, excellent training, and cultural prestige associated with serving a full-time mission. Illustratively, C. S. Lewis once observed: "There have been men before now who got so interested in proving the existence of God that they came to care nothing for God Himself . . . as if the good Lord had nothing to do but *exist!* There have been some who were so occupied in spreading Christianity that they never gave a thought to Christ. Man! Ye see it in smaller matters. Did ye never know a lover of books that with all his first editions and signed copies had lost the power to read them? Or an organiser of charities that had lost all love for the poor? It is the subtlest of all the snares."[15] Elaborate programming, although not inherently wrong, can sometimes blur the essence of the message.

In this regard, it is interesting to note what the missionaries of the Book of Mormon taught as their missionary discussions. Often we see that they taught the simple core doctrines of the gospel. In Alma 18:36–39 we learn that these missionaries taught what Elder Bruce R. McConkie called the three pillars of eternity—the doctrines of the Creation, the Fall, and the Atonement. We have been told by prophets that these central doctrines are interrelated and form the very foundation of our Father in Heaven's wonderful plan of redemption.[16] Section 20 of the Doctrine and Covenants contains an excellent summary statement of the doctrines contained in the Book of Mormon (see D&C 20:11–31). Included in this summary are the doctrines of the Creation, Fall, and Atonement. How intriguing that the Lord highlights for us in a modern revelation the importance of these three preeminent doctrines that were taught anciently by missionaries in the Book of Mormon. Our modern missionaries are invited to receive their endowment before they begin full-time service and are encouraged to attend the temple often while in the Missionary Training Center. It is by no means a coincidence that the very essence of the endowment, as far as doctrinal instruction goes, centers on these three doctrinal pillars—the Creation, the Fall, and the Atonement. Thus, it appears that the Lord's pedagogy for training missionaries has not changed. Certain methods of missionary training may change and fluctuate over time, but the doctrine never will.

### Build Relationships without Ulterior Motives

Later in the account of Alma 17 the scene of action switches to the missionary labors of Ammon in the land of Ishmael. After being detained and brought before King Lamoni, Ammon is asked by the king if he desires to live amongst the Lamanites: "And Ammon said unto him: Yea, I desire to dwell among this people for a time; yea, and perhaps until the day I die. And it came to pass that king Lamoni was much pleased with Ammon, and caused that his bands should be loosed; and he would that Ammon should take one of his daughters to wife. But Ammon said unto him: Nay, but I will be thy servant. Therefore Ammon became a servant to king Lamoni. And it came to pass that he was set among other servants to watch the flocks of Lamoni, according to the custom of the Lamanites" (vv. 23–25). Successful missionaries quickly learn that it is important to be true friends and servants to those we teach, without any ulterior motives. Elder Neal A. Maxwell counseled: "It is important in our relationships with our fellowmen that we approach them as neighbors and as brothers and sisters rather than coming at them flinging theological thunderbolts."[17] Likewise, Elder

M. Russell Ballard gave this admonition: "That is our doctrine—a doctrine of inclusion. That is what we believe. That is what we have been taught. Of all people on this earth, we should be the most loving, the kindest, and the most tolerant because of that doctrine. . . . May I suggest three simple things we can do to avoid making others in our neighborhoods feel excluded? First, get to know your neighbors. Learn about their families, their work, their views. Get together with them, if they are willing, and do so without being pushy and without any ulterior motives. Friendship should never be offered as a means to an end; it can and should be an end unto itself."[18] In other words, we should be friends with those not of our faith because it is simply the right thing to do! Let the baptisms take care of themselves.

## CONCLUSION

These are but a few of the principles relating to successful missionary work as found in the Book of Mormon. Many more are waiting to be discovered. The Book of Mormon not only can bring us closer to Christ, but it can help us bring others to Him. By abiding by its precepts, we all can become missionaries who teach the gospel "with power and authority of God" (Alma 17:3). Elder McConkie stated that God "has placed in our hands the most effective, compelling, and persuasive missionary tool ever given to any people in any age. The name of this tool is the Book of Mormon."[19] Not only is the Book of Mormon a tool to convert investigators, but likewise it can be a powerful manual to prepare missionaries for great success in the mission field. What a valuable treasure the Lord has given us in this magnificent record!

President Benson's challenge is one we should never forget: "I challenge our Church writers, teachers, and leaders to tell us more Book of Mormon conversion stories that will strengthen our faith and prepare great missionaries. Show us how to effectively use it as a missionary tool, and let us know how it leads us to Christ and answers our personal problems and those of the world."[20] May we as parents, teachers, and leaders use the Book of Mormon as such a tool as we prepare our valiant youth to serve in the vineyard of the Lord.

## NOTES

1. Boyd K. Packer, "The Word of Wisdom: The Principle and the Promises," *Ensign,* May 1996, 17.

2. Richard G. Scott, "Acquiring Spiritual Knowledge," *Ensign,* November 1993, 86; emphasis added.

3. Ezra Taft Benson, "The Power of the Word," *Ensign,* May 1986, 81.

4. Elder Delbert L. Stapley, in Conference Report, October 1951, 123.

5. Ezra Taft Benson to author on July 10, 1985, in Salt Lake City.

6. Ezra Taft Benson, as quoted in "Testimony Best Mission Preparation," *Church News,* July 10, 1993, 7.

7. Jeffrey R. Holland, "Missionary Work and the Atonement," *Ensign,* March 2001, 14–15.

8. Robert L. Millet, *Alive in Christ: The Miracle of Spiritual Rebirth* (Salt Lake City: Deseret Book, 1997), 86.

9. Ezra Taft Benson, *Teachings of Ezra Taft Benson* (Salt Lake City: Bookcraft, 1988), 190.

10. Robert E. Wells, "Adventures of the Spirit," *Ensign,* November 1985, 28.

11. *Called to Serve,* video, The Church of Jesus Christ of Latter-day Saints.

12. Jeffery R. Holland, in Conference Report, April 2001, 15–16.

13. As quoted in Richard H. Cracroft, "Preach the Gospel . . . and If Necessary, Use Words," *BYU Magazine,* Fall 2002.

14. Holland, "Missionary Work and the Atonement," 10–11.

15. C. S. Lewis, *The Great Divorce* (New York: HarperCollins 2001), 73–74.

16. Russell M. Nelson, "Constancy amid Change," *Ensign,* November 1993, 33.

17. Neal A. Maxwell, *Neal A. Maxwell Quote Book,* ed. Cory H. Maxwell (Salt Lake City: Bookcraft, 2001), 212.

18. M. Russell Ballard, in Conference Report, October 2001, 45.

19. Bruce R. McConkie, in Conference Report, April 1961, 38.

20. Ezra Taft Benson, "Flooding the Earth with the Book of Mormon," *Ensign,* November 1988, 5.

# 17

# HOW TO BE RECLAIMED FROM THE FALL OF ADAM

## Frank F. Judd Jr.

When Alma the Younger returned to Zarahemla following his mission to the Zoramites, "he caused that his sons should be gathered together, that he might give unto them every one his charge, separately, concerning the things pertaining to righteousness" (Alma 35:16). The Book of Mormon contains a significantly larger amount of counsel from Alma to his wayward son Corianton than to Helaman and Shiblon.

Within Alma's teachings, we discover a concise explanation of the Fall of Adam and three elements necessary to reclaim each individual from the Fall, namely, death, the Atonement, and the Resurrection. This chapter will discuss the Fall of Adam and these three elements in Alma's teachings to Corianton and also in the inspired teachings of modern apostles and prophets. This chapter will conclude that we can control only one of the three elements necessary to reclaim mankind from the Fall: whether we use the Atonement to repent of our sins and forgive others.

---

Frank F. Judd Jr. is an assistant professor of ancient scripture at Brigham Young University.

## WRITTEN FOR OUR DAY

The Book of Mormon is "a just and a true record" (3 Nephi 5:18), but it is by no means an exhaustive history. The prophets who wrote and compiled the Book of Mormon stated that they could include only a very small portion of what happened among their people (see Jacob 3:13; Words of Mormon 1:5; Helaman 3:14; 3 Nephi 5:8; 3 Nephi 26:6; Ether 15:33). These prophet-writers carefully selected the material they incorporated into the record. Concerning the small plates, Nephi stated: "The *fulness of mine intent* is that I may persuade men to *come unto the God of Abraham,* and the God of Isaac, and the God of Jacob, and *be saved.* Wherefore, the things which are pleasing unto the world I do not write, but the things which are pleasing unto God and unto those who are not of the world" (1 Nephi 6:4–5; emphasis added; see also 2 Nephi 4:15).

In other words, Nephi and other Book of Mormon prophets included information by inspiration that would lead readers to come unto Christ and be saved. President Ezra Taft Benson summarized this truth: "The Book of Mormon . . . was written for our day. The Nephites never had the book; neither did the Lamanites of ancient times. It was meant for us. . . . Under the inspiration of God, who sees all things from the beginning, [Mormon] abridged centuries of records, choosing the stories, speeches, and events that would be most helpful to us. . . . *We should constantly ask ourselves, 'Why did the Lord inspire Mormon (or Moroni or Alma) to include that in his record? What lesson can I learn from that to help me live in this day and age?'*"[1]

Thus, one of the most important approaches to the Book of Mormon is to study its stories and doctrines and then apply its principles to the situations we encounter in our daily activities. While knowledge of the Book of Mormon is important, such knowledge is ultimately hollow unless used to live better lives.[2] Concerning the Book of Mormon, the Prophet Joseph Smith taught that "a man would get nearer to God by abiding by its precepts than by any other book."[3] Consequently, throughout the following discussion of the Fall of Adam and the three elements necessary to be reclaimed from it, this chapter will suggest valuable ways we might incorporate these important principles into our own lives to become more effective disciples of Jesus Christ.

## "THE VIRTUE OF THE WORD OF GOD"

When Alma the Younger learned that the Zoramites were "perverting the ways of the Lord" (Alma 31:1), he resolved to reclaim them from their state of wickedness. Alma took two of his younger sons, Shiblon and Corianton, on his mission among the Zoramites (see Alma 31:7). Alma carefully considered what approach he might take with the Zoramites: "The preaching of the word had a great tendency to lead the people to do that which was just—yea, it had had more powerful effect upon the minds of the people than the sword, or anything else, which had happened unto them—therefore Alma thought it was expedient that they should try the *virtue* of the word of God" (Alma 31:5; emphasis added).[4]

The use of the word *virtue* is noteworthy. We don't know what Nephite word was on the plates, but by inspiration Joseph Smith felt that *virtue* was the best translation. The primary definition of *virtue* in the 1828 Webster's Dictionary is "strength."[5] Thus, rather than trying to enforce obedience by the sword—or any other means—Alma felt inspired to employ the strength or power of divine persuasion that comes from preaching the pure truths of the word of God.

President Boyd K. Packer has taught that the doctrines of the gospel have power to change people's lives: "True doctrine, understood, changes attitudes and behavior. The study of the doctrines of the gospel will improve behavior quicker than a study of behavior will improve behavior. . . . That is why we stress so forcefully the study of the doctrines of the gospel."[6] It is true that a study of human psychology or sociology is worthy of our attention and can yield helpful insights. But the mere understanding of basic information about human behavior or environment does not contain the necessary power or strength to change lives. When people understand the basic doctrines of the gospel, such as the Fall and the Atonement, they will be more likely to change their behavior to conform to the truths of the gospel. Alma had so much faith in this principle that it guided not only his missionary actions but also his parenting strategy. Rather than reject or force his son, Alma taught Corianton the pure doctrines of the gospel to help change his life—cultivating opportunities to hear the word of God. This highlights the importance of opening up our souls to the word of God through repeated studying, pondering, and teaching.

Corianton's choices in the mission field had revealed his carnal nature—boasting, neglecting his ministry, and ultimately going after the harlot Isabel (see Alma 39:2–4). Alma emphatically told his son concerning Isabel: "She did steal away the hearts of many; but this was no excuse for thee, my son. Thou shouldst have tended to the ministry wherewith thou wast entrusted" (Alma 39:4). Not only was Corianton's bad example an embarrassment to his family, but it also frustrated the work Alma had set out to accomplish. As Alma lamented, "When they saw your conduct they would not believe in my words" (Alma 39:11).

This principle can be applied to our own lives. The example we set for others really does matter. Elder Marvin J. Ashton observed: "You don't know how many people are looking at you and copying you. . . . Others are watching you—often unannounced—and they don't want you to let them down. They're going to emulate you, follow your example. . . . How great it is to have others see our performance, our conduct, and be lifted and led by the pattern we set!"[7]

Alma explained he was going to preach the very message Corianton should have taught the Zoramites: salvation through the Atonement of Jesus Christ. "And now, my son, I would say somewhat unto you concerning the coming of Christ. Behold, I say unto you, that it is he that surely shall come to take away the sins of the world; yea, he cometh to declare glad tidings of salvation unto his people. And now, my son, this was the ministry unto which ye were called, to declare these glad tidings unto this people" (Alma 39:15–16).

While counseling his sons, Alma perceived that Corianton was very concerned with a few key points of doctrine, including the coming of Christ, the Resurrection, the law of restoration, and the justice of God against sinners (see Alma 39:17; 40:1; 41:1; 42:1). Corianton seems to have been attempting to use a misunderstanding of some doctrines to justify his wicked actions. Alma warned Corianton: "Deny the justice of God no more. Do not endeavor to excuse yourself in the least point because of your sins" (Alma 42:30). In particular, Corianton seems to

have misunderstood, or at least underestimated, the heavy consequences for evil actions. Alma told his son, "Ye do try to suppose that it
is injustice that the sinner should be consigned to a state of misery"
(Alma 42:1).

Likewise, as mortals, we regularly fall short of perfection and may
be tempted to rationalize our shortcomings. Rather than make excuses
for our own imperfect conduct, it is much better to accept responsibility and put forth renewed effort to improve our behavior. As President
Gordon B. Hinckley taught, "It is better to obey than to rationalize."[8]
Throughout Alma's counsel, we read the heartfelt declaration of pure
doctrine from a loving father to a wayward son in hopes that Corianton
would also, like some of the Zoramites, be persuaded by "the virtue of
the word of God" (Alma 31:5) and come unto Christ.

## THE EFFECTS OF THE FALL

Like any good parent, Alma sought first to understand and then to
instruct. At the beginning of Alma chapter 42, Alma states that he knew
Corianton was concerned about the "justice of God in the punishment
of the sinner" (Alma 42:1). Corianton apparently felt that it was "injustice that the sinner should be consigned to a state of misery" (Alma
42:1). To clarify and explain this important issue, Alma taught
Corianton about the Fall. President Benson seems to have described
Corianton's situation when he declared: "Just as a man does not really
desire food until he is hungry, so he does not desire the salvation of
Christ until he knows why he needs Christ. No one adequately and
properly knows why he needs Christ until he understands and accepts
the doctrine of the Fall and its effect upon all mankind. And no other
book in the world explains this vital doctrine nearly as well as the Book
of Mormon."[9]

Robert J. Matthews has explained that "the Book of Mormon testifies that the Fall is a companion doctrine with the Atonement. . . . In
other words, to teach the Atonement without understanding the Fall
is to offer medication without knowing of the malady, to present a solution without pointing out the problem."[10] So that Corianton might
more fully understand the Atonement of Jesus Christ, Alma first
explained to him the doctrine of the Fall.

When Adam and Eve were in the Garden of Eden, they partook of the fruit of the tree of knowledge of good and evil, and "they were driven out of the garden of Eden, to till the earth" (2 Nephi 2:19).[11] God had created Adam and Eve "in a state of innocence" in which "they knew no sin" (2 Nephi 2:23). Therefore, as Elder Bruce R. McConkie taught: "It is proper and according to the scriptural pattern to speak of the *transgression of Adam,* but not the *sin of Adam.* . . . Knowledge of good and evil is an essential element in the commission of sin, and our first parents did not have this knowledge until after they had partaken of the fruit of the tree of knowledge of good and evil."[12]

As a result of their transgression, Adam and Eve "became lost forever, yea, they became fallen man" (Alma 42:6). But the Fall was no accident, nor was it a tragedy. Father Lehi concluded, "Adam fell that men might be; and men are, that they might have joy" (2 Nephi 2:25). Elder Orson F. Whitney described the Fall in the following terms: "The fall had a twofold direction—downward, yet forward. It brought man into the world and set his feet upon progression's highway."[13] In other words, rather than being a tragedy that mankind should lament and condemn, the Fall was part of God's plan for His children.

President Brigham Young once taught: "How did Adam and Eve sin? Did they come out in direct opposition to God and to His government? No. But they transgressed a command of the Lord, and through that transgression sin came into the world. The Lord knew they would do this, and He had designed that they should."[14]

The transgression of Adam and Eve brought both physical and spiritual consequences to themselves and to all mankind. Adam and Eve were "cut off both temporally and spiritually from the presence of the Lord" (Alma 42:7), and this Fall "brought upon all mankind a spiritual death as well as a temporal" death (Alma 42:9).[15]

### Physical Death

Adam and Eve and all mankind inherited the ability to die physically. In the Garden of Eden, God warned Adam and Eve not to eat of the fruit of the tree of knowledge of good and evil, "for in the day thou eatest thereof thou shalt surely die" (Moses 3:17). Alma explained to Corianton that after they partook of the forbidden fruit, if Adam and

Eve had then partaken of the fruit of the tree of life, they "would have lived forever" on earth in a sinful state, "and the great plan of salvation would have been frustrated" (Alma 42:5). Thus, as Alma stated, "it was appointed unto man to die" (Alma 42:6). This appointment granted to mankind a temporary time on earth "to repent, yea, a probationary time, a time to repent and serve God" (Alma 42:4).

## Spiritual Death

Adam and Eve and all mankind became separated from the presence of God and experienced what is called a spiritual death. Samuel the Lamanite taught that because of the Fall, we are "cut off from the presence of the Lord" and "are considered as dead, both as to things temporal and to things spiritual" (Helaman 14:16). In the Garden of Eden, our first parents were in the presence of God, subject to the will of God. But when they were cast out and separated from God's presence, they "became subjects to follow after their own will" (Alma 42:7).

## RECLAMATION FROM THE FALL

Having explained the doctrine of the Fall, Alma emphasized the fact that the Fall created a nearly hopeless situation for mankind. As a consequence of the Fall, all mankind would become "miserable, being cut off from the presence of the Lord" (Alma 42:11). Hugh W. Nibley concluded: "The Fall has put us into a state of corruption in which it would be disastrous to remain. . . . Nobody wants to live forever in a sewer."[16] The purpose of life, however, is "that they might have joy" (2 Nephi 2:25). The Prophet Joseph Smith emphasized this principle in his famous statement: "Happiness is the object and design of our existence."[17] Because the purpose of our existence on earth is to experience joy and happiness, but the Fall brought misery, "it was expedient that mankind should be reclaimed from this spiritual death" (Alma 42:9).

But how could mankind be reclaimed from this dreadful situation? Alma shared three primary elements necessary for mankind to be reclaimed from the Fall: death, the Atonement of Jesus Christ, and the Resurrection from the dead.

## Death

First, in order to be reclaimed from the Fall, we must die. As ironic as it may sound, death is an essential part of life. Jacob, brother of Nephi, declared, "Death hath passed upon all men, to fulfill the merciful plan of the great Creator" (2 Nephi 9:6). Elder Joseph B. Wirthlin taught, "We know that death is a necessary transition. It will come sooner or later to each of us."[18]

What does the necessary step of death accomplish? Alma explained to Corianton that "the spirits of all men, whether they be good or evil, are taken home to that God who gave them life" (Alma 40:11). In other words, death facilitates the solution to our physical separation from God—eventually everyone is brought back into the presence of God to be judged. Jacob taught, "When all men shall have passed from this first death unto life, insomuch as they have become immortal, they must appear before the judgment seat of the Holy One of Israel" (2 Nephi 9:15). Without our own death, we—like Adam and Eve if they had partaken of the fruit of the tree of life—would remain on earth in our sinful condition, forever separated from the presence of God.

Perhaps Alma, because of his years of experience in life and war, was more grateful for mortal probation than was Corianton, who is described as young and in need of counsel from his brothers (see Alma 39:10). As we grow older, many of us experience vivid reminders that death is an inescapable and unpredictable part of life. For some, this awareness prompts an adoption of the hedonistic attitude, "Eat, drink, and be merry, for tomorrow we die" (2 Nephi 28:7).

For those seeking true happiness, however, such reminders motivate a more urgent and immediate reliance on the Atonement, for the ability to die and to return to the presence of God will not help reclaim us from our fallen condition unless we are clean. Alma taught this important truth to Corianton: "No unclean thing can inherit the kingdom of God" (Alma 40:26; see also 1 Nephi 10:21; Alma 11:37; 3 Nephi 27:19; Moses 6:57). Those who are unclean at their judgment will again be separated from God's presence—permanently.[19]

## The Atonement

The second element necessary to reclaim mankind from the Fall is the Atonement of Jesus Christ. Alma declared: "The plan of redemption could not be brought about, only on conditions of repentance of men in this probationary state. . . . And thus we see that all mankind were fallen, and they were in the grasp of justice; yea, the justice of God, which consigned them forever to be cut off from his presence. And now, the plan of mercy could not be brought about except an atonement should be made" (Alma 42:13–15).[20]

Elder Dallin H. Oaks aptly summarized this important principle: "In the course of mortality, we would become subject to death, and we would be soiled by sin. To reclaim us from death and sin, our Heavenly Father's plan provided us a Savior, whose atonement would redeem all from death and pay the price necessary for all to be cleansed from sin on the conditions he prescribed."[21] Thus, only through taking advantage of the blessings of the Atonement by repenting of our own sins and forgiving others can we be clean and confident in that inevitable "interview" with God at the judgment bar.[22]

## The Resurrection

Being clean and passing our interview with God will also not completely reclaim us from our fallen condition unless we have a resurrected body. Therefore, the third and final element necessary to reclaim mankind from the Fall is the Resurrection from the dead. Alma taught: "It is requisite that all things should be restored to their proper order. Behold, it is requisite and just, according to the power and resurrection of Christ, that the soul of man should be restored to its body, and that every part of the body should be restored to itself" (Alma 41:2).

Concerning this issue, Alma further taught his son that "the atonement bringeth to pass the resurrection of the dead; and the resurrection of the dead bringeth back men into the presence of God" (Alma 42:23).

Having a resurrected body is necessary to experience complete happiness—the ultimate purpose of life. The Lord declared this fundamental truth in modern revelation: "For man is spirit. The elements are eternal, and spirit and element, inseparably connected, receive a fulness of joy; and when separated, man cannot receive a fulness of joy" (D&C 93:33–34; see also D&C 38:17). The Prophet Joseph Smith taught: "We came to this earth that we might have a body and present it pure before God in the celestial kingdom. The great principle of happiness consists in having a body."[23] He further testified: "God has appointed a day in which He will judge the world, and this He has given an assurance of in that He raised up His Son Jesus Christ from the dead—the point on which the hope of all who believe the inspired record is found for their future happiness and enjoyment."[24]

Why must a person have a resurrected body to receive a full amount of joy? Modern revelation declares that the dead who are separated from their physical bodies look upon "the long absence of their spirits from their bodies as a bondage" (D&C 138:50; see also D&C 45:17). Elder Melvin J. Ballard explained this concept more fully: "I grant you that the righteous dead will be at peace, but I tell you that when we go out of this life, leave this body, we will desire to do many things that we cannot do at all without the body. We will be seriously handicapped, and we will long for the body; we will pray for the early reunion with our bodies. We will know then what advantage it is to have a body."[25]

Thus, the three crucial elements necessary to be completely reclaimed from the Fall are death, so that we might return to the presence of God; the Atonement, so that we might be clean when we are reunited with God; and the Resurrection, so that we might receive a fulness of joy—the purpose of life.[26]

## THE EFFECT OF THE WORD

Alma the Younger knew that the most effective way to bring a person to Christ was through the simple but powerful preaching of "the word of God" (Alma 31:5). This seems to have been Alma's strategy not only among the wicked Zoramites but also with his own wayward son, Corianton. After Alma taught his son concerning the elements necessary to be reclaimed from the Fall, he pleaded with his son to apply these important teachings to his own life, saying, "May God grant unto you even according to my words" (Alma 42:31). Alma instructed Corianton to return to his missionary service and follow the pattern that his father had just demonstrated: "And now, O my son, ye are called of God to preach the word unto this people. And now, my son, go thy way, declare the word with truth and soberness, that thou mayest bring souls unto repentance, that the great plan of mercy may have claim upon them" (Alma 42:31).

By recommissioning Corianton to the mission field, Alma once again demonstrated his faith in the Atonement—both for his son and for those he was called to serve.

Corianton seems to have taken his father's teachings seriously, for he did indeed return to preach the gospel among the people (see Alma 43:1–3). Mormon subsequently declared: "There was continual peace among them, and exceedingly great prosperity in the church because of their heed and diligence which they gave unto the word of God, which was declared unto them by Helaman, and Shiblon, and Corianton, and Ammon and his brethren, yea, and by all those who had been ordained by the holy order of God, being baptized unto repentance, and sent forth to preach among the people" (Alma 49:30).[27]

Corianton's courageous repentance changed his life and brought many of his fellow Nephites unto Christ. Not only did he learn from his father, but he also applied the Atonement to his life and actively lived the gospel.

## CONCLUSION

How might modern disciples apply the principles that Alma explained to his son Corianton? A close examination of the teachings above reveals the proper course of action. Of the three elements necessary to reclaim mankind from the Fall, then, the only one that mankind can have any control over is whether to take advantage of the blessings of the Atonement of Jesus Christ. Death will come to "all men" (2 Nephi 9:6), in the due time of the Lord. Further, every person who has ever lived upon the earth, whether good or evil, will eventually be resurrected (see Alma 11:43–44).[28]

Therefore, the focus of our daily activities should be repenting of our own sins and forgiving others of their sins. Concerning the vital necessity of each of us applying the Atonement of Jesus Christ to our lives, Hugh W. Nibley concluded: "There are only two things in this world that we can do very well. We can't build very good buildings—

they come falling down after a few years. We can't build very big dams—they get washed out after a while. We can't paint perfect pictures. We can't do anything very perfectly. But the two things we can do perfectly are to *repent* and *forgive*. Forgive ourselves, forgive other people, and come to the Lord, to return to him with full purpose of heart."[29]

The most important thing that we can do in this life is to follow the example set in the Book of Mormon and humbly take advantage of the blessings of the Atonement of Jesus Christ through repentance and forgiveness. As the people of King Benjamin declared, we should "apply the atoning blood of Christ that we may receive forgiveness of our sins, and our hearts may be purified" so that we may be "filled with joy, having received a remission of [our] sins" and have "peace of conscience, because of the exceeding faith which [we have] in Jesus Christ" (Mosiah 4:2–3).

---

## NOTES

1. Ezra Taft Benson, *A Witness and a Warning* (Salt Lake City: Deseret Book, 1988), 19–20; emphasis added.

2. Jacob warned, "But to be learned is good if they hearken unto the counsels of God" (2 Nephi 9:29). President David O. McKay taught that correctly applying information is the key difference between having knowledge and having wisdom: "Gaining knowledge is one thing and applying it, quite another. Wisdom is the right application of knowledge; and true education—the education for which the Church stands—is the application of knowledge to the development of a noble and Godlike character" (*Gospel Ideals* [Salt Lake City: Deseret Sunday School Union Board, 1957], 440).

3. Joseph Smith, *History of the Church of Jesus Christ of Latter-day Saints,* ed. B. H. Roberts, 2nd ed. rev. (Salt Lake City: Deseret News, 1950), 4:461.

4. This was no empty rhetoric for Alma, having personally led his people into tremendous battles (see Alma 2:16–38). Following his experiences in battle, Alma gave up his position as chief judge so that he might devote himself to preaching the gospel among his people, "seeing no way that he might reclaim them save it were in bearing down in pure testimony against them" (Alma 4:19).

5. See Noah Webster, *An American Dictionary of the English Language* (New York: S. Converse, 1828), s.v. "virtue."

6. Boyd K. Packer, "Little Children," *Ensign,* November 1986, 17; see also Henry B. Eyring, "The Power of Teaching Doctrine," *Ensign,* May 1999, 73–75; and Virginia H. Pearce, "Trying the Word of God," *Ensign,* May 1995, 89.

7. Marvin J. Ashton, "We Believe in Being Honest," *New Era,* September 1983, 4.

8. Gordon B. Hinckley, "Pillars of Truth," *Ensign,* January 1994, 6. Compare also the counsel of Elder Robert D. Hales: "We cannot excuse our conduct because of the actions of our friends or because of the pressure they place upon us. Do you know how to recognize a true friend? A real friend loves us and protects us" ("The Aaronic Priesthood: Return with Honor," *Ensign,* May 1990, 40).

9. Benson, *A Witness and a Warning,* 33.

10. Robert J. Matthews, "Fall of Adam and Eve, the," in *Book of Mormon Reference Companion,* ed. Dennis L. Largey (Salt Lake City: Deseret Book, 2003), 265.

11. See the accounts in Genesis 3:1–24; Moses 3:15–17; 4:5–31; Abraham 5:8–13.

12. Bruce R. McConkie, *Mormon Doctrine,* 2nd ed. (Salt Lake City: Bookcraft, 1966), 804; see also Dallin H. Oaks, "Sins and Mistakes," *Ensign,* October 1996, 62–67.

13. Orson F. Whitney, *Cowley and Whitney on Doctrine* (Salt Lake City: Bookcraft, 1963), 287.

14. Brigham Young, in *Journal of Discourses* (London: Latter-day Saints' Book Depot, 1854–86), 10:312.

15. See Robert J. Matthews, "Resurrection," *Ensign,* April 1991, 9.

16. Hugh W. Nibley, "The Atonement of Jesus Christ, Part 1," *Ensign,* July 1990, 18.

17. Joseph Smith, *Teachings of the Prophet Joseph Smith,* comp. Joseph Fielding Smith (Salt Lake City: Deseret Book, 1976), 255.

18. Joseph B. Wirthlin, "The Time to Prepare," *Ensign,* May 1998, 16.

19. Samuel the Lamanite explained, "Whosoever repenteth the same is not hewn down and cast into the fire; but whosoever repenteth not is hewn down and cast into the fire; and there cometh upon them again a spiritual death, for they are cut off again as to things pertaining to righteousness" (Helaman 14:18).

20. See also the words of Amulek, Alma's missionary companion, who had been taught the gospel by Alma: "It is expedient that an atonement should be made; for according to the great plan of the Eternal God there must be an atonement made, or else all mankind must unavoidably perish; yea, all are hardened; yea, all are fallen and are lost, and must perish except it be through the atonement which it is expedient should be made" (Alma 34:9). Nephi's brother Jacob similarly testified, "I know if there should be no atonement made all mankind must be lost" (Jacob 7:12).

21. Dallin H. Oaks, "The Great Plan of Happiness," *Ensign,* November 1993, 72.

22. Ironically, it is through the blood of the Savior that we clean our own garments from the bloody stain of sin (see Alma 5:21–22).

23. Smith, *Teachings of the Prophet Joseph Smith,* 181.

24. Smith, *Teachings of the Prophet Joseph Smith,* 62.

25. Melvin J. Ballard, *Crusader for Righteousness* (Salt Lake City: Bookcraft, 1966), 213.

26. See also John S. Tanner, "The Body as a Blessing," *Ensign,* July 1993, 8.

27. At the end of the book of Alma, after the wars between the Nephites and Lamanites had ended, Corianton assisted in bringing provisions to the Nephites who had migrated northward (see Alma 60:13).

28. Even the sons of perdition will be resurrected, although their resurrected bodies and their eternal destiny will be devoid of any glory. Concerning the final state of the sons of perdition, the Lord has stated, "*All the rest* shall be brought forth by the resurrection of the dead, *through the triumph and the glory of the Lamb*" (D&C 76:39; emphasis added).

29. Hugh W. Nibley, as quoted in John W. Welch, "Understanding the Sermon at the Temple; Zion Society," in Hugh W. Nibley, *Teachings of the Book of Mormon* (Provo, UT: FARMS, 1993), 4:161–62.

# 18

# THE ATONEMENT OF JESUS CHRIST: "GLAD TIDINGS OF GREAT JOY"

## *Michael L. King*

The Book of Mormon teaches the power of the Atonement with greater light and understanding than any other book. One reason we have been repeatedly invited to read daily from the Book of Mormon is that it plainly teaches the Atonement's application in our lives and shows its effects on those who truly come unto Christ and "apply [His] atoning blood" (Mosiah 4:2). Of all the principles and doctrines outlined for us to abide by in the Book of Mormon, none brings more joy than the Atonement of Jesus Christ. Nephi declares with great clarity the intent of the writers of the Book of Mormon: "For we labor diligently to write, to persuade our children, and also our brethren, to *believe in Christ, and to be reconciled to God;* for we know that it is by grace that we are saved, after all we can do. . . . And we talk of Christ, we *rejoice* in Christ, we preach of Christ, we prophesy of Christ, and we write according to our prophecies, that our children may know to *what source they may look for a remission of their sins*" (2 Nephi 25:23, 26; emphasis added).

---

*Michael L. King is a Church Educational System coordinator in Corpus Christi, Texas.*

In teaching the Atonement, the Book of Mormon prophets make plain the agonies of Christ's suffering in our behalf (see Alma 7:11–13; Mosiah 3:7; 2 Nephi 2:21; 1 Nephi 11; Mosiah 14). They make equally clear, however, that the intent of the Atonement is to lift our hearts and minds to the joy that comes as a result of applying the atoning blood in our lives so that we might "sing the song of redeeming love" (Alma 5:26). Just as God's church in the latter days does not use the cross as a symbol of faith, the Book of Mormon emphasizes the life-giving power of the Atonement, not merely the agony of what Christ suffered. In the limited pages of this chapter, we will look to see the "glad tidings of great joy" (Mosiah 3:3) taught by the Book of Mormon prophets. Not only do they lift our minds with hope that we can receive a remission of our sins through the Atonement, but they also show us how to apply the atoning blood in our lives to allow His love and saving power to reach us. This leads us to "come unto Christ, and be perfected in him" (Moroni 10:32), that we may obtain a fullness of joy.

Many years ago I witnessed a presentation on the Atonement that focused solely on the suffering of Christ, including a graphic display of the agony of crucifixion. I left feeling that in seeing only the suffering, we had lost the love and missed the message of the Atonement. Since that time I have struggled to put into words the hope, love, and joy I have felt as I have studied the Atonement from the pages of the Book of Mormon. I have come to see that finding joy in the Atonement is something that must be understood in the heart and not with some kind of scholarly understanding. It is a personal journey that we each must pursue for ourselves.[1] The Atonement by nature is *infinite,* but hope and joy come through its redeeming power only as our connection to God becomes *intimate.* President Boyd K. Packer stated, "You should learn while you are young that while the Atonement of Christ applies to humanity in general, the influence of it is individual, very personal, and very useful. Even to you beginners, an understanding of the Atonement is of immediate and very practical value in everyday life."[2]

In my teenage years, I had a close friend who, like many of us, did not yet understand the full joy of the Atonement. When sixteen years old, he had a dream in which he met a heavenly personage in a deserted city park. In the visions of the night, the personage looked him in the eye, embraced him, and told him that he had some difficult trials to face in his life. He told this young man that he would need to remember the love and joy he felt at this moment and know that the Savior knew, understood, and loved him.

About six months later, this young man was driving with some friends when a momentary lapse in judgment caused a terrible accident, rolling the car several times. All of his friends were seriously injured, one barely clinging to life in an intensive-care unit. During the week that followed, the young man fasted that his friend would live. He spent entire nights praying, seeking the Savior's healing power to preserve the life of his friend. He returned again and again to the park where his dream had taken place, hoping beyond hope that he would receive some sort of divine answer to his pleadings.

Then his friend passed away. In despair, the young man lost faith for a time. He felt the Lord had not answered his prayers. He felt alone, abandoned, and separated from God by the guilt that he felt over causing the death of one of his best friends.

Eventually, with support from family and friends and after much searching of the scriptures, he found the reconciliation he had been seeking. He came to understand that through the Atonement, death was not the end for his friend. He was reminded of the Savior's love and came to see that His Atonement was not just for sin, but for mistakes, guilt, and the challenges of the heart. He at last understood that the Atonement provides an enabling power to our lives that allows us to go forward with faith and feel joy once again.

## JOY IN THE BEGINNING

From our first beginnings, Christ's Atonement gave us hope that we could come to earth and overcome the challenges of this mortal existence and obtain a fullness of joy (see Alma 13:1–12). Living in the presence of God, we learned that without a physical body we could not receive a fulness of joy (see D&C 93:29–35). To obtain a body, we would need to come to earth and experience mortality. As the plan unfolded regarding the need for a Savior and the separation that would take place because of sin, we became fully aware of the unlimited capacity required of Him who would fulfill the role of Redeemer. When

Christ stood to accept the role as Savior, it was not simply the offering of a kind, wishful brother. Through the eons and eternities, He alone had lived fully every word that our Father in Heaven had instructed, and He had attained a fullness of light. Not only was He willing to perform the role of Redeemer but He also possessed the ability to fulfill such an infinite task. He was in very deed the Word of God (see John 1:1–3).

Some of us showed exceeding great faith in the Word and the redemption that would come through Christ's Atonement. As spirit children of God, we were witnesses of His infinite goodness. We felt His great love for us. With this evidence as the foundation of our faith, we chose to follow Him. We exercised faith in His ability to fulfill God's plan and were thus allowed to come to earth. We knew He was the only one with the infinite capacity and love to do as He promised. From the foundation of the world, Christ was prepared to redeem all those who would believe on His name that we might receive joy (see Alma 22:13–15). Elder Bruce R. McConkie explains: "He who was beloved and chosen from the beginning then became the Lamb slain from the foundation of the world; he was then chosen and foreordained to be the One who would work out the infinite and eternal atonement. 'Behold, I am he who was prepared from the foundation of the world to redeem my people,' he said to the brother of Jared. 'Behold, I am Jesus Christ.' (Ether 3:14.) And so before mortal men were, before Adam fell that men might be, before there was mortality and procreation and death—before all this, provision was made for the redemption."[3]

The knowledge of Christ's atoning power taught to us in our premortal existence penetrated deep into the fiber of our spirits and became engraved in the spiritual countenances of those who believed in Christ (see Alma 5:14). This knowledge provided a light for all of us who chose to follow our Father's plan and enabled us to discern good from evil in order to see our way through our mortal existence. With this light, we took courage and were confident that we could make the journey to earth and return home to our Father. The Light of Christ was given to every one of us that we might be persuaded to "lay hold upon every good thing" so that we could become as our Father in Heaven (see Moroni 7:15–25). It was this knowledge planted deep in our souls that caused the morning stars to sing together and all the sons of God to shout for joy (see Job 38:6–7).

## THAT WE MIGHT HAVE JOY

With the hope of eternal glory and the joy of Christ's light within, all who followed God's plan have been permitted to receive a body and come to earth. To learn the lessons of godliness, however, it was necessary that an opposition be provided. Though the truth of Christ was embedded in our hearts, a veil was placed upon our minds so that we could learn to choose for ourselves whether we would follow that light within us. From the beginning, the Lord God had given unto us our agency so we could act for ourselves. We could not act for ourselves unless we had opposition from which to choose (see 2 Nephi 2:11, 15–16). To introduce choice into the world, Adam and Eve were provided with the fruit of the tree of knowledge of good and evil in opposition to the fruit of the tree of life. When they partook of the forbidden fruit, the Fall made it possible for us to come to the earth to obtain joy "through the great Mediator of all men" (2 Nephi 2:27). The Fall did not introduce joy into the world, but as a result of the Fall, Adam, Eve, and the rest of mankind can know the joy of redemption through the Atonement of Christ (see Moses 5:10–11).

We cannot truly understand or appreciate the Atonement until we first understand the Fall. President Ezra Taft Benson taught, "Just as a man does not really desire food until he is hungry, so he does not desire the salvation of Christ until he knows why he needs Christ. No one adequately and properly knows why he needs Christ until he understands and accepts the doctrine of the Fall and its effect upon all mankind."[4] Without trying to expound all of the doctrinal implications of the Fall, we must use the Fall to gain some perspective relative to our need for the Atonement.

Alma the Younger uses this approach in teaching his wayward son, Corianton (see Alma 41–42). He taught that when Adam partook of the fruit, man "became lost forever, yea, they became fallen man, . . . cut off both temporally and spiritually from the presence of the Lord; and thus we see they became subjects to follow after their own will" (Alma 42:6–7). Alma further teaches that man "had become carnal, sensual, and devilish, by nature. . . . If it were not for the plan of redemption, . . . as soon as they were dead their souls were miserable, being cut off from the presence of the Lord. And now, there was no means to reclaim men from this fallen state, which man had brought upon himself because of his own disobedience" (Alma 42:10–12). At the conclusion of his teachings, Alma reassured his son that because of the Atonement, the effects of the Fall could be completely overcome and mercy could claim all who will come and "partake of the waters of life freely" (Alma 42:27).

While Adam's Fall brought us into a world filled with the nature and disposition to do evil, it is our conscious following of that nature that causes us to fall and separates us from God. Preaching to the priests of King Noah, Abinadi taught: "All mankind [became] carnal, sensual, devilish, knowing evil from good, subjecting themselves to the devil. Thus all mankind were lost; and behold, they would have been endlessly lost were it not that God redeemed his people from their lost and fallen state. But remember that *he that persists in his own carnal nature, and goes on in the ways of sin and rebellion against God, remaineth in his fallen state* and the devil hath all power over him. Therefore he is as though there was no redemption made, being an enemy to God" (Mosiah 16:3–5; emphasis added).

In our carnal and fallen state, our sinful nature becomes contrary to that God who gave us life and offends the spirit inside of us, robbing us of joy. Alma explains that "all men that are in a state of nature, or . . . in a carnal state, are in the gall of bitterness and in the bonds of iniquity; they are without God in the world, and they have gone contrary to the nature of God; therefore, they are in a state contrary to the nature of happiness" (Alma 41:11). You cannot do wrong and feel right. Without Christ's Atonement for our sins, our spirits would become subject to the devil, and "we [would] become devils, angels to a devil, to be shut out from the presence of our God, and to remain with the father of lies, in misery, like unto himself" (2 Nephi 9:9). With no Atonement to overcome our spiritual death, we would be left forever in a state of misery.

Without the Atonement, the effects of the Fall would be total and irrevocable. Mankind would be lost temporally and spiritually, without resurrection or repentance, forever separated from God. The "natural man" would remain an "enemy to God . . . forever and ever" without the power to become a saint (Mosiah 3:19). Thus estranged, we would be unable to become at one with God and obtain any kind of joy. Truly there had to be an infinite Atonement to overcome the effects of the Fall and make us at one again with God, bringing us a fullness of joy.

Throughout the Book of Mormon, the Atonement is taught side by side with the precept of the Fall (see 2 Nephi 2, 9; Mosiah 3–4, 13–16, 27; Alma 11–12, 33–34, 36, 41–42), showing clearly that Christ's Atonement has overcome the effects of the Fall for all who will take advantage of its redeeming power. Understanding and abiding by this precept can give us the strength to overcome the challenges that come as a part of our mortal existence and experience the joy provided by the enabling power of Christ.

## THE JOY OF RESURRECTION

Physical death is one of the great challenges that we all face in mortality. Through the Resurrection, Christ overcame the separation caused by death (see 2 Nephi 9:4; Alma 42:23; Helaman 14:15–17), making us at one again physically with our Heavenly Father and giving us the "oil of joy for mourning" (Isaiah 61:3). Since one individual and not each individual person brought death upon mankind, one individual is responsible for overcoming that death (see 1 Corinthians 15:20–22).[5] The Resurrection blesses all the children of God who ever had or would come to earth to gain a physical body (see Alma 11:42–45). This doctrine provides great hope and comfort to all of us who have lost loved ones, just as in the case of my young friend mentioned earlier (see also Alma 28:12).

## ABILITY TO SUCCOR HIS PEOPLE

Along with overcoming the physical death brought about through Adam's Fall, Christ can also overcome the effects of our personal fall that we bring upon ourselves through sin. While having been taught this idea from our youth, many of us may wonder how Christ can truly understand and atone for our sins when during His mortal journey, Christ lived without ever going against the divine light inside Him. We are told in modern revelation, "He received not of the fulness at first, but *continued from grace to grace,* until he received a fulness" (D&C 93:13; emphasis added). Without ever sinning, how then was He to comprehend all that we feel and experience and thus be able to atone for our sins and give help in time of need?

Just as Moses had been shown all the inhabitants of the earth by the Spirit of God (see Moses 1:27–28), in one of the most supremely intimate aspects of the Atonement, Christ was shown all those for whom He would atone (see Mosiah 14:10; 15:10–12). Elder Merrill J. Bateman taught, "The Atonement involved more than an infinite mass of sin; it entailed an infinite stream of individuals with their specific needs."[6] To see and understand according to the Spirit, however, was not sufficient for the Atonement Christ sought to make in our behalf. After comprehending all things by the Spirit, Christ also suffered *according to the flesh* the afflictions, temptations, sins, pain, infirmities, and sicknesses of all mankind, "that he may know *according to the flesh how to succor his people*" (Alma 7:12; emphasis added).

Christ's suffering "according to the flesh" allowed him to comprehend every person and every need so that He could make peace between God and us. The "at-one-ment" worked in both directions. Before the Atonement could make us at one with God again, *Christ had to be at one with us,* sharing in all of our sorrows, sins, disappointments, and heartaches. Yet with all of the temptations, trials, and adversity of the world upon Him while in the Garden of Gethsemane, Christ "resisted unto blood" (Hebrews 12:4) that He might not let sin into His being. In the words of Elder Neal A. Maxwell, "Jesus partook of history's bitterest cup without becoming bitter!"[7] It is from this perspective that Paul tells us, "We have not an high priest which cannot be touched with the feeling of our infirmities [or unable to sympathize with our frailties and imperfections]; but was in all points tempted like as we are, *yet without sin*" (Hebrews 4:15; emphasis added). Only by passing beneath all things could Christ lift us out of all things, showing us how to live in a godly way through every circumstance of mortality (see D&C 88:6).

To pay the price for sin, He had to first comprehend all things and then overcome all things. Christ's infinite payment encompassed all that each individual in the whole of mankind would suffer. Such suffering caused even a God "to tremble because of pain, and to bleed at every pore" (D&C 19:18). He paid more than any person would need or require. Justice was to be completely satisfied for every person who would come unto Christ. In suffering the agony of Gethsemane and the cross,[8] His flesh became "subject even unto death, the will of the Son being swallowed up in the will of the Father . . . giving the Son power to make intercession for the children of men" (Mosiah 15:7–8). Isaiah added, "He hath borne our griefs, and carried our sorrows; . . . he was wounded for our transgressions; . . . the chastisement of our peace was upon him; and with his stripes we are healed" (Isaiah 53:3–5). This principle brings us joy in the knowledge that there is someone who knows and understands all that we can possibly suffer and can help us to overcome.

## THE BROKEN HEART

Although the Book of Mormon teaches us the magnitude of Christ's suffering, it is not the Lord's desire that we merely feel sorry for what He suffered or simply cause us to fear the retribution of unrepentant sin. True comprehension of the Atonement from the perspective of His sufferings breaks our hearts so that we become humble, teachable, and willing to repent, filled with the hope that "joy cometh in the morning" (Psalm 30:5). Unfortunately, many of us misunderstand this idea and choose to beat ourselves up for what we have caused the Savior to suffer. Instead of coming to Him with a broken heart and contrite spirit, we shrink from His healing arms, which are outstretched to provide us comfort and protection from the law of justice (see 2 Nephi 2:6–10; 7:1–2; 3 Nephi 10:4–6; Alma 42:12–23). We clench our fists and determine that we will never again cause Him such pain. Instead of becoming one with Him in our hurtful state, we attempt to make it right on our own. We somehow try to pay the price of sin for ourselves rather than cause Him to suffer. We ache to pay for that which we have done that we might be clean.

Eternal law, however, does not allow the offering of something imperfect to pay for imperfection. We are unable to pay the full price necessary to be made whole. It is true that we may suffer because of our sins, and we may even suffer for our sins, but we cannot, in the end, remove our sins. Because we are still unclean, the punishment that is affixed to answer the ends of the law of justice requires that we be cut off from the presence of God (see 2 Nephi 2:5–10; 1 Nephi 15:24). We are trapped. We find ourselves "in the grasp of justice, . . . consigned . . . forever to be cut off from his presence" (Alma 42:14). Lost and cut off, we plead for mercy, but mercy requires an infinite sacrifice to satisfy justice and pay the price that we cannot pay. Elder Bruce R. McConkie taught:

> This, then, is the doctrine of the divine Sonship. It took our Lord's mortal and his immortal powers to work out the atonement, for that supreme sacrifice required both death and resurrection. There is no salvation without death, even as there is no salvation without resurrection. Thus Amulek, speaking of this "great and last sacrifice," says it could not be "a human sacrifice; but it must be an infinite and eternal sacrifice. Now there is not any man that can sacrifice his own blood which will atone for the sins of another." (Alma 34:10–11.) Man cannot resurrect himself; man cannot save himself; human power cannot save another; human power cannot atone for the sins of another. The work of redemption must be infinite and eternal; it must be done by an infinite being; God himself must atone for the sins of the world.[9]

Truly, "there was no other good enough to pay the price of sin."[10] Only through the infinite offering of Christ can our garments be "washed white through the blood of the Lamb" (Alma 13:11). With beautiful and heart-breaking light, President Boyd K. Packer declares: "There are times you cannot mend that which you have broken. . . . Perhaps the damage was so severe that you cannot fix it no matter how desperately you want to. Your repentance cannot be accepted unless there is a restitution. If you cannot undo what you have done, you are trapped. . . . Restoring what you cannot restore, healing the wound you cannot heal, fixing that which you broke and you cannot fix is the very purpose of the atonement of Christ. When your desire is firm and you are willing to pay the 'uttermost farthing,' *the law of restitution is suspended.*

Your obligation is transferred to the Lord. He will settle your accounts."[11]

As we come unto Christ with true godly sorrow, He settles our accounts with the law of justice, making our garments white, or in other words, we become clean so that guilt is swept away (see Enos 1:4–8). God does not desire that we continually harrow ourselves up by the memory of our sins but desires that we accept His mercy in our behalf. The prophet Zenos taught, "Thou art angry, O Lord, with this people, because they will not understand thy mercies which thou hast bestowed upon them because of thy Son" (Alma 33:16).

Through the eternal gift of the Atonement, mercy can indeed satisfy the demands of justice and encircle us in the "arms of safety" (Alma 34:16). Unlike the gift of resurrection, however, which comes freely and universally to all in overcoming the physical effects of Adam's Fall, this gift must be obtained by following the path outlined by the Savior. This path consists of the basic principles of the gospel. First, we must exercise faith that He is both able and willing to atone for us (see Alma 33:1, 22–23). Next, we must come unto Him with a broken heart and contrite spirit and be willing to do whatever is necessary to obtain mercy and forgiveness (see Alma 22:13–15). We must then willingly enter into a covenant with Him to always remember Him and keep His commandments (see Mosiah 5:5–9). As we enter, live, and renew our covenants, we receive the baptism of fire, or the gift of the Holy Ghost, which brings a remission of our sins (see 2 Nephi 31:10–18). Coming to Him this way, we feel and comprehend His healing power both in our minds and in our hearts. We "remember [our] pains no more" and are "harrowed up by the memory of [our] sins no more" (Alma 36:19), leaving us filled with unspeakable joy.

## THE RECONCILED HEART

As we follow the path outlined by the Savior to obtain His mercy and have our sins remitted, our hearts are reconciled unto God and our divine potential is restored. We become His sons and daughters, striving once again to be as He is. These feelings are expressed in a poem called "Reconciled":

*The veil is parted, allowing me in; the light of God shows what is within*
*This hallowed room within my soul where godliness dwells and I am whole.*
*From the world's call I am free, and I see the me I want to be;*
*On holy ground I ponder long the path to which I truly belong.*
*Am I to be a celestial soul? Or merely dream of a godly goal?*
*Then He appears and I can see—to be like Him is what I should be,*
*But I see reflected in His eyes what my soul cannot disguise,*
*The things I've done that marred my soul; I'm less than godly, incomplete—*
    *not whole.*
*There comes an ache into my heart—He knows, He sees, my ugly part.*
*I begin to turn my face away—What can I do, what can I say?*
*I've tried so hard to heed the call to follow Him, but still I fall.*
*With head bowed low, I humbly plea, "Please, dear Lord, have mercy on me!"*
*Then I feel His love; I see His face; I feel His arms in warm embrace.*
*Healing light fills my soul, and once again I'm godly—I am whole.*
*The godly child that lies within is now pure and free from sin,*
*Reconciled to God above by atoning power and the Savior's love.*[12]

This cleansing and removal of sin leaves us filled with humility and gratitude to a loving Savior. Certainly He has atoned for our sins in every sense of the word. Both the Hebrew (*kâphar*) and the Greek (*katallagē*) words for *atonement* help us to understand the Savior's role in overcoming sin and reconciling us to God.[13] Forgiveness alone, however, does not leave us finished, complete, and filled with the joy we came to earth to obtain (see 2 Nephi 2:25; 31:19). In the final judgment, it is not simply a cover for our sin that we seek in repenting through the Atonement. For a complete and full restitution to our godly nature, not only must the sin be removed but our desire for the sin, or carnal nature, must be removed and the divine nature we possessed before our fall must be restored.

Elder Bruce C. Hafen taught: "The Savior asks for our repentance not merely to compensate him for paying our debt to justice, but also as a way of inducing us to undergo the process of development that will make our nature divine, giving us the capacity to live the celestial law. The 'natural man' will remain an enemy to God forever—even after paying for his own sins—unless he also 'becometh a saint through the atonement of Christ the Lord, and becometh as a child.' . . . The Atonement does more than pay for our sins. It is also the agent through which we develop a saintly nature."[14]

At our deepest level, we desire a literal change of our nature that unites us with God, making us as He is. In modern English, the Christian intent of the word *atonement* means literally "the state of union with God in which man exemplifies the attributes of God."[15] This kind of union must reach infinitely to every cell of our body, every thought of our mind, and every desire of our heart. Our spiritual genes desire the state of holiness that we witnessed in the beginning with the Father. We desire to have the "natural man" removed and be brought to a "divine nature" (see Mosiah 3:19; 2 Peter 1:3–4). It is this change of our nature—more than a change in desires—that goes beyond our own capacity. Such a change can only be brought about by an infinite atonement.

President David O. McKay taught: "Human nature *can* be changed, here and now." He continued, "You can change human nature. No man who has felt in him the Spirit of Christ even for half a minute can deny this truth. . . . You do change human nature, your own human nature, if you surrender it to Christ. Human nature can be changed here and now. Human nature has been changed in the past. Human nature must be changed on an enormous scale in the future, unless the world is to be drowned in its own blood. And only Christ can change it."[16]

Herein lies the key to understanding the Atonement. Without its infinite power, not only would we not be able to return to the presence of our Heavenly Father, which is made possible through the Resurrection and forgiveness of sin (see Helaman 14:15–16; Mormon 9:12–13), we would also not have the power to change our nature and therefore could not overcome our inevitable misery in this life or the life to come. Overcoming this natural state and obtaining true joy is more than having the sins committed during our mortal existence removed through repentance. We must have a mighty change of heart that changes our countenance and brings us to hungering and thirsting after righteousness, to true discipleship, and to the process of becoming like Christ in every way.

## THE MIGHTY CHANGE OF HEART

As one embraces the true meaning of the Atonement, the Spirit of the Lord allows us in a very spiritually real sense to feel the Savior's embrace and see His love for us in His eyes. Rather than only seeking the Savior at times of repentance, we seek the Lord daily in personal experiences. The heart of the word *Atonement* is "one." It is in the one-on-one experiences in the scriptures that our lives are truly changed (see 3 Nephi 11:14–17). The Atonement becomes an intimate personal relationship when we come unto Him and seek His healing power, whatever the circumstance may be (see 3 Nephi 17:5–22). While we cannot physically experience the feelings of the Savior, by the same spirit that opened the minds of Nephi, Jacob, Isaiah and other prophets we can experience spiritual oneness with the Savior and feel His love for us. By the spirit we can allow His light into our most intimate and difficult challenges and allow Him to show us all things that we must do. It is in these intimate moments that we have a chance to feel His love for us in every fiber of our soul and experience a mighty change of heart, bringing true joy in its wake.

The people of King Benjamin experienced this mighty change of heart. Directed by an angel to speak to his people so that they might be filled with joy, King Benjamin taught that "with power, the Lord Omnipotent . . . shall come down from heaven, . . . and lo, he cometh unto his own, that salvation might come unto the children of men even through faith on his name" (Mosiah 3:5, 9). He showed them the fallen condition to which they had come. After hearing his teachings, the people viewed themselves in their carnal state and pleaded with one voice, "O have mercy, and apply the atoning blood of Christ that we may receive forgiveness of our sins, and our hearts may be purified" (Mosiah 4:2).

These people understood that it was not enough simply to be forgiven of sin. They also understood that payment for sin is not the same as removal of the sinful nature, which causes people to sin. They wanted their hearts changed so that they no longer had any desire for sin. King Benjamin taught them what they must do to always rejoice and retain a remission of their sins. Following their heartfelt plea, "the Spirit of the Lord came upon them, and they were filled with joy, having received a remission of their sins, and having peace of conscience, because of the exceeding faith which they had in Jesus Christ" (Mosiah 4:3). Through the mighty change of heart that had been wrought by the Spirit of the Lord, they had "no more disposition to do evil, but to do good continually" (Mosiah 5:2).

This change in our nature causes us to shake at the very appearance of sin and to look upon sin with abhorrence (see 2 Nephi 4:31; Alma 13:12). We are sanctified through the offering of the body of Jesus Christ and receive "boldness to enter into the holiest by the blood of Jesus, by a new and living way, which he hath consecrated for us, through the veil, that is to say, his flesh; . . . having our hearts sprinkled from an evil conscience" (Hebrews 10:19–22). The Lord gives us a new heart so that we may walk in His laws and live the ordinances that He has given us (see Ezekiel 11:19–20; 36:25–28).

## PURE LOVE OF CHRIST

How is it possible to effect such a change in the very heart and nature of an individual? What touches a heart so deeply and completely that it not only becomes broken but also changed in its very desires, becoming sanctified and pure, eradicating all desire for sin?

While pondering the Atonement of Jesus Christ, we often focus on what He suffered and the pains He bore. Though His infinite suffering on our behalf may cause our hearts to break, it is not focusing upon His sufferings that will ultimately cause our hearts to become sanctified and godly and bring us joy. Only through experiencing and comprehending God's love for us can we take on the divine nature of our Father. In His godly, eternal personage is the very radiance of love (see 1 John 4:7–19). This life-changing, godly love is manifested to us in two ways: through our Father's love in offering His Only Begotten Son and also through the Savior's love in giving Himself as a willing sacrifice on our behalf (see 2 Nephi 26:24). The Holy Ghost is the great testator of this eternal love felt for us by the Father and the Son. As the Spirit directs our thoughts relative to the Atonement, we feel and comprehend Their love which softens even the hardest of hearts and changes the natural man into a saint. It is in comprehending and experiencing this love through the Spirit that the infinite power of the Atonement brings a change to our natures and joy to our souls.

Mormon instructs us that this love, known as charity, never fails, that it is the "pure love of Christ, and it endureth forever" (Moroni 7:47). He admonishes us to pray unto our Father in Heaven "with all the energy of heart, that [we] may be filled with this love, which he hath bestowed upon all who are true followers of his Son, Jesus Christ; that [we] may *become the sons of God;* that when he shall appear we shall *be like him,* for we shall see him as he is; that we may have this hope; that we may *be purified even as he is pure*" (Moroni 7:48; emphasis added). Experiencing charity, the true motive behind the Atonement, is truly a matter of the heart. Books may attempt to teach it, but it is not until the Spirit of the Lord touches our hearts that we truly experience this love. Once we feel this love, our hearts are changed and we are eternally bound to our Father through the Savior, and according to the Apostle Paul, there is nothing that can separate us from that love (see Romans 8:35–39; see also Romans 8:1–34).

## PROPHETIC JOY

The Book of Mormon witnesses the experiences of many prophets who tasted of this life-changing love of the Savior and obtained joy. Through their writings, the Spirit conveys the eternal love of the Savior and our Father in Heaven, allowing us to feel the joy that it brings. While many prophets might be cited, we will look briefly at the testimony of a few who became intimately acquainted with the Savior, tasted of His love, and taught the joyful message of the Atonement.

Lehi experienced this love and joy in his first vision (see 1 Nephi 1:14) and then again in the vision of the tree of life. In the latter experience, he spoke of the sweetness of the fruit that filled his soul "with exceedingly great joy" and "was desirable above all other fruit" (1 Nephi 8:12). He knew, however, that it was not enough for his family to hear his explanation of what he felt, so he beckoned for them to come and partake of the fruit for themselves. Lehi's experience teaches us that the love of God must be experienced individually to fill us with joy.

Abinadi taught that while Christ was making His offering in our behalf, He saw His seed, or those who had looked to Him for a remission of their sins. He testified that "these are they who have pub-lished peace, who have brought good tidings of good" (Mosiah 15:14). When we open our hearts to the love that He felt for us while paying for the very sins that were causing Him such anguish, we join our voice to all those who publish peace and bring good tidings of good (see Mosiah 15:13–18). We sing with the angels "good tidings of great joy, which shall be to all people" (Luke 2:10). We are among those who have experienced the great love of God for all His children and are filled with joy.

Alma the Younger came to understand this joy while he lay uncon-scious for three days. After being "racked, even with the pains of a damned soul" (Alma 35:16), his mind caught hold of his father's teach-ings regarding the coming of Jesus Christ and His Atonement for sin. He longed for healing and cried within his heart to have the atoning power applied in his behalf. Echoing the imagery of the tree of life, Alma repeatedly refers to the exquisite and sweet joy that he *tasted* upon receiving this mighty change of heart. Once penetrated by the infinite love of the Savior, Alma's "soul was filled with joy as exceeding as was [his] pain!" (Alma 36:20). Alma no longer desired to be "extinct both soul and body" (v. 15), but his soul longed to be at one with God.

## PERFECTED IN CHRIST

The Atonement of Jesus Christ is indeed the power to cover a mul-titude of sins, and it is the only way that we can have our sins remitted. But it is more—much more. It is the power by which Christ can effect an actual change in our nature so that we become celestial *by nature* that our joy might be full. The very process of perfection happens through the power of the Atonement of Christ, which is manifested to us through His Spirit. This atoning power overcomes any of those things which rob us of joy in this life: hard feelings that have caused years of separation in families, offenses given or taken, the hurt of a lost loved one, the damage done by abuse and neglect. It is indeed infinite in its capacity to overcome all things, but we must come unto Him and invite the healing power of the Atonement into our lives through repentance. As we worthily partake of the sacrament, Christ's designated reminder of the Atonement, we are promised that we will always have His Spirit to be with us. This Spirit testifies to our hearts of His love and atoning power to overcome whatever tribulations may come so that we might have joy (see John 16:33). Without tasting the joy of the Spirit, we find ourselves continually returning to past sins, to past hurt feelings, and to longings for the things of this telestial world. When the spirit of His infinite Atonement permeates our hearts, we lose all desire for anything that separates us from feeling God's love and gain the joy spoken of by the prophets of the Book of Mormon. This joy is to be found not just after we depart this life but also as we continue on our journey in mortality (see Mosiah 2:41).

In his final chapter to the Book of Mormon, Moroni taught that we must "come unto Christ, and *be perfected in him,* and deny [ourselves] of all ungodliness; . . . and love God with all [our] might, mind and strength, then is his grace sufficient for [us], that by his grace [we] may be *perfect in Christ,* . . . if [we] by the grace of God are perfect in Christ, and deny not his power, then are [we] sanctified . . . *through the shedding of the blood of Christ*" (Moroni 10:32–33; emphasis added). Through the grace provided by the Atonement of Christ, we become possessed of the very attributes of God and are at last at one with Him in heart, in mind, and in nature, having a fulness of joy.

---

NOTES

1. These thoughts are expressed beautifully by Ella Wheeler Wilcox in her poem "Gethsemane," quoted by Vaughn J. Featherstone, "'However Faint the Light May Glow,'" in *Ensign,* November 1982, 72–73.

2. Boyd K. Packer, "Washed Clean," *Ensign,* May 1997, 9.

3. Bruce R. McConkie, *A New Witness for the Articles of Faith* (Salt Lake City: Deseret Book, 1985), 110–11.

4. Ezra Taft Benson, "The Book of Mormon and the Doctrine and Covenants," *Ensign,* May 1987, 83–87.

5. Joseph F. Smith, *Gospel Doctrine* (Salt Lake City: Deseret Book, 1977), 69.

6. Merrill J. Bateman, as quoted in W. Jeffrey Marsh, "The Living Reality of the Savior's Mercy," in *Jesus Christ, Son of God, Savior,* ed. Paul H. Peterson, Gary L. Hatch, and Laura D. Card (Provo, UT: Religious Studies Center, Brigham Young University, 2002), 162.

7. Neal A. Maxwell, "Enduring Well," *Ensign,* April 1997, 7.

8. Bruce R. McConkie, "The Purifying Power of Gethsemane," *Ensign,* May 1985, 10.

9. Bruce R. McConkie, *A New Witness for the Articles of Faith* (Salt Lake City: Deseret Book, 1985), 111–12.

10. "There Is a Green Hill Far Away," *Hymns* (Salt Lake City: The Church of Jesus Christ of Latter-day Saints, 1985), no. 194.

11. Boyd K. Packer, "The Brilliant Morning of Forgiveness," *Ensign,* November 1995, 19–20.

12. Poem by the author, July 24, 2002.

13. In the Old Testament, *atonement* comes from the Hebrew word *kâphar,* which means literally "to cover . . . ; to expiate or condone, to placate or cancel." The New Testament Greek word, *katallagē* means "restoration to (the divine) favor:—atonement, reconciliation" (see *Strong's Exhaustive Concordance of the Bible, Hebrew and Chaldee Dictionary,* 57, ref. 3722, and *Greek Dictionary of the New Testament,* 40, ref. 2643).

14. Bruce C. Hafen, *The Broken Heart: Applying the Atonement to Life's Experiences* (Salt Lake City: Deseret Book, 1989), 8.

15. *Webster's Encyclopedic Unabridged Dictionary of the English Language* (New York: Portland House, 1989), 95.

16. David O. McKay, *Stepping Stones to an Abundant Life* (Salt Lake City: Deseret Book, 1971), 23, 127.

# 19

# THE MERITS OF CHRIST: FALLEN HUMANITY'S HOPE FOR REDEMPTION

## Michael J. Fear

As a teacher of youth, I occasionally begin a class by asking the students if they would like to receive what they deserve at the judgment day. The initial response of a few is in the affirmative, but after thinking it over for a moment the class generally concludes that they want something more than they "deserve" when it comes to an eternal reward. While this view might reflect the natural desire to get something for nothing, I believe it also reflects the inward feeling in each of us that holiness, or righteousness, is unattainable without divine assistance. In other words, we are "prone to wander, Lord, [we] feel it, prone to leave the God [we] love."[1]

The Book of Mormon affirms that without the love, mercy, and merits of Christ, our reward in the eternities is not very desirable. Jacob insisted that were it not for the redemption of Christ, we would become "angels to [the] devil, to be shut out from the presence of our God, and to remain with the father of lies, in misery, like unto himself" (2 Nephi 9:9). In such a state, "we shall not dare to look up to our God"

Michael J. Fear is an instructor at the Ogden Utah Institute of Religion.

(Alma 12:14) but would rather be put out of His presence forever. Alma felt this shame and horror of getting what he deserved as he struggled under the consciousness of his own guilt and desired banishment instead of coming back into the presence of God to be judged (see Alma 36:12–16).

Understanding men and women's inability to merit salvation through their own efforts can lead one to rely "alone upon the merits of Christ" (Moroni 6:4). Nephi put it this way: "O Lord, I have trusted in thee, and I will trust in thee forever. I will not put my trust in the arm of flesh; for I know that cursed is he that putteth his trust in the arm of flesh. Yea, cursed is he that putteth his trust in man" (2 Nephi 4:34). Nephi had seen his weak and fallen condition and realized that without the strength of the Lord, he would not be able to overcome the world and his own personal struggles (see 2 Nephi 4:17–19, 26–30). When we see clearly that we are lost and that we need Him, we can be led to rely on His goodness and His grace in our lives.[2] This reliance on the merits of Christ involves more than simply passive belief. It includes recognizing our fallen nature and finding access to grace through making and keeping sacred covenants.

## THE FALL

One of the foundational doctrines taught in the Book of Mormon is the doctrine of the Fall. It clearly states that the gulf between fallen humanity and a "perfect, just God" (Alma 42:15) is insurmountable without assistance. Lehi taught that "no flesh . . . can dwell in the presence of God, save it be through the merits, and mercy, and grace of the Holy Messiah" (2 Nephi 2:8). Aaron likewise instructed the king of the Lamanites that "since man had fallen he could not merit anything of himself; but the sufferings and death of Christ atone for their sins, through faith and repentance, and so forth" (Alma 22:14). Our inability to merit, or deserve, salvation is a result of the Fall and its consequences.

When discussing the Fall, it is important to distinguish between traditional Christianity's teaching of "original sin" and the restored doctrine of the Fall as taught in the Book of Mormon. For centuries, traditional Christianity has held the belief that little children are somehow tainted and unclean from birth because of the transgression of Adam and Eve. John Calvin taught that "even infants bringing their condemnation with them from their mother's womb, suffer not for another's, but *for their own defect.*"[3] John Wesley described the nature of the human race as having a "total loss of righteousness and true holiness which we sustained by the sin of our first parent."[4] This attitude about our nature, including the nature of little children, led to practices such as infant baptism as well as a pessimistic view of human nature that seemed to dominate the thinking of Christian scholars and leaders for centuries.[5]

In contrast to this view of a corrupt race, latter-day scripture acknowledges the weakness of humanity without condemning the innocent. The Savior told Mormon through revelation that "little children are whole, for they are not capable of committing sin; wherefore the curse of Adam is taken from them in me" (Moroni 8:8). Mormon also taught that "little children are alive in Christ, even from the foundation of the world" (Moroni 8:12). We further learn from a revelation to the Prophet Joseph Smith that "the Lord said unto Adam: Behold I have forgiven thee thy transgression in the Garden of Eden" (Moses 6:53). And also that "the Son of God hath atoned for original guilt, wherein the sins of the parents cannot be answered upon the heads of the children, for they are whole from the foundation of the world" (Moses 6:54).

The Book of Mormon insists that little children and those who "are without the law" are not accountable for their sins because of the merits of Christ and therefore are innocent before God (see Mosiah 3:11, 16; Moroni 8:22). At the same time, those who have reached the years of accountability are guilty of their own sins, which make them unclean. This distinction between the innocence of youth and the accountability of parents is made clear in the Book of Mormon. "This thing shall ye teach—repentance and baptism unto those who are accountable and capable of committing sin; yea, teach parents that they must repent and be baptized, and humble themselves as their little children, and they shall all be saved with their little children" (Moroni 8:10). This exalting of little children was also taught by the Savior while He was in mortality: "At the same time came the disciples unto Jesus, saying, Who is the greatest in the kingdom of heaven? And Jesus called a little child unto him, and set him in the midst of them, and said, Verily I say unto you, Except ye be converted, and become as little children, ye shall not enter into the kingdom of heaven. Whosoever therefore shall humble himself as this little child, the same is greatest in the kingdom of heaven" (Matthew 18:1–4).

Even though little children are not condemned by the Fall, all of us are affected by it. This effect shows up most noticeably in the "natural man" as the Book of Mormon calls it (Mosiah 3:19), or "carnal nature" (Mosiah 16:5). By nature, fallen humanity is prone to sin and susceptible to the weakness and temptations of the flesh. King Benjamin taught, "The natural man is an enemy to God, and has been from the fall of Adam, and will be, forever and ever, unless he yields to the enticings of the Holy Spirit, and putteth off the natural man and becometh a saint through the atonement of Christ the Lord, and becometh as a child, submissive, meek, humble, patient, full of love" (Mosiah 3:19). The Lord taught Adam, "Inasmuch as thy children are conceived in sin, even so when they begin to grow up, sin conceiveth in their hearts, and they taste the bitter, that they may know to prize the good. And it is given unto them to know good from evil; wherefore they are agents unto themselves, and I have given unto you another law and commandment. Wherefore teach it unto your children, that all men, everywhere, must repent, or they can in nowise inherit the kingdom of God, for no unclean thing can dwell there, or dwell in his presence" (Moses 6:55–57). From these verses it is apparent that through conception the seeds of a fallen nature are transferred to Adam and Eve's posterity. These seeds do not condemn children, for the Savior's Atonement, as mentioned previously, covers for them. However, as the seeds of sin and death germinate in this fallen world, they grow up to take root in men and women's hearts.

"Because of the fall our natures have become evil continually," the brother of Jared observed (Ether 3:2). We therefore need to have "this wicked spirit rooted out of [our] breast, and receive [Christ's] spirit" (Alma 22:15). After experiencing a change of heart, Alma testified: "The Lord said unto me: Marvel not that all mankind, yea, men and women . . . must be born again; yea, born of God, changed from their carnal and fallen state, to a state of righteousness, being redeemed of God, becoming his sons and daughters; and thus they become new creatures; and unless they do this, they can in nowise inherit the kingdom of God" (Mosiah 27:25–26).

The Book of Mormon further demonstrates the danger of remaining in this state once we have become accountable and begin to sin. Abinadi taught, "He that *persists* in his own carnal nature, and *goes on* in the ways of sin and rebellion against God, *remaineth* in his fallen state and the devil hath all power over him. Therefore he is as though there was no redemption made, being an enemy to God" (Mosiah 16:5; emphasis added). One does not become natural through any particular action but rather as a result of being born into this fallen world and becoming accountable before God.

Though the Fall created a gulf between God and humanity, it was part of the plan from the beginning. Elder Bruce C. Hafen of the Seventy taught:

> The Lord restored His gospel through Joseph Smith because there had been an apostasy. Since the fifth century, Christianity taught that Adam and Eve's Fall was a tragic mistake, which led to the belief that humankind has an inherently evil nature. That view is wrong—not only about the Fall and human nature, but about the very purpose of life.
>
> The Fall was not a disaster. It wasn't a mistake or an accident. It was a deliberate part of the plan of salvation. We are God's spirit "offspring," sent to earth "innocent" of Adam's transgression. Yet our Father's plan subjects us to temptation and misery in this fallen world as the price to comprehend authentic joy. Without tasting the bitter, we actually *cannot* understand the sweet. We require mortality's discipline and refinement as the "next step in [our] development" toward becoming like our Father.[6]

The Fall is therefore a blessing: a step down, yet a step forward on the road to becoming what our Heavenly Father wants us to become.[7]

## OBEDIENCE AND COVENANTS

President Joseph F. Smith taught that "obedience is the first law of heaven."[8] However, there would be no salvation in obeying the law were it not for Christ. Abinadi insisted that "salvation doth not come by the law alone; and were it not for the atonement, which God himself shall make for the sins and iniquities of his people . . . they must unavoidably perish, notwithstanding [obedience to] the law" (Mosiah 13:28). Even Adam, though he was obedient to the commands issued by the voice of the Lord from Eden, still required an angel to come and teach him the purpose for his obedience and the name by which salvation would be available to his posterity (see Moses 5:4–9).

Obedience is a central part of the Father's plan of salvation as championed by Christ. By obedience we declare our love for the Lord (see John 14:15) as well as declare our allegiance to the Master we desire to serve (see Mosiah 5:13–15). Obedience is likewise one of the first covenants we make, both through baptism as well as through other sacred ordinances. King Benjamin's people expressed their willingness to follow Christ: "We are willing to enter into a covenant with our God to do his will, and to be obedient to his commandments in all things that he shall command us, all the remainder of our days" (Mosiah 5:5). Such a commitment to obey His words is vital to both relying on His merits and accessing the power that comes to His sons and His daughters through faith on His name.

Covenants are the Lord's appointed way of allowing His children access to His grace. Elder John A. Widtsoe taught: "When ordinances are performed, blessings are received which give power to man, power that belongs to the everyday affairs of this life as to a future life. It is not merely knowledge; not merely consecration; not merely a labeling, so to speak; but the actual conferring of power that may be used every day."[9]

The Book of Mormon has many examples of this pattern of covenant making and the subsequent power that flows into the life of a covenant person. One example is the people of King Benjamin. Upon hearing the gospel taught by their king, this group of good people—remember they had obediently traveled to the temple and had brought sacrifices to offer according to the law of Moses (see Mosiah 2:1–6)—

viewed themselves in their lost and fallen state and saw clearly that they were powerless without divine assistance. They cried out, "O have mercy, and apply the atoning blood of Christ that we may receive forgiveness of our sins, and our hearts may be purified; for we believe in Jesus Christ, the Son of God" (Mosiah 4:2).

It was then, as the Spirit entered into their hearts and their prayers were answered, that they received strength and assistance (see Mosiah 5:2–5). The Spirit also changed their hearts; they were born again as children of Christ, by covenant. As King Benjamin described it, "And now, because of the covenant which ye have made ye shall be called the children of Christ, his sons, and his daughters; for behold, this day he hath spiritually begotten you; for ye say that your hearts are changed through faith on his name; therefore, ye are born of him and have become his sons and his daughters" (Mosiah 5:7).

## CONCLUSION

The doctrine of the merit of Christ as taught in the Book of Mormon is a hopeful doctrine, but to accept it requires humility. It requires us to consider ourselves as "fools before God" (2 Nephi 9:42), as fallen and lost children who have no hope on our own of ever returning to a perfect Father's presence. At the same time, it is a liberating doctrine, for when it settles in our heart we can truly "lay aside the things of this world, and seek for the things of a better" (D&C 25:10). We can move our hope from *our* righteousness to *His*. In this way we can be confident and not in constant doubt about our own salvation. This is a critical step if we are to serve Him and our fellow beings here on the earth. If our own salvation is a matter of doubt, we cannot extend the kind of mercy, generosity, and forgiveness that we could if we were confident in our salvation through His merits.

Recognition of our inability to merit any good thing on our own (see Mosiah 2:21), as well as recognition of the Savior's all-sufficient merits, reveals a key to our salvation. It is His goodness, His sacrifice, His righteousness that merit an inheritance for the children of God. His merits and grace are both redemptive and reconstructive to fallen humans. His plan is developmental, and through reliance on His merits we can be saved, which Joseph Smith explained, is to be "assimilated into their [the Father and Son's] likeness."[10] Without access to His grace and His merits, such a change in fallen men and women would not be possible. With His merits and grace, however, we can become "just men [and women] made perfect through Jesus the mediator of the new covenant, who wrought out this perfect atonement through the shedding of his own blood" (D&C 76:69). Such is the debt we owe to Him and such is His gift to us, if we will rely "alone upon the merits of Christ, who [is] the author and the finisher of [our] faith" (Moroni 6:4).

---

## NOTES

1. "Come Thou Fount of Every Blessing," *Hymns* (Salt Lake City: The Church of Jesus Christ of Latter-day Saints, 1948), no. 70.

2. "Just as a man does not really desire food until he is hungry, so he does not desire the salvation of Christ until he knows why he needs Christ. No one adequately and properly knows why he needs Christ until he understands and accepts the doctrine of the Fall and its effect upon all mankind" (Ezra Taft Benson, "The Book of Mormon and the Doctrine and Covenants," *Ensign,* May 1987, 85).

3. John Calvin, *Institutes of the Christian Religion,* trans. Henry Beveridge (Grand Rapids, MI: Eerdmans, 1989), 2:1:8; emphasis added.

4. John Wesley, "Original Sin" (1759) in *The Sermons of John Wesley: An Anthology,* ed. Albert C. Outler and Richard P. Heitzenrater (Nashville: Abingdon Press, 1991), 334.

5. Augustine was one of the first to have such a view and his teachings spread effectively throughout Christianity (see Bruce L. Shelley, *Church History in Plain Language* [Nashville: Thomas Nelson Publishers, 1995], 129–31).

6. Bruce C. Hafen, "The Atonement: All for All," *Ensign,* May 2004, 97.

7. Elder Orson F. Whitney taught, "The Fall had a twofold direction— downward, yet forward. It brought man into the world and set his feet upon progression's highway" (*Cowley and Whitney on Doctrine,* comp. Forace Green [Salt Lake City: Bookcraft, 1963], 287).

8. Joseph F. Smith, in *Journal of Discourses* (London: Latter-day Saints' Book Depot, 1854–86), 16:247–48.

9. *The Message of the Doctrine and Covenants,* ed. G. Homer Durham (Salt Lake City: Bookcraft, 1969), 161.

10. Joseph Smith, *Lectures on Faith* (Salt Lake City: Deseret Book, 1985), 7:16.

*20*

---

# "PROPER ORDER": A POWERFUL PRECEPT OF THE BOOK OF MORMON

## *Brian K. Ray*

As the Second Coming of Jesus Christ draws near, the world appears to be caught in an intensifying maelstrom of chaos and confusion. In contrast to the personal and societal turmoil of the latter days, the Book of Mormon teaches that order can and must be achieved through Jesus Christ and His gospel. In fact, order—and the need for order—is one of the great precepts of the Book of Mormon.

By definition, order means being in the proper relationship or arrangement.[1] In a gospel context, order is found in enjoying a harmonious relationship with God. This chapter will examine what the Book of Mormon teaches about order, how students of the Book of Mormon can order their lives, and the related doctrines of ordination and ordinances.

### ORDER

The importance of the precept of order is evident in its repetition throughout the Book of Mormon and other sacred scriptures. In quoting the prophet Isaiah, Nephi taught his people that establishing order

---

*Brian K. Ray is a seminary principal and teacher in Mesa, Arizona.*

would be one of Jesus Christ's divine functions: "For unto us a child is born, unto us a son is given; and the government shall be upon his shoulder; and his name shall be called, Wonderful, Counselor, The Mighty God, The Everlasting Father, The Prince of Peace. Of the increase of government and peace there is no end, upon the throne of David, and upon his kingdom *to order it,* and to establish it with judgment and with justice from henceforth, even forever. The zeal of the Lord of Hosts will perform this" (2 Nephi 19:6–7; emphasis added). One need only look to the manner in which the Savior interacts with mankind and with His earthly institutions to learn much about order. His truly is a "house of order" (D&C 88:119; see also D&C 109:8; 132:8, 18), and following His teachings and example will bring order to any life or organization.

King Benjamin, Book of Mormon prophet and political leader, admonished his people to "see that all these things are done in wisdom and order; for it is not requisite that a man should run faster than he has strength. And again, it is expedient that he should be diligent, that thereby he might win the prize; therefore, all things must be done in order" (Mosiah 4:27). A life that is out of order is certainly not a Christlike life. An ordered life is one that places the Redeemer and His gospel foremost. President Howard W. Hunter explained that although we may naturally want things the other way around, order and progression come from having Jesus Christ first in our lives: "Living members put Christ first in their lives, knowing from what source their lives and progress come. There is a tendency for man to put himself in the center of the universe and expect others to conform to his wants and needs and desires. Yet nature does not honor that erroneous assumption. The central role in life belongs to God. Instead of asking him to do our bidding, we should seek to bring ourselves into harmony with his will, and thus continue our progress as a living member."[2]

One of the precious examples of order contained in the Book of Mormon is its description of nature, namely how celestial bodies follow the order established by the Creator. The abridger of the Nephite records, the prophet Mormon, addressed this astronomical order when describing the night wherein there was no darkness when the Savior was born: "And it came to pass that there was no darkness in all that night, but it was as light as though it was mid-day. And it came to pass that the sun did rise in the morning again, according to its proper order; and they knew that it was the day that the Lord should be born, because of the sign which had been given" (3 Nephi 1:19). The prophet Alma the Younger presented the order of heavenly bodies as evidence of God's reality to the sign-seeking Korihor: "Even the earth, and all things that are upon the face of it, yea, and its motion, yea, and also all the planets which move in their regular form do witness that there is a Supreme Creator" (Alma 30:44). Much can be learned from the planets that rotate around the sun in proper order. Modern revelation teaches that the earth will receive a celestial glory because it abides by the laws and order given to it by the Creator (see D&C 88:25–26). President James E. Faust taught that principles of order and obedience should govern the lives of men and women just as they govern celestial bodies:

> Consider the earth itself. It was formed out of matter and in the beginning was empty, desolate, and dark. Then came order as God commanded that the light should be divided from the darkness. God's command was obeyed, and the earth had its first day, followed by its first night. Then God ordered the creation of the atmosphere. He organized the sun, the moon, and the stars to shine in their appropriate times and seasons. After a series of commands and obedience to commands, the earth not only became habitable but beautiful. . . .
>
> This earth on which we dwell is an individual planet occupying a unique place in space. But it is also part of our solar system, an orderly system with . . . planets, asteroids, comets, and other celestial bodies that orbit the sun. Just as the earth is a planet in its own right, so each of us is an individual in our own sphere of habitation. We are individuals, but we live in families and communities where order provides a system of harmony that hinges on obedience to principles. Just as order gave life and beauty to the earth when it was dark and void, so it does to us.[3]

Consider what the adverse effects on mankind would be if the earth were not obedient to the laws governing its motion. The Book of

Mormon peoples were examples of how order, or the lack thereof, has a profound effect on individuals and societies. The blessed state of the Nephites approximately twenty-five years after the birth of Christ is a stark contrast to the ugly, horrifying circumstances immediately preceding the Nephites' destruction. Mormon commented that many years earlier, after having gained a monumental victory over the Gadianton robbers and having returned to their own lands, the Nephites enjoyed great peace and prosperity because their lives were in order: "Thus they did establish peace in all the land. And they began again to prosper and to wax great; and the twenty and sixth and seventh years passed away, and there was great order in the land; and they had formed their laws according to equity and justice. And now there was nothing in all the land to hinder the people from prospering continually, except they should fall into transgression" (3 Nephi 6:3–5). Sadly, this same group of Nephites who enjoyed the blessings of an ordered life fell into pride and wickedness, and only the most righteous survived the destruction incident to the Lord's Crucifixion.

While chronicling the cyclical nature of the Nephite civilization from righteousness and order to wickedness and chaos and back again, Mormon was eyewitness to his people's nadir. Mormon lamented the Nephite descent into self-ruin to his son, Moroni:

> O the depravity of my people! They are without order and without mercy. Behold, I am but a man, and I have but the strength of a man, and I cannot any longer enforce my commands.
>
> And they have become strong in their perversion; and they are alike brutal, sparing none, neither old nor young; and they delight in everything save that which is good; and the suffering of our women and our children upon all the face of this land doth exceed everything; yea, tongue cannot tell, neither can it be written.
>
> And now, my son, I dwell no longer upon this horrible scene. Behold, thou knowest the wickedness of this people; thou knowest that they are without principle, and past feeling; and

their wickedness doth exceed that of the Lamanites. (Moroni 9:18–20)

The destruction of the Nephites provides a chilling exclamation point to a precept that is repeated often throughout the record: order brings blessings of peace and prosperity, while disorder brings misery and despair. Elder L. Tom Perry taught that happiness and order are parallel precepts: "The gospel of Jesus Christ teaches hope and opportunity. To find the happiness we are seeking and rid ourselves of fear, we must be prepared to follow the system and order the Lord has established for His children here on earth."[4]

To bring order to our lives, President Boyd K. Packer taught that it is important to understand the origins of the word. The word *order* means a row, a rank, a series, or a regular arrangement.[5] In context of the gospel, we are in order if we are in harmony with, aligned with, and in the proper arrangement and relationship to God. The scriptural image of the strait and narrow path vividly depicts this principle (see 1 Nephi 8:20; 2 Nephi 31:18–19; Helaman 3:29). Certainly we cannot move very far along this strait and narrow path without coming in line with the end goal—a place in our Father's kingdom. And considering the imagery of the iron rod in Lehi's vision (see 1 Nephi 8), one can visualize travel along the strait and narrow path taking place in single-file lines, another example of order according to the word's definition. President Packer also taught that there are other words related to *order,* both etymologically and theologically, that help in our efforts to put our lives in order: *ordinance* and *ordination.* A study of the related principles of *ordinance* and *ordination* in prophetic teachings and how they bring order can facilitate practical, personal application of those principles.

## ORDINANCES

One of the clearest descriptions of the interrelatedness of *order, ordinance,* and *ordination* is found in Alma's teachings to Zeezrom and others in the land of Ammonihah. Alma taught that men were foreordained in the premortal existence to be ordained in mortality according to their faithfulness and explained to these apostates how ordination to the priesthood made possible the saving ordinances and order (see

Alma 13). Throughout Alma's teachings in Alma 13, the word *order* is used fourteen times, forms of the word *ordain* are used seven times, and *ordinance* or *ordinances* appear three times.[6] Alma's exposition on *order*—in concert with those of other prophets, both ancient and modern—underscores the profound nature of this precept.

An ordinance is a sacred rite through which an individual makes covenants with God. Etymologically, *ordinance* means to "put in order" or "regulate."[7] The ordinances of the gospel help individuals maintain order in their lives in several ways. One way is found in the teachings of the prophet Abinadi. Abinadi explained to King Noah and his priests that the law of Moses alone could not provide salvation but that salvation only comes through the "redemption of God" (Mosiah 13:32). Abinadi taught that the ordinances of the law of Moses served a special purpose: "Therefore there was a law given them, yea, a law of performances and of ordinances, a law which they were to observe strictly from day to day, to keep them in remembrance of God and their duty towards him" (Mosiah 13:30). While referring specifically to the law of Moses, Abinadi's teaching applies to all ordinances. Ordinances, and their attendant covenants, serve to remind us of our "duty to God" after having received them (see Alma 7:22).

The power of ordinances to remind—and, consequently, to order—is evident in the ordinance of the sacrament. President David O. McKay highlighted this principle as follows: "Order, reverence, attention to divine promises—the promise to enter into the fold of Christ, to cherish virtues mentioned in the gospel of Christ, to keep them ever in mind, to love the Lord wholeheartedly, and to labor, even at the sacrifice of self, for the brotherhood of man—these and all kindred virtues are associated with the partaking of the sacrament. It is good to meet together and especially to renew our covenants with God in that holy sacrament."[8]

Ultimately, faithfulness to ordinances helps those who have entered into such to remain close to God and worthy of His blessings. The Savior's quotation of Malachi to the Nephites gives emphasis to this principle. The Lord reminds His people that even though they have drifted from Him through unrighteous actions, He will draw close to them to the degree that they draw close to Him. "Even from the days of your fathers ye are gone away from mine ordinances, and have not kept them. Return unto me and I will return unto you, saith the Lord of Hosts" (3 Nephi 24:7). While some failed to see and understand the connection between being faithful to ordinances and the blessings of the Lord—"It is vain to serve God, and what doth it profit that we have kept his ordinances and that we have walked mournfully before the Lord of Hosts?" (3 Nephi 24:14)—the righteous recognized and remembered how maintaining order in their lives by keeping the ordinances brings the blessings of heaven and leads to exaltation: "Then they that feared the Lord spake often one to another, and the Lord hearkened and heard; and a book of remembrance was written before him for them that feared the Lord, and that thought upon his name. And they shall be mine, saith the Lord of Hosts, in that day when I make up my jewels; and I will spare them as a man spareth his own son that serveth him. Then shall ye return and discern between the righteous and the wicked, between him that serveth God and him that serveth him not" (3 Nephi 24:16–18).

Those same promises and blessings are available to the Saints of this dispensation. Those who bring order to their lives by participating in and remaining faithful to the saving ordinances will one day return to the presence of the Father and receive a place in His kingdom. An additional result of spiritual orderliness will be peace in our Savior, a veritable "anchor to the souls of men" (Ether 12:4).

## ORDINATION

Integral to the precepts of order and ordinances is the principle of ordination. In large measure, the Lord calls upon His people to assist in providing the blessings of order in individual lives, especially in relation to ordinances. God delegates His authority—the priesthood—to worthy male members of His Church and charges them with the responsibility of shepherding His children and performing the saving ordinances for them. There is no other way for ordinances—and the subsequent spiritual order—to take place without the authority of His priesthood. Elder Robert L. Simpson taught: "With all of the soberness of my soul, I declare that God's house is a house of order. His holy purposes are not carried out by man's whim or fancy but, rather, in this church which bears his name, sacred ordinances can only be performed by proper authority."[9]

The Book of Mormon plainly teaches the profound importance of priesthood ordination in God's plan. According to Alma's testimony to Zeezrom, those ordained to the Melchizedek Priesthood are given the sacred responsibility to care for the sons and daughters of God and to help bring order to their lives. "Now they were ordained after this manner—being called with a holy calling, and ordained with a holy ordinance, and taking upon them the high priesthood of the holy order, which calling, and ordinance, and high priesthood, is without beginning or end" (Alma 13:8). This same principle was taught in modern times by Elder Bruce R. McConkie: "The Melchizedek Priesthood is the highest and holiest order ever given to men on earth. It is the power and authority to do all that is necessary to save and exalt the children of men. It is the very priesthood held by the Lord Jesus Christ himself and by virtue of which he was able to gain eternal life in the kingdom of his Father."[10]

The Book of Mormon outlines several examples of how those who are ordained bring order. First, as mentioned, ordination provides the power and authority to perform ordinances. For example, authority was given by the Savior and His prophets to baptize and administer the sacrament (see 3 Nephi 7:25; 18:5). Second, ordination to the priesthood can also include the opportunity to preside over God's Church (see Mosiah 25:19; Alma 6:1). President Brigham Young taught that governing is one of the great purposes of the priesthood: "The Priesthood . . . is [the] perfect order and system of government, and this alone can deliver the human family from all the evils which now afflict its members, and insure them happiness and felicity hereafter."[11]

Those who preside are given keys to direct the work and ensure that ordinances are performed according to the proper order. President James E. Faust explained the function of priesthood keys in establishing order:

> Priesthood is the greatest power on earth. Worlds were created by and through the priesthood. To safeguard this sacred power, all priesthood holders act under the direction of those

who hold the keys of the priesthood. These keys bring order into our lives and into the organization of the Church. For us, priesthood power is the power and authority delegated by God to act in His name for the salvation of His children. Caring for others is the very essence of priesthood responsibility. It is the power to bless, to heal, and to administer the saving ordinances of the gospel. Righteous priesthood authority is most needed within the walls of our own homes. It must be exercised in great love. This is true of all priesthood holders—deacon, teacher, priest, elder, high priest, patriarch, Seventy, and Apostle.[12]

Third, priesthood ordination gives to the ordained the responsibility and the authority to teach and preach to the members of God's Church. After having gathered those who believed in the words of Abinadi and baptized them, the prophet Alma put the Church of God in order. To accomplish that purpose, Alma, "having authority from God, ordained priests; even one priest to every fifty of their number did he ordain to preach unto them, and to teach them concerning the things pertaining to the kingdom of God" (Mosiah 18:18). Moroni's final instructions before concluding the Nephite record include details about the procedure and the purpose for ordaining priesthood holders to teach and preach: "In the name of Jesus Christ I ordain you to be a priest, (or, if he be a teacher) I ordain you to be a teacher, to preach repentance and remission of sins through Jesus Christ, by the endurance of faith on his name to the end. Amen. And after this manner did they ordain priests and teachers, according to the gifts and callings of God unto men; and they ordained them by the power of the Holy Ghost, which was in them" (Moroni 3:3–4).

We find safety in following the counsel of those ordained to preside and to preach, especially those sustained as prophets, seers, and revelators. A spiritually ordered life will be the result of obedience to their teachings. Elder L. Tom Perry explained, "Prophets through the ages have taught us to be obedient to the laws of the Lord, and these laws are the foundation of our existence here and will bring order out of chaos."[13] The importance of following the counsel of the duly ordained was reiterated by Elder Henry B. Eyring: "There seems to be no end to the Savior's desire to lead us to safety. And there is constancy in the way He shows us the path. He calls by more than one means so that it will reach those willing to accept it. And those means always include sending the message by the mouths of His prophets, whenever people have qualified to have the prophets of God among them. Those authorized servants are always charged with warning the people, telling them the way to safety."[14]

## CONCLUSION

Jacob, one of the early Book of Mormon prophets, counseled his Nephite brethren to "reconcile [themselves] to the will of God" (2 Nephi 10:24). *Reconciliation* connotes a return to a previous position, an elimination of differences between two beings, literally "to sit again with" God.[15] Reconciliation and order both have reference to an individual's position in relation to God. Jacob taught unmistakably that it is only in and through Jesus Christ that order and reconciliation are possible. He encouraged his people to "come unto the Lord, the Holy One. . . . Behold, the way for man is narrow, but it lieth in a straight course before him, and the keeper of the gate is the Holy One of Israel; and he employeth no servant there; and there is none other way save it be by the gate" (2 Nephi 9:41). Again, the imagery of the strait and narrow path is both beautiful and profound and adds to our understanding of order. We bring spiritual order to our lives by entering the narrow path (see 2 Nephi 31:16–21). We do so through sacred ordinances such as baptism and confirmation performed by one duly ordained. Order is increased as we continue along the path toward God by obedience, successive ordinances, and enduring well the vicissitudes of mortality. Conversely, deviations from the path result in a loss of order, or turmoil, confusion, and sorrow. Ultimately, the order that comes from being on the narrow path, or being in line or harmony with God, will result in a sweet reunion with—reconciliation with—the Father and the Son, who stand "with open arms to receive [us]!" (Mormon 6:17).

The precept of order in the Book of Mormon is one of the plain and precious truths contained therein. The Book of Mormon teaches that to successfully put our lives in order, we must do so through the proper application of gospel principles, through participation in and faithfulness to the saving ordinances, and through the blessings of the priesthood bestowed by those who have been properly ordained. It is through these processes that we bring ourselves into harmony, in order or in line with, the will of our Heavenly Father through the Atonement of His Son and our Savior, Jesus Christ. Applying this beautiful precept will assist disciples to enjoy the blessings of peace and stability in this life and exaltation in the world to come.

---

NOTES

1.  See Robert K. Barnhart, ed., *Chambers Dictionary of Etymology* (New York: Larousse Kingfisher, Chambers, 1988), s.v. "order." Additionally, the words *precept* and *order* are etymologically related.

2.  Howard W. Hunter, "Am I a 'Living' Member?" *Ensign,* May 1987, 17–18.

3.  James E. Faust, "Obedience: The Path to Freedom," *Ensign,* May 1999, 45–46.

4.  L. Tom Perry, "When Ye Are Prepared, Ye Shall Not Fear," *Ensign,* November 1981, 37.

5.  See Boyd K. Packer, *Things of the Soul* (Salt Lake City: Bookcraft, 1996), 186; see also Boyd K. Packer, *The Holy Temple* (Salt Lake City: Bookcraft, 1980), 144–45; see also Barnhart, *Chambers Dictionary of Etymology,* s.v. "order," "ordinance," "ordain."

6.  See Richard Dilworth Rust, *Feasting on the Word: The Literary Testimony of the Book of Mormon* (Salt Lake City: Deseret Book, 1997), 129–30.

7.  Barnhart, *Chambers Dictionary of Etymology,* s.v. "ordinance."

8.  David O. McKay, *Gospel Ideals* (Salt Lake City: Deseret Book, 1954), 147.

9.  Robert L. Simpson, "The Most Vital Information," *Ensign,* November 1974, 46.

10.  Bruce R. McConkie, "The Doctrine of the Priesthood," *Ensign,* May 1982, 33.

11.  Brigham Young, *Discourses of Brigham Young,* comp. John A. Widtsoe (Salt Lake City: Deseret Book, 1954), 130.

12.  James E. Faust, "Power of the Priesthood," *Ensign,* May 1997, 41.

13.  L. Tom Perry, "Family Traditions," *Ensign,* May 1990, 20.

14.  Henry B. Eyring, "Finding Safety in Counsel," *Ensign,* May 1997, 24.

15.  Russell M. Nelson, "The Atonement," *Ensign,* November 1996, 34.

## 21

# PROPHETIC PRINCIPLES FOR BUILDING ZION

## *Neal W. Kramer*

*Blessed are they who seek to bring forth my Zion.*
—1 NEPHI 13:37

W hen we think of the doctrine of Zion[1] as taught in the Book of Mormon, our minds often turn to 4 Nephi.[2] The book describes in a few verses a society organized around the principles taught by the Savior to a righteous remnant of Nephites and Lamanites at the temple in Bountiful. Some important characteristics of this community of Christians were love of God, faith, family, hope, peace, security, and happiness. Indeed, Mormon powerfully asserts that "there could not be a happier people among all the people who had been created by the hand of God" (4 Nephi 1:16). Imagine that! This Book of Mormon Zion had been foretold from the time Lehi and his family left Jerusalem. In preparation for that great day, crucial principles about Zion were regularly taught by prophets like King Benjamin and Alma the Elder. But the Book of Mormon was written for our day to assist us

*Neal W. Kramer is a part-time instructor in the English Department at Brigham Young University.*

in preparing for the building of our Zion. And so the Book of Mormon calls us to come unto Christ and take upon us His name by building Zion, which is founded on the principles of equality, unity, covenants, and priesthood organization.

## EQUALITY

Equality is a prerequisite for Zion. It is a formidable principle because it can be achieved only through consecration and sacrifice. Equality has a wide variety of definitions, which include parity, fairness, impartiality, and egalitarianism. Mormon offers a more specific definition of Zion: all persons in the community "imparting to one another both temporally and spiritually according to their needs and their wants" (Mosiah 18:29). It suggests not so much sameness as individualism restrained by righteousness. This conception of equality begins with a fundamentally true principle: we are all children of Heavenly Father, and we may all become "the children of Christ" (4 Nephi 1:17). In turn, this principle is consistent with Nephi's teaching that "all are alike unto God" (2 Nephi 26:33). In similar terms, the Apostle Peter explained that "God is no respecter of persons" (Acts 10:34).

Old Testament prophets also regularly taught that righteousness requires that no person be given special treatment. They taught that respect derives more from who we are than from what we have acquired. In matters of justice, the commandment is clear: "Thou shalt not respect the person of the poor, nor honour the person of the mighty" (Leviticus 19:15).

And the Apostle James teaches that "if ye have respect to persons, ye commit sin, and are convinced of the law as transgressors" (James 2:9). This teaching suggests that worldly titles and all the honors and regalia associated with them are inimical to the Zion concept of equality. President Spencer W. Kimball taught that the "Lord has made a vibrant contrast between the honors of the world and the honors which can come to the soul."[3] In Zion there can be no unrighteous distinctions among the children of Christ. Zion honors only heavenly accomplishments.

Mormon underlines the truth of this principle by highlighting what happens when unrighteous distinctions enter a society and some are arbitrarily respected more than others. Speaking of the people during Alma the Younger's rule as chief judge, Mormon states, "Alma saw the wickedness of the church, and he saw also that the example of the church began to lead those who were unbelievers on from one piece of iniquity to another, thus bringing on the destruction of the people. Yea, he saw great inequality among the people, some lifting themselves up with their pride, despising others, turning their backs upon the needy and the naked and those who were hungry, and those who were athirst, and those who were sick and afflicted" (Alma 4:11–12). It should come as no surprise that the actions of members of the Church, supposed believers, were especially damning. Even nonbelievers were aware of the righteous standard the prophets had laid down. When people in the Church gave up their commitment to righteousness, it opened the floodgates for others to accept iniquity in the form of recognition, success, and pride as the keys to happiness.

In 3 Nephi, Mormon again assesses the causes of wickedness in Nephite society and makes a similar diagnosis. "Now the cause of this iniquity of the people was this—Satan had great power, unto the stirring up of the people to do all manner of iniquity, and to the puffing them up with pride, tempting them to seek for power, and authority, and riches, and the vain things of the world" (3 Nephi 6:15). A crucial feature of unrighteous respect for persons is the desire for power. Once power has been achieved, inequality will not be far behind. Those people are iniquitous who, under the influence of Satan, strive for power, seek for personal status, recognize their friends with dishonest honors or awards, and reward the special interests of people who enrich them while shunning those who cannot pay.

As President Kimball taught, "The enemies of faith know no God but force, no devotion but the use of force."[4] Abuse of authority almost naturally follows the acquisition of power. The Prophet Joseph Smith taught, "We have learned by sad experience that it is the nature and disposition of almost all men, as soon as they get a little authority, as they suppose, they will immediately begin to exercise unrighteous dominion" (D&C 121:39). Laws may then be prejudicially enforced, with the poor and the weak often incarcerated for inconsequential acts. Such authority may then be employed to pervert the good, to "call evil good, and good evil, . . . put darkness for light, and light for darkness, . . . [and] put bitter for sweet, and sweet for bitter" (2 Nephi 15:20; see also Isaiah 5:20). And what will be their reward? The vain things of the world: mansions, luxury cars, yachts, rare books, fine art, extravagant jewels and apparel, fame, and so on.

President Marion G. Romney contrasted these desires and practices with "a willingness to forego luxuries, prayerful consideration of all major purchases, and learning to live within our means."[5] The prophet Jacob added that this vanity arises because "ye suppose that ye are better than they" (Jacob 2:13).

A principle of equality parallel to the denial of unrighteous status distinctions is the erasure of a society in which some are obviously rich and others are obviously poor. The anti-Christ Nehor was a firm advocate of the belief that the rich are better than the poor. As a consequence, Alma the Younger spent much of his career fighting against the impact on the Church of Nehorism, a term I coined to name the ideology of the "order of the man who slew Gideon," or Nehor (Alma 2:1). Nehor's career started with beginning "to be lifted up in the pride of his heart, and to wear very costly apparel, yea, and even began to establish a church after the manner of his preaching" (Alma 1:6). He founded a church based on popularity, the ability of the wealthy to give him large amounts of money, and his ability to use his own costly apparel to create the impression of superiority over the true church led by Alma the Younger.

When Alma saw "all their inequality, [he] began to be very sorrowful; nevertheless the Spirit of the Lord did not fail him" (Alma 4:15). This led to his leaving the judgment seat to combat the teachings of Nehor by "preach[ing] the word of God unto them, to stir them up in remembrance of their duty, and that he might pull down, by the word of God, all the pride and craftiness and all the contentions which were among his people, seeing no way that he might reclaim them save it were in bearing down in pure testimony against them" (Alma 4:19).

Alma and his companions later visited the Zoramites, who were by then a spiritual catastrophe. Alma's "heart was grieved; for . . . they were a wicked and perverse people. . . . Their hearts were lifted up unto great boasting, in their pride" (Alma 31:24–25). In mighty prayer he asked the Lord for "success" in his efforts to combat the Zoramites' commitment to "costly apparel, and their ringlets, and their bracelets, and their ornaments of gold, and all their precious things which they are ornamented with." For Alma saw that "their hearts [were] set upon them" and that they viewed their wealth as confirmation of their righteousness and their special status in God's eyes: "They cry unto thee and say—We thank thee, O God, for we are a chosen people unto thee, while others shall perish" (Alma 31:32, 28).

The immediate consequence of the Zoramite perversion of Zion was the rejection of the poor. As Nehor had taught, if costly apparel and financial support for the ministry were crucial to a true church, then surely the Church would not minister to the poor. It would cater solely to the rich, those who could pay the price of admission.

In fact, the Zoramites created an environment in which the poor were "despised of all men because of their poverty." The Zoramite poor reported to Alma that they had been rejected "more especially by our priests; for they have cast us out of our synagogues which we have labored abundantly to build with our own hands; and they have cast us out because of our exceeding poverty" (Alma 32:5).

The Zoramites had decided that God's chief blessings were gold, silver, fine clothes, and extravagant places of worship. The prophets taught otherwise: "Behold, doth he [God] cry unto any, saying: Depart from me? Behold, I say unto you, Nay; but he saith: Come unto me all ye ends of the earth, buy milk and honey, without money and without price" (2 Nephi 26:25). There are no economic requirements for those who come to Zion.

Alma urged his people to reject Nehorism and the persecution it generated. He fostered and built a society based on principles of Zion. In this society, priests supported themselves: "And when the priests left their labor to impart the word of God unto the people, the people also left their labors to hear the word of God. And when the priest had imparted unto them the word of God they all returned again diligently unto their labors; and the priest, not esteeming himself above his hearers, for the preacher was no better than the hearer, neither was the teacher any better than the learner; and thus they were all equal, and they did all labor, every man according to his strength." Together they worked hard to erase the distinction between rich and poor: "And they did impart of their substance, every man according to that which he had, to the poor, and the needy, and the sick, and the afflicted; and they did not wear costly apparel, yet they were neat and comely" (Alma 1:26–27). When the Book of Mormon Zion had been built after the coming of the Savior, "there were not rich and poor, bond and free, but they were all made free, and partakers of the heavenly gift" (4 Nephi 1:3). They were equal.

## UNITY

A second principle of Zion closely related to equality is unity. Words commonly associated with unity include *harmony, agreement, accord,* and *unanimity.* A more specific definition of unity is "an undivided or unbroken completeness or totality with nothing wanting."[6] In the Book of Mormon Zion, "they were in one, the children of Christ, and heirs to the kingdom of God" (4 Nephi 1:17). Their lives were characterized by singleness of purpose, deep faith in Christ and His gospel, love for family, and equality. In a revelation to the Prophet Joseph Smith, the Savior emphasized the importance of unity: "If ye are not one ye are not mine" (D&C 38:27). If we are not one, we cannot live in Zion, for a Zion people are "of one heart and one mind, and [dwell] in righteousness" (Moses 7:18).

As he did with equality, Mormon often shows us the value of unity by giving examples of the causes and effects of disunity. One especially damaging cause is contention and disputation (see 4 Nephi 1:17). When the Savior visited the Nephites, He taught that "the devil . . . is the father of contention, and he stirreth up the hearts of men to contend with anger, one with another" (3 Nephi 11:29). He also commanded the righteous that "there shall be no disputations among you, as there have hitherto been; neither shall there be disputations among you concerning the points of my doctrine, as there have hitherto been" (3 Nephi 11:28). According to Lehi, a primary purpose of scripture, especially the Book of Mormon, is stopping contention. In the patriarchal blessing Lehi gave his son Joseph, who was born in the wilderness, he promised, "That which shall be written by the fruit of thy loins, and also that which shall be written by the fruit of the loins of Judah, shall grow together, unto the confounding of false doctrines and laying down of contentions, and establishing peace among the fruit of thy loins . . . saith the Lord" (2 Nephi 3:12). The sowing of discord was a constant problem among the Nephites and was a primary cause of their ultimate demise.

The Book of Mormon anti-Christs and their followers were especially adept at sowing contention. The lawyer Zeezrom, for example, was a follower of Nehor, and Mormon describes him as "a man who was expert in the devices of the devil, that he might destroy that which was good" (Alma 11:21). Like other judges and lawyers in Ammonihah, he "did stir up the people to riotings, and all manner of disturbances and wickedness, that they might have more employ, that they might get money."

Being adept at these skills, he stirred up "the people against Alma and Amulek" (Alma 11:20). He sought to intimidate, threaten, weaken, and confuse the prophets by plying the tools of his trade. His first challenge to Alma and Amulek was the temptation of money. As we have already seen, the Nehors put great stock in money, which conferred on them greater status. The essence of priestcraft is to teach false (or even true) doctrine in the pursuit of wealth and power.[7] And so Zeezrom tempted Amulek: "Behold, here are six onties of silver, and all these will I give thee if thou wilt deny the existence of a Supreme Being" (Alma 11:22).

When Amulek refused the money, Zeezrom tried false doctrine, by asking Amulek to deny the Atonement. "Shall [the Son of God] save his people in their sins?" (Alma 11:34). Amulek again demurs. Zeezrom's question is cunning in its subtlety and chilling in its effect. Nehor had taught "that all mankind should be saved at the last day, and that they need not fear nor tremble, but that they might lift up their heads and rejoice; for the Lord had created all men, and had also redeemed all men; and, in the end, all men should have eternal life" (Alma 1:4). This is the false doctrine of universal salvation without repentance, a doctrine that strongly denounces the doctrine of Christ (see 3 Nephi 11:31–39).

In light of Nehor's false teachings, Zeezrom's temptation proclaims that men do not need a redeemer, hearkening back to the premortal

Council in Heaven, where Satan sought to preempt the Atonement: "I will redeem all mankind, that one soul shall not be lost" (Moses 4:1).

Amulek, understanding the temptation, undermines its cunning premise by bearing powerful, clear testimony of the Savior: "And he shall come into the world to redeem his people; and he shall take upon him the transgressions of those who believe on his name; and these are they that shall have eternal life, and salvation cometh to none else" (Alma 11:40). Prophets seek to build Zion by replacing deception with testimony and contention with conversion.

A second feature of unity, as described in the Book of Mormon, comes by "following the light from above."[8] This of course means simply that we follow the Savior and not another leader or teacher from the world. The prophet Nephi reveals what the Savior requires: "Follow thou me. Wherefore, my beloved brethren, can we follow Jesus save we shall be willing to keep the commandments of the Father?" (2 Nephi 31:10).

In contrast, the anti-Christs reject the Zion teaching of living according to the word of God and following Christ. A strong example of rejecting the ways of God and replacing them with the ways of the world is Korihor. Korihor's pernicious teachings reflect Nehor's founding principle "that every priest and teacher ought to become popular" (Alma 1:3). That is, the measure of the truth of a man's teaching depends on how closely it coincides with what people want to hear rather than what God has commanded.

Korihor takes the principle of popularity to its logical conclusion, which is that mankind needs no redemption, and therefore, there is no God. "Why do ye look for a Christ?" he seems to ask. "Why waste your hopes on redemption, when the world and all its pleasure, goods, and power lie before you?" The question relies on the premise that "every man fare[s] in this life according to the management of the creature; therefore every man prosper[s] according to his genius, and that every man conquer[s] according to his strength; and whatsoever a man [does is] no crime." Korihor sought thoroughly to remove God from life. He deplored religion as something entirely produced by wicked men who seek "to usurp power and authority over [their followers], to keep them in ignorance, that they may not lift up their heads" (Alma 30:17, 23).

Korihor's alternative was simple: reject revelation, splinter into competing groups, live for the moment. In other words, reject Zion and the revelation that is its lifeblood. President Boyd K. Packer has taught that those standing "on Zion's hill" can "see continuing revelation, open to the Church and to each individual member."[9]

Unity is also a principle of Zion because it produces peace. At the end of his reign, King Mosiah appeals to his people to reject being ruled by kings, who have too much power, and instead choose "wise men to be judges, that will judge this people according to the commandments of God" (Mosiah 29:11). The purpose of this change is straightforward: "to establish peace throughout the land, that there should be no wars nor contentions, no stealing, nor plundering, nor murdering, nor any manner of iniquity" (Mosiah 29:14). Mosiah's teachings thus clarify what the Nephites most want and almost never achieve—peace.

In the Book of Mormon, the principles of disunity feed the ever-hungry, never-satisfied monster of war. Mormon himself is profoundly troubled by the consequences of war that he witnessed. He laments, "It is impossible for the tongue to describe, or for man to write a perfect description of the horrible scene of the blood and carnage which was among the people, both of the Nephites and of the Lamanites; and every heart was hardened, so that they delighted in the shedding of blood continually" (Mormon 4:11). He condemns people who cause war, such as Amalickiah, Gidgiddoni, Zarahemna, Ammoron, Amlici. He praises people who rise up against the truly wicked and defend their families even to the shedding of their own blood, like Helaman, Captain Moroni, Teancum, Lachoneus. And he introduces us to the Anti-Nephi-Lehies, a people once so immersed in the wicked traditions of their war-like ancestors that after their conversion they refuse to risk committing such sins by taking up arms. Mormon speaks of these people with deep respect: "When these Lamanites were brought to believe and to know the truth, they were firm, and would suffer even unto death rather than commit sin; and thus we see that they buried their weapons of peace, or they buried the weapons of war, for peace" (Alma 24:19). The Anti-Nephi-Lehies were truly converted and chose to live for Zion. In our own day, Elder Russell M. Nelson has urged that peace will come "if leaders and citizens of nations would apply the teachings of Jesus Christ. Ours could then be an age of unparalleled peace and progress." Unified commitment to building Zion can replace war and contention with the true peace of Christ.[10]

## COVENANTS

Zion cannot be built without making covenants. In fact, "'Zion cannot be built up,' the Lord said, 'unless it is by the principles of the law of the celestial kingdom.' The covenant of consecration is central to this law."[11] Covenants allow equality and unity to be maintained, nourished, and perpetuated. Covenant-makers are peacemakers. The covenants bind each partaker to a community of the pure in heart, dispelling feelings of isolation and loneliness and generating a profound sense of belonging.[12] Covenants allow us to belong to Christ and to each other. In the Book of Mormon Zion, covenants helped create a society where "the people were all converted unto the Lord," "they had all things common among them," "they were all made free," "they did heal the sick, and raise the dead, and cause the lame to walk, and the blind to receive their sight, and the deaf to hear," "they did build cities," and "they were married, and given in marriage, and were blessed according to the multitude of the promises which the Lord had made unto them" (4 Nephi 1:2, 3, 5, 7, 11). As 4 Nephi teaches, covenants place all who make them in a position to receive blessings as promised to them by God.[13]

King Benjamin described some specific ways in which his people, builders of Zion, were to keep the covenant (and thereby receive God's blessings) through which they would be "called the children of Christ, his sons, and his daughters" (Mosiah 5:7). These saints had "the Spirit of the Lord [come] upon them, and they were filled with joy, having received a remission of their sins, and having peace of conscience, because of the exceeding faith which they had in Jesus Christ." In that condition, they were prepared to be taught how to live after such a glorious experience. The measure of their faithfulness would be their actions: "If you believe all these things see that ye do them" (Mosiah 4:3, 10). King Benjamin then describes what must be done. A Zion people must live in peace. They must be just and fair, their labors and transactions defined by honesty and integrity (Mosiah 14:13). They must take responsibility for happy family life, including teaching their children about Zion and the covenants that bind it together (Mosiah 4:14–15).

King Benjamin also taught, in the words of President Marion G. Romney, that "caring for the poor is a covenantal obligation."[14] He does so by presenting us with a "hard saying" (John 6:60): "Ye will not suffer that the beggar putteth up his petition to you in vain, and turn him out to perish" (Mosiah 4:16). Because it is very difficult to know what is fair or just with regard to a beggar, a Zion people must not say, "The man has brought upon himself his misery; therefore I will stay my hand, and will not give unto him of my food, nor impart unto him of my substance that he may not suffer, for his punishments are just" (Mosiah 4:17).

This grand call is not simply a request to drop coins into a beggar's cup. It requires the full extension of hospitality, sustenance, and succor to those in need. It makes Zion a place where the failed and forlorn are raised up again, where "independence, self-respect, dignity, and self-reliance will be fostered, and free agency maintained."[15] Christ changes the poor by lifting them out of poverty and into the dignified world of the self-reliant, whatever the cost. This same principle requires that even the poor will carry in their hearts the willingness to give. King Benjamin's teachings emphasize that for Zion to flourish the covenants made upon entry must be nourished and kept (see Mosiah 4:24). The intensity of such an enterprise may become so overwhelming that we find ourselves trapped in our own expectations. Therefore, King Benjamin concludes with the admonition that "all these things are [to be] done in wisdom and order"; the efforts of making and keeping covenants in Zion must be organized and administered (Mosiah 4:27).

## PRIESTHOOD ORGANIZATION

Once the covenants have been made and Zion communities have been founded, Book of Mormon prophets follow priesthood principles to maintain Zion by putting "the priesthood of God to work."[16] This means organizing quorums, defining responsibilities, and teaching priesthood holders their duty (see D&C 107). The work and the workers are bound together by covenant (see D&C 84:33–40). The priesthood is the organization and the power through which Zion principles are implemented. When the Savior visited the Nephites and Lamanites,

He called men to whom He gave power to baptize in His name (see 3 Nephi 11:21). He taught them the specific manner in which to baptize and taught them the proper words and actions by which to perform the ordinance (see 3 Nephi 11:23–27). He organized them into a quorum with a designated leader (see 3 Nephi 12:1). He taught them true doctrine, from which they should not diverge. He introduced them to all present and urged the multitude to listen carefully to what they taught. He instituted the ordinance of the sacrament (see 3 Nephi 18:1–11). He prayed that the Father would allow them to receive the Holy Ghost (see 3 Nephi 19:20–21). He left them to run His Church in His absence (see 3 Nephi 27:5–12). The priesthood holders, the power, and the ordinances combined constituted the priesthood, the mortar that would hold the bricks of Zion together.

Such a conjunction of people and power cannot function as a loose collection of individuals who follow their own impulses, doing whatever they choose. We must belong to the Savior's true Church, which involves structure, leadership, cooperation, and united effort in a common purpose to maintain and expand Zion.[17] Priesthood organization encompasses all of that and more. Before the Savior's coming, other prophets had also organized Church communities in order to build Zion. Their experience helps us to see more clearly how this is to be achieved.

After Alma the Elder and his people were baptized, they formed a fledgling Zion community. Alma baptized them all by virtue of the "authority" he had received "from the Almighty God" (Mosiah 18:13). All these people together constituted "the church of Christ" (Mosiah 18:17). Using the same authority from God that had enabled him to baptize the group, Alma then called and ordained priests. Each priest was given responsibility over fifty members of the Church of Christ. Priests were to teach their flocks "concerning the things pertaining to the kingdom of God," which comprised the teachings of Alma and what "had been spoken by the mouth of the holy prophets" (Mosiah 18:19). They focused on the basic principles of the gospel: "Repentance and faith on the Lord, who had redeemed his people" (Mosiah 18:20). They were to maintain unity by "having one faith and one baptism, having their hearts knit together in unity and in love one towards another."

This tiny group was thereby enabled to become "the children of God" (Mosiah 18:21–22). The priesthood was the authority to baptize, organize, preach, and teach. The men who did this work were priests. The institutions and organizations auxiliary to their core callings increased their ability to do their work effectively. People thereby empowered by God were able to organize and persevere, binding their flocks together by covenants and ordinances and teaching them true and fundamental principles of the gospel of Jesus Christ (see Mosiah 18:29). But such a community must also provide its members with incentives to continue to grow, organizing times and places for study, designing curriculum, providing opportunities for fellowship and service, and so on.[18] Priesthood organization allowed this to happen in wisdom and in order, as the experience of Alma the Elder demonstrates.

Once Alma the Elder had led his people back to Zarahemla, he established a church there as well. In this church strict rules were established for priests and teachers. In keeping with the practice of King Benjamin, who had "labored with [his] own hands" rather than be supported by his people, priests were required to work to support themselves and their families (Mosiah 2:14). King Benjamin had very clearly explained his reasons for the practice. He believed that he could not serve his people if, in fact, they were "laden with taxes" in order to pay him a salary or provide him and those around him with unnecessary royal luxury.[19] From this, we learn that work must be central to Zion.[20] First of all, Zion must be built, and only organized work directed by the priesthood will achieve that. But Zion will also expand; it will never be a static and passive society (see D&C 42:42). Hard work and effort will characterize its people, because they "believe not only in the gospel of spiritual salvation, but also in the gospel of temporal salvation."[21] The Book of Mormon teaches that each person worked, "every man according to his strength." In Alma we read that "the priests left their labor to impart the word of God unto the people, [and] the people also left their labors to hear the word of God." Beyond this, a priest was taught to maintain personal humility, "for the preacher was no better than the hearer, neither was the teacher any better than the learner" (Alma 1:26). Worldly status or wealth was not attached to the priesthood, nor was wealth or status a prerequisite for church service. In Zion, the practices and attitudes of priests and teachers along with covenants hold the community together. Therefore, priesthood organization is the backbone of Zion; without it, Zion cannot flourish.

## CONCLUSION

Book of Mormon prophets convincingly teach us to desire to build and expand Zion and to "look forward with one eye" to the day of its completion (Mosiah 18:21). They explain to us what Zion is and which practices will help us work toward it. They also teach us that Zion can now be built up by living the doctrines of the gospel of Jesus Christ and joining His Church. For Latter-day Saints, such a life must be characterized by equality, unity, covenants, and priesthood organization. Careful study of the Book of Mormon will help us to become more deeply committed to building Zion, The Church of Jesus Christ of Latter-day Saints, the kingdom of God. We will learn from the example of past righteous peoples how this is to be done, step by step. If we do not understand what is required in order to seek Zion, we will never be able to labor for Zion. But if we do not go to work, our understanding will surely be antiseptic and academic. All who understand the principles taught by Book of Mormon prophets must therefore learn to work together in this greatest of all causes. As Nephi records, "Blessed are they who shall seek to bring forth my Zion" (1 Nephi 13:37). I pray that we may be among them.

---

## NOTES

1. I rely on a definition of Zion offered by Elder Bruce R. McConkie: "Be it remembered that Zion is people; Zion is the pure in heart; Zion is the saints of the living God" (*The Millennial Messiah: The Second Coming of the Son of Man* [Salt Lake City: Deseret Book, 1982], 293). I am writing about Zion as the Church of Christ.

2. See Andrew C. Skinner, "Zion Gained and Lost: Fourth Nephi as the Quintessential Model," in Monte S. Nyman and Charles D. Tate, eds., *Fourth Nephi through Moroni, from Zion to Destruction* (Provo, UT: Religious Studies Center, Brigham Young University, 1995), 289–302.

3. Spencer W. Kimball, "Seeking Eternal Riches," *Ensign*, May 1976, 107.

4. Kimball, "Seeking Eternal Riches," 107.

5. Marion G. Romney, "Principles of Temporal Salvation," *Ensign*, April 1981, 6.

6. Dictionary.com, Princeton University, s.v. "unity," http://dictionary. reference.com/browse/unity (accessed January 15, 2007).

7. See Dallin H. Oaks, "Why Do We Serve?" *Ensign,* November 1984, 13.

8. Marion G. Romney, "Unity," *Ensign,* May 1983, 17.

9. Boyd K. Packer, "On Zion's Hill," *Ensign,* November 2005, 71, 73.

10. Russell M. Nelson, "'Blessed Are the Peacemakers,'" *Ensign,* November 2002, 41.

11. Keith B. McMullin, "Come to Zion! Come to Zion!" *Ensign,* November 2002, 96.

12. See Bruce C. and Marie K. Hafen, *The Belonging Heart: The Atonement and Relationships with God and Family* (Salt Lake City: Deseret Book, 1994).

13. See Marion G. Romney, "Gospel Covenants," *Ensign,* May 1981, 43.

14. Marion G. Romney, "Caring for the Poor—A Covenantal Obligation," *Ensign,* November 1978, 87.

15. R. Quinn Gardner, in "I Have a Question," *Ensign,* March 1978, 20.

16. Harold B. Lee, "Admonitions for the Priesthood of God," *Ensign,* January 1973, 104.

17. N. Eldon Tanner, "The Greatest Brotherhood," *Ensign,* May 1977, 46.

18. See L. Tom Perry, "What Is a Quorum?" *Ensign,* November 2004, 23–25.

19. In this, King Benjamin stands in direct contrast to the wicked King Noah (see Mosiah 11:24).

20. See Harold B. Lee, "Strengthen the Stakes of Zion," *Ensign,* July 1973, 2–6.

21. Joseph F. Smith, *Gospel Doctrine* (Salt Lake City: Deseret Book, 1978), 208.

## 22

# "THE PURE LOVE OF CHRIST": THE DIVINE PRECEPT OF CHARITY IN MORONI 7

## Matthew O. Richardson

While conversing with members of the Quorum of the Twelve at Brigham Young's home, the Prophet Joseph Smith stated that "a man would get nearer to God by abiding by [the Book of Mormon's] precepts, than by any other book."[1] The Book of Mormon provides several important insights more clearly than any other record.[2]

Consider, for example, the precept, or doctrine, of charity.[3] The most developed scriptural writings of charity are found in the New Testament and the Book of Mormon. The Apostle Paul's letter to the Corinthians is similar in many ways to the contents of Mormon's sermon on charity.[4] Because of the similarities, one may wonder how the precepts of charity contained in the Book of Mormon could bring us nearer to God than even Paul's writings on the same subject. A closer inspection of Mormon's sermon reveals an understanding and foundation that will, if abided by, actually get a person nearer to God than by abiding by more superficial forms of charity.

Rather than being satisfied with describing what charity is *like*,

---

*Matthew O. Richardson is an associate professor of Church history and doctrine at Brigham Young University.*

Mormon provides a straightforward definition of what charity actually *is*. With simple and absolute clarity, Mormon defines charity as "the pure love of Christ" (Moroni 7:47). Like all definitions of charity, Mormon's interpretation places divine love at the very core. Thus, some may feel that the Book of Mormon precept of charity really doesn't differ all that much from the other scriptural or traditional definitions. "It's still all about love," they may point out, "and everything else is only decoration." But Mormon's definition is much more than decoration. It is explicit rather than implicit, particularly in the way he connects charity inseparably to Christ.

Some may ask, Can you really go wrong with love—in any form? But Mormon taught that "if ye have not charity, ye are nothing" (Moroni 7:46) and that "whoso is found possessed of it [charity] at the last day, it shall be well with him" (Moroni 7:47). Obviously, saying that charity is important is an understatement. But what if people *understate* charity and are left with a form that isn't even the same charity Mormon spoke of? What if the present understanding of charity has already shifted from the divine precept taught in the Book of Mormon?

## CONTEMPORARY CHARITY

As malicious acts of terror become more common and as indiscriminate violence spreads, government leaders have called for a renewed sense of charity, or love, toward humanity as a whole. David Cameron, Britain's Conservative Party leader, for example, felt that showing "a lot more love" would be the best long-term solution to crime and antisocial behavior.[5] Most people like Cameron's approach and believe that love does have its far-reaching benefits. Society's confidence in love should not be surprising, for our culture has practically adopted the song "All You Need Is Love" as a prescription for most of its problems. And certainly the Apostle Paul taught that charity was the greatest of all virtues (see 1 Corinthians 13:13).

In Paul's letter to Timothy, he wrote of the conditions of our day: "This know also, that in the last days perilous times shall come," and he described a world filled with people who are proud, disobedient, unholy, traitors, liars, and immoral (see 2 Timothy 3:1–7). Included in Paul's list of perils is "having a form of godliness, but denying the power thereof," and Paul concludes, "from such turn away" (v. 5). Some may question how perilous "having a form of godliness, but denying the power thereof" could really be. To understand the possible peril of this particular circumstance, we could ask, in what ways do we embrace "forms of godliness" but deny its source of power?

Consider how easily society embraces forms of godliness while, at the same time, vehemently opposes any type of connection with God. Typically society readily accepts the acts of Jesus Christ—kindness, compassion, promotion of peace, understanding, and love—but will not acknowledge any serious connection these acts have with Christ and His doctrines or precepts. "For many," wrote Robert L. Millet, professor of ancient scripture at Brigham Young University, "the doctrine of Christ has been replaced by the ethics of Jesus."[6] Thus, some enjoy the "ethical" aspects of the ministry of Jesus but cannot tolerate the doctrinal teachings of the divine Christ. In short, they love the *form* of godliness but despise the power thereof, namely, God. It is in this sense that charity is really little more than a "form of godliness" and is disconnected from its power—the divine.

This disconnect can also be seen in the etymology of *charity*. Technically, the English word *charity* is derived from adaptations from the Old French *charité*, based on the Latin *cartatem*. Scripturally, the Vulgate New Testament derived *charity* from the Latin *caritas*, while Greek versions are based on *agape*. All these terms are roughly translated as *love*. It is true that many other words describing aspects of love have also been used to define *charity*. Words like *benevolence, affection, kindness,* or *esteem* all come to mind. Even though every word either originated from some form of the term *love* or was associated with it, it should be pointed out that in earlier times, these definitions of charity were framed under the rubric of divine love. In short, the early word sources for *charity* were connected, in some way, with the divine Christ.[7]

Unfortunately, the meaning of charity has transformed over the years. By A.D. 1225, charity continued to include terms like *love, kindness, affection, generosity,* and *goodness* but had lost some of its obvious religious connection.[8] Sadly, the gap between charity's affiliation with the divine was widened by the 1300s, when charity became the term of choice for the act of giving alms, service, or compassion to the needy. By the late

1600s, the definition of charity morphed into an institutional context describing organizations that rendered such services as "charitable institutions."[9]

Please understand that this is not an attempt to minimize or vilify love, kindness, compassion, generosity, or ethics in any way. In truth, these are admirable traits and necessary for a healthy society. Surely some could care less whether charity was connected to the divine as long as it provided practical, beneficial service to mankind. On the other hand, some feel that because these acts are good then a person exhibiting these behaviors will still come closer to God whether they intended to or not. But while these practical and even biblical ideas of charity have favorable results, even the slightest disconnect with the divine stalls our progression.

While Mormon did teach that all things which are good come from God (see Moroni 7:12), he was more specific as his speech continued: "Every thing which inviteth to do good, and *to persuade to believe in Christ,* is sent forth by the power and gift of Christ; wherefore ye may know with a perfect knowledge it is of God" (Moroni 7:16; emphasis added). We must remember that charity has a designed purpose: to persuade people to believe in Christ. This recalls President Gordon B. Hinckley's advice: "It is not enough just to be good. You must be good for something."[10] It also underscores Elder Bruce C. Hafen's teaching that "service to others will surely bring us closer to God, especially when motivated by an unselfish sense of personal compassion. But even such desirable service will not of itself complete our relationship with God, because it will not by itself result in the bestowal of the complete attributes of godliness."[11]

Thus, even with good intentions, forms of godliness without its true source of power may provide some measure of reward; they are ultimately ineffective in helping us become as Christ truly is. Perhaps this is what C. S. Lewis meant when describing affection, friendship, intimate love, and charity as good but, when disconnected from the divine, being "unworthy to take the place of God by the fact that they cannot even remain themselves and do what they promise to do without God's help."[12] Without God's help, charity will, at best, bring us closer to our fellowmen. While this is good and worthy, it does not necessarily help us come nearer to God, and we forfeit divine possibilities. Paul warned of such "forms of godliness" and cautioned us to turn away or flee because these subtle misconceptions are the sort that creep in and lead the silly away. Sadly, such are "ever learning, and never able to come to the knowledge of the truth" (2 Timothy 3:7).

Clearly, the precept of charity taught in the Book of Mormon is not really the same charity so often discussed today. It is only what Elder Neal A. Maxwell called a "particularized charity," or "the pure love of Christ," that will serve us well in the last days.[13] The precept of charity as contained in the Book of Mormon is particular in that it is divinely connected and can never be reduced to mere ethical behavior—as good as ethics may seem. Because it is divinely connected, charity must be understood from a godly perspective that, in turn, has divine expectations and outcomes making possible divine empowerment to change.

## THE LOVE OF CHRIST

Because the Book of Mormon's precept of charity is a "particularized" type of love, it is vital to understand exactly what the phrase "love of Christ" means. A narrow interpretation of this phrase yields only two meanings: (1) the "love of Christ," meaning Christ's love, or the love that comes *from* Christ, and (2) the "love of Christ," meaning the love *we have for* Christ.

### Love from Christ

In considering the first interpretation, we are to understand that those who have charity have actually received pure love *from* Christ. Naturally, Christ loves all mankind and those who have the love *from* Christ feel of His abiding comfort and know of His deep affection for each of us. But there is a deeper, more direct, and necessary way we partake of the love *from* Christ. John taught that God's love for the world is embodied in Jesus Christ. "In this was manifested the love of God toward us, because that God sent his only begotten Son into the world, that we might live through him." He continues, "Herein is love, not that we loved God, but that he loved us, and sent his Son to be the propitiation for our sins" (1 John 4:9–10).

It appears that we receive God's love by receiving the Savior and

His Atonement. Christ taught, "He that receiveth me receiveth my Father" (D&C 84:37). Likewise, Christ's love for us directly parallels God's love for us. Moroni, as he spoke to the Savior, said, "I remember that thou hast said that thou hast loved the world, even unto the laying down of thy life for the world, that thou mightest take it again to prepare a place for the children of men" (Ether 12:33). Moroni then said, "I know that this love which thou hast had for the children of men is charity" (Ether 12:34). Charity, in this context, is the love *from* Christ and is embodied in Christ's teachings and Atonement. "It is through the love and mercy of the Son of God for humanity," President Joseph Fielding Smith testified, "that this redemption comes."[14]

King Benjamin taught that salvation was possible "only in and through the name of Christ, the Lord Omnipotent" (Mosiah 3:17). Both King Benjamin and Mormon taught, those who receive the love *from* Christ receive the Redemption of Christ and become His children (see Mosiah 5:7; Moroni 7:48; D&C 34:3). Thus, it is only as we accept the love *from* Christ as manifest in the Atonement that we become His children—His sons and daughters—and it is clear that becoming His children requires entering into sacred covenants (see Mosiah 5:5–7). Mormon, in his sermon dealing with charity, also emphasized Christ's teachings to "repent . . . and come unto me, and be baptized in my name, and have faith in me, that ye may be saved" (Moroni 7:34). Because the love *from* Christ is manifest in the Atonement and because it is only through the Atonement and covenant ordinances that we can become the children of Christ and be saved, it makes perfect sense that Mormon taught that "whoso is found possessed of it [charity, or the pure love of Christ] at the last day, it shall be well with him" (Moroni 7:47).

### Love for Christ

When we possess the love *from* Christ, we discover "a mighty change in us, or in our hearts, that we have no more disposition to do evil, but to do good continually" (Mosiah 5:2). In this change, we obtain "a new heart filled with charity" that comes only "through the Atonement."[15] A heart filled with the love *from* Christ greatly changes our disposition and our love *for* Christ. "We love him," John wrote, "because he first loved us" (1 John 4:19). As we receive the Atonement, we begin to feel a pure love *for* Christ. Obviously, this is more than just affection, appreciation, or admiration. The pure love *for* Christ envelopes us. It requires all our might, mind, and strength (see Moroni 10:32).

In Mormon's sermon, he urged us to pray to be "filled with this love [charity, or the pure love of Christ]" (Moroni 7:48). If we are really *filled* with a pure love *for* Christ, we are required to give all our heart, and it doesn't take long to find that we have very little room for anything else but Christ. It is ironic that when the Savior was born into mortality, the inns were filled, leaving no room for Him. While today there is still little room for the Savior in the world, there is ample room for Him in the hearts of those who possess a pure love *for* Him. Those with charity have room in their hearts for the Savior, but they have very little room for anything else. In this complete condition, they possess "an eye single to the glory of God" (D&C 4:5), or, in other words, Christ fills them and there is no room for pride, self-aggrandizement, or avarice.

## "LOVE ONE ANOTHER"

Some may ask, "What about loving others? Isn't that part of the love of Christ?" After all, those who love Christ have been commanded to keep His commandments (John 14:13), and Jesus taught that the first great commandment is to "love the Lord thy God with all thy heart, and with all thy soul, and with all thy mind." He then added, "And the second is like unto it, Thou shalt love thy neighbor as thyself" (Matthew 22:37–39). According to this, those who keep the first great commandment and possess a love *for* Christ must love others *as* Christ loves them (see John 13:34). In truth, however, this is not accomplished by obedience and obligation alone.

As we receive the pure love of Christ—meaning the love *from* Christ (the Atonement), which in turn generates our love *for* Christ—our disposition is changed. Our love for others results more from this change than from dutifully keeping His commandments alone.

Consider, for example, Lehi's experience when partaking of the fruit of the tree of life, which represented the "love of God." As Lehi received Christ's love *for him* (meaning partaking of the fruits of Christ), his own love *for Christ* increased. "As I partook of the fruit thereof," Lehi said of this experience, "it filled my soul with exceedingly great joy"

(1 Nephi 8:12). The product of Lehi's experience was a manifestation of love for others. "Wherefore," Lehi explained, "I began to be desirous that my family should partake of it also" (1 Nephi 8:12).

Another example of this process was when Enos, the son of Jacob, was hunting in the woods. After Enos received the love *from* Christ and was forgiven, he stated, "I began to feel a desire for the welfare of my brethren, the Nephites; wherefore, I did pour out my whole soul unto God for them" (Enos 1:9). This charity continued to swell, and his love for the Lamanites increased.

Finally, consider that same pattern when the sons of Mosiah repented and felt the love *from* Christ. Following this experience, "they were desirous that salvation should be declared to every creature, for they could not bear that any human soul should perish. . . . And thus did the Spirit of the Lord work upon them" (Mosiah 28:3–4).

Note that in all three examples, those possessing the pure love of Christ through the Atonement didn't feel compelled or pressured to "love one another," as Christ commanded (John 13:34). They were changed creatures, and their love for others was directly connected to receiving the pure love *from* Christ. "The Atonement in some way, apparently through the Holy Ghost," Elder Hafen wrote, "makes possible the infusion of spiritual endowments that actually change and purify our nature, moving us toward that state of holiness or completeness we call eternal life or Godlike life." He then insightfully concludes, "At that ultimate stage we will exhibit divine characteristics not just because we think we should but because that is the way we are."[16]

## "PURE LOVE OF CHRIST"

Mormon did not define charity simply as the "love of Christ" but as the "*pure* love of Christ." Consider two lessons taught by this specific wording. First, love and Christ are inseparable. In other words, charity is the *pure* "love of Christ," the genuine form of His love. It is the real thing, not counterfeit or even diluted.

### Pure Love and Christ

In some ways, this has already been addressed, at least in regards to how the etymology of charity and love has progressively diluted any affiliation with the divine. But to truly understand the *pure* love of Christ, we must consider Mormon's precept of charity again—at least, from a different vantage point. Mormon's sermon on charity was delivered to those "of the church" who were "peaceable followers of Christ" (Moroni 7:3) rather than those who did not believe in Jesus or might naturally mistake acts of ethical behavior as acts of charity. As such, this sermon places heavy responsibility on the followers of Christ to take care to understand and exercise charity in its purest form. Thus, followers of Christ must never juxtapose love (in whatever form) with the love of Christ. I recall, for example, a member bearing testimony of the power of love. The testimony was sincere and heartfelt. Yet other than closing in the name of Christ, there was no mention of Jesus Christ or the gospel. In short, this was a fine testimonial of the power of love, but it was not a testimony of the power of the love *of Christ.* In no way am I implying that this member did not bear pure testimony; the member did not, however, bear testimony of the pure love of Christ. Please know it is not my intent to be critical or even judge the acceptability or value of any member's testimony. It is, however, my intent to provide a practical illustration of how easy it is for the *pure* love of Christ to be diluted by members and thus forfeit its promised power.

Consider another subtle dilution to understand the pure love of Christ. It is not uncommon for members to define charity as "Christlike" love. While this descriptor may be mostly correct, charity is not *like* Christ's love, it *is* Christ's love. This reminds me of counterfeit watches sold on big-city street corners at a fraction of the cost of the genuine product. These watches bear the name, logo, color, and styling of their genuine counterparts. Some fakes are better than others and include real gold, diamonds, and leather. They are sure to impress those that cannot discriminate between the genuine brand name and its counterfeit. Some feel that the fakes keep time just as well as the real thing, and so a multimillion-dollar racket continues to thrive. But though these watches may look *like* the real thing and even keep time *like* the real thing, in the end, the value of the counterfeit watch will *never* be the same *as* the real thing. In this way, the term *Christlike love* may approximate *the love of Christ,* but it does not possess the same value or power as *the pure love of Christ.* The Book of Mormon precept of charity is pure and not counterfeit, and charity is not something that looks *like*, sounds *like*, acts *like*, or even feels *like* Christ's love—it *is* Christ's love.

In truth, it is impossible for us to even love *like* Christ on our own. Charity is not attainable by our own power, dedication, or personal development. Mormon taught that charity is *bestowed* by God upon those who "pray unto the Father with all the energy of heart" to "be filled with this love [pure love of Christ]" and "are true followers of his Son, Jesus Christ" and "become the sons of God" (Moroni 7:48). As such, it is impossible to even practice *Christlike* love without some connection with Christ.

### Pure Love and Behavior

The second lesson gleaned when considering the *pure* love of Christ is that our behaviors must also be pure. According to Mormon, the peaceable followers of Christ would be known by their works. In fact, their works reveal their truest character. "For I remember the word of God which saith by their works ye shall know them," Mormon taught. He continued, "If their works be good, then they are good also" (Moroni 7:5). Mormon also taught that if we "offereth a gift, or prayeth unto God, except he shall do it with real intent it profiteth him nothing" (Moroni 7:6). When it comes to charity, at least in its purest form, our behavior is more than just "talking the talk."

Incongruent behavior dilutes charity to the point that it is no longer charity—at least charity in its most pure form as defined in Mormon's sermon. "Some people wear masks of decency and outward righteousness," President James E. Faust warned, "but live lives of deception, believing that, like Dr. Jekyll, they can live a double life and never be found out."[17] The inner conflict President Faust refers to is, of course, from Robert Louis Stevenson's 1888 best-selling novel *The Strange Case of Dr. Jekyll and Mr. Hyde*. Stevenson's work describing the struggle between the good and evil within the same man was so moving that the characters of his novel actually became a mainstream phrase ("Jekyll and Hyde") for describing incongruent behavior.

It is hypocritical to profess charity but act in ways contrary to those professed principles. It is also deeply disturbing that virtue could ever be the front for vice, but unfortunately it isn't very surprising when such activities actually take place. Consider the Houston-based energy company Enron. By the end of its sixth consecutive year of having been named "America's Most Innovative Company" by *Forbes* magazine, Enron plunged into bankruptcy due to legal entanglements involving unprecedented fraud and corruption. In Jekyll-and-Hyde fashion, Enron executives and employees read a sixty-four-page "Code of Ethics" manual and penned their signatures certifying personal agreement and compliance long before they were found guilty of spurious behavior.[18]

When people have pure charity, it is unlikely that their behavior is determined by a situation or current temptation. Rather than being a code of conduct or a skill set of learned ethics, pure charity is literally a manifestation of our character—who we are rather than just what we do. Elder C. Max Caldwell said that charity "is an internal condition that must be developed and experienced in order to be understood. We are possessors of charity when it is a part of our nature."[19]

## CONCLUSION

When we receive the pure, undiluted love *from* Christ (which comes only through the Atonement of Christ and by entering into sacred ordinances) and the pure, undiluted love *for* Christ (which empowers our ability to keep His commandments and love others just as Christ loves us), we experience a mighty change and we *become* as Christ is. "When he [Christ] shall appear," Mormon concluded in his profound sermon, "we shall be like him, for we shall see him as he is; that we may have this hope; that we may be purified even as he is pure" (Moroni 7:48).

Because the ultimate purpose of charity is to cause us to become as Christ is, we must never mistake charity for its counterfeits—regardless of how good and important they may seem. Only when charity is inseparably connected with Jesus Christ can the real outcome be realized—to be as He is. In this light, when Mormon preached that a man "must needs have charity; for if he have not charity he is nothing" (Moroni 7:44), one can see that a man without charity really is *nothing* like Jesus Christ.

## NOTES

1. Joseph Smith, *History of the Church of Jesus Christ of Latter-day Saints,* ed. B. H. Roberts, 2nd ed. rev. (Salt Lake City: Deseret Book, 1976), 4:461.

2. It should be remembered that the ancient texts are not necessarily represented in their original or even intended forms. Joseph Smith taught, "I believe the Bible as it read when it came from the pen of the original writers. Ignorant translators, careless transcribers, or designing and corrupt priests have committed many errors" (*Teachings of the Prophet Joseph Smith,* comp. Joseph Fielding Smith [Salt Lake City: Deseret Book, 1976], 327). Nephi reminded us that "plain and precious things were taken away" from scriptural texts (see 1 Nephi 13:25–29).

3. Precepts, by definition are more than ideas or concepts. Precepts are official or authorized instructions, directions, rules, or mandates. In other words, a precept is typically seen as something official or authorized. In this way, some may liken a precept with a doctrine.

4. See Bruce R. McConkie, *Mormon Doctrine,* 2nd ed. (Salt Lake City: Bookcraft, 1966), 122.

5. "UK Youth Need More Love, Says Conservative Leader," *Taipei Times,* July 12, 2006.

6. Robert L. Millet, "A Divine Deterrent to Creeping Relativism," in *LDS Marriage and Family Relations* (Dubuque, IA: Kendall/Hunt, 1998), 26.

7. *The Oxford English Dictionary,* 2nd ed. (New York: Oxford University Press, 1989), s.v. "charity."

8. *The Oxford English Dictionary,* see s.v. "charity," 2.a.

9. *The Oxford English Dictionary,* see s.v. "charity," 4b, 5, 6.

10. Gordon B. Hinckley, "Stand Up for Truth," in *Speeches* (Provo, UT: Brigham Young University, 1997), 22.

11. Bruce C. Hafen, *The Broken Heart: Applying the Atonement to Life's Experiences* (Salt Lake City: Deseret Book, 1989), 197.

12. C. S. Lewis, *The Four Loves* (New York: Harcourt, 1960), 166.

13. Neal A. Maxwell, *Notwithstanding My Weakness* (Salt Lake City: Deseret Book, 1981), 47.

14. Joseph Fielding Smith, *Answers to Gospel Questions* (Salt Lake City: Deseret Book, 1963), 4:58.

15. Henry B. Eyring, *To Draw Closer to God* (Salt Lake City: Deseret Book, 1997), 71.

16. Bruce C. Hafen, *The Broken Heart: Applying the Atonement to Life's Experiences* (Salt Lake City: Deseret Book, 1989), 18.

17. James E. Faust, "The Enemy Within," *Ensign,* November 2000, 46.

18. Brian Cruver, *Anatomy of Greed* (New York: Carroll and Graf, 2002), 329–31, 333, 346.

19. C. Max Caldwell, "Love of Christ," *Ensign,* November 1992, 30.

# INDEX